MW00698563

Bad Bridget

ABOUT THE AUTHORS

Elaine Farrell is a Reader in the School of History, Anthropology, Philosophy and Politics at Queen's University Belfast.

Leanne McCormick is a Senior Lecturer in the School of Arts and Humanities at Ulster University.

Bad Bridget

Crime, Mayhem and the Lives of
Irish Emigrant Women

ELAINE FARRELL AND
LEANNE McCORMICK

SANDYCOVE

an imprint of

PENGUIN BOOKS

SANDYCOVE

UK | USA | Canada | Ireland | Australia
India | New Zealand | South Africa

Sandycove is part of the Penguin Random House group of companies
whose addresses can be found at global.penguinrandomhouse.com.

First published 2023
001

Copyright © Elaine Farrell and Leanne McCormick, 2023

The moral right of the authors has been asserted

BAD BRIDGET is a registered trademark of The Queen's University Belfast. All rights reserved.

Set in 13.5/16pt Garamond MT Std
Typeset by Jouve (UK), Milton Keynes
Printed and bound in Great Britain by Clays Ltd, Elcograf S.p.A.

The authorized representative in the EEA is Penguin Random House Ireland,
Morrison Chambers, 32 Nassau Street, Dublin D02 YH68

A CIP catalogue record for this book is available from the British Library

ISBN: 978–1–844–88581–7

www.greenpenguin.co.uk

Penguin Random House is committed to a
sustainable future for our business, our readers
and our planet. This book is made from Forest
Stewardship Council® certified paper.

For Andrew and James, and Aedan and Clio.
Our littlest loves.

Contents

Acknowledgements

We've been working on the Bad Bridget project for many years and have lots of people to thank. For generous financial support to complete this research, we wish to thank the Arts and Humanities Research Council UK (grant AH/M008649/1). We are also grateful to Queen's University Belfast and Ulster University for financial and other support. Leanne would like to acknowledge the British Academy for support from grant SG132451.

We crossed the Atlantic many times to find records of Irish women who left the island a century or two before us. We are indebted to staff at the many archives, libraries and repositories who facilitated and aided our research, including at the Archives of Ontario; City of Toronto Archives; Archives of the Roman Catholic Archdiocese of Toronto, especially Erin Bienert; the Sisters of St Joseph Archive, Toronto, especially Linda Wicks; American Antiquarian Society; Boston City Archives; Boston Public Library; Massachusetts Historical Society; Massachusetts Archives, especially Caitlin Jones; Massachusetts Judicial Archives; University Archives and Special Collections, Joseph P. Healey Library, University of Massachusetts Boston, particularly Jessica R. Holden; New York Historical Society; New York Municipal Archives; New York Public Library; New York State Archives; New York Society for the Prevention of Cruelty to Children, particularly Joseph Gleason; Public Record Office of Northern Ireland, especially Stephen

Scarth; and the McClay Library, Queen's University Belfast, especially Deborah Wilson.

Several research assistants have aided our work in different ways over the past few years. We are particularly indebted to Leanne Calvert, who was a brilliant postdoctoral research fellow on the project for twelve months, inputting data, crunching numbers and lending the Bad Bridget project her Twitter expertise! We are also very thankful to our rainy-day researcher, Liam Farrell, to our comma queen, Debbie McCormick, and to Bridget Harrison for data entry in the summer of 2019.

Our Bad Bridget advisory committee kept us right across the duration of the project, and we're very grateful for their valuable input: Enda Delaney, Don MacRaild, Mary O'Dowd and Diane Urquhart. Our colleagues at Queen's University Belfast, Ulster University and beyond have been generous with their advice and support. We especially want to acknowledge Ciara Breathnach, Sarah-Anne Buckley, Kate Byrne, Arunima Datta, Liz Dawson, Cara Delay, Frank Ferguson, Helen Jackson, Laura Kelly, Liam Kennedy, Maria Luddy, Fearghal McGarry, Jennifer Redmond, Nik Ribianszky, Ian Thatcher, Keira Williams, Mike Wilson and Nerys Young. We're also very thankful to those who have been involved in our other Bad Bridget endeavours that have helped shape this book, particularly Paddy Fitzgerald, Catherine Griffin, Colm Heatley, Zara McBrearty, Andrew McDowell, Victoria Millar, Megan Parker-Johnson and Dermot Tierney. We're grateful to those who organized academic and public Bad Bridget talks, to those who came to hear us speak and to all our wonderful Bad Bridget Twitter followers.

For editorial input and guidance, we are indebted to the team at Penguin, and particularly Brendan Barrington, who kept us from writing an academic book and overdoing the statistics! And to Conor Reidy of Silverview Editing for compiling our index.

Our parents, siblings and partners have been listening to Bad Bridget stories for years and have been unfailingly supportive and encouraging, and have at least pretended to be interested some of the time. Andrew and Yiannis deserve particular mention for the many miles, both literal and figurative, they have travelled on the Bad Bridget journey – we appreciate them all. Our children have provided plenty of distraction and constantly disrupted the research and writing process. But we wouldn't have it any other way!

Introducing Bad Bridget

Bridget Jones was born in Ballykinave, near Claremorris, County Mayo, on 18 July 1888, one of twelve children. Her family called her Delia, short for Bedelia, an Irish variant of Bridget. Neither of Delia's parents could write. Delia and her siblings all attended school when they could, but their labour was often needed at home or on their small twelve-acre farm.[1]

When Delia was eight, her father died from a stomach ulcer. This left Ellen as the sole parent to children ranging in age from seventeen years to four months, and it likely influenced Delia's withdrawal from school a few months later, around the time that she made her Confirmation. Years later, Delia reflected that her childhood home 'was always comfortable in every way' and the 'family always happy together'. But her childhood was not without further tragedy. Two of her siblings died in infanthood, and when she was a teenager an older brother was fatally injured by a train.

When Delia was around fifteen, her older sister, Mary, who was by then living in Massachusetts, paid for her passage to the US, and they were later joined there by a younger sister, Margaret. Two of Delia's older brothers also emigrated, to England and Canada, and two younger brothers joined the British Army, serving in France during the First World War. The youngest sister, Ella, remained at home to look after their ageing mother.

Delia and her siblings were among at least 7.5 million people who emigrated from Ireland between 1815 and 1914.[2] Ireland was the only European country to have fewer people at the end of this period than at the beginning.[3] Emigration peaked in the 1840s and 1850s, when a potato blight brought starvation to a population largely dependent on the crop. Between 1845 and 1855, around two and a half million emigrants departed Ireland, more than had left across the previous 250 years.[4] That flood of emigration continued into the post-Famine decades as generation after generation of Irish-born inhabitants left the island.

The number of girls and women involved in this exodus was remarkable. One in three emigrants from Ireland was female in the 1820s, increasing to around one in two between 1845 and 1885. Thereafter, up to the 1920s, a majority of Irish emigrants was female.[5] This was at a time when immigrants who entered the United States were predominantly male.[6] The vast majority of Irish emigrant girls and women arrived in North America unmarried.[7]

At around fifteen years old, Delia was young when she emigrated, but not exceptionally so: more than half of Irish emigrants from 1880 to 1916 were between fifteen and twenty-five years old.[8] They often travelled alone, as Delia did.[9] In 1883, the Children's Aid Society in New York observed that it was 'surprising to find how many young girls cross the ocean alone or perhaps with some home neighbor who is unable to do much for them when they land'.[10] In 1897, a journalist from *The New York Times* who observed 'large importation of Kathleens, Eileens, Delias, and Norahs' arriving at the port noted: 'The remarkable fact is that most of the young women come across without any attendant. Their passages are prepaid by relatives in this country, and they confidently expect to be met on arrival.'[11] In our research we came across girls as young as seven years old crossing the Atlantic without relatives.

Unaccompanied girls and women faced specific challenges. Teenager Mary Ward left her widowed mother in Wexford and emigrated to Massachusetts on the *James Foster Jr.* in September 1864. She was treated on arrival for syphilis. She was certain she had caught it from a crew member, Robert Stafford, on board the ship because she had 'been with no other man'.[12] It is not clear if Ward's relationship with Stafford was consensual, but female steerage passengers in the 1840s and 1850s were sometimes subjected to sexual assault.[13] A concerned clergyman wrote to philanthropist Vere Foster from Carrick-on-Shannon, County Leitrim, in 1881, expressing support for some kind of chaperone scheme for emigrating girls: 'I fully concur that something should be done to protect girls both on the passage and on their arriving for I fear there is a terrible amount of destruction done to poor unsuspecting girls in both places.'[14]

Most emigrants in the Famine and post-Famine years travelled on the back of the labour of a relative or friend already in North America – a phenomenon known as chain migration. Other migrants were funded by their Ireland-based families, often in anticipation that the outlay would later be returned in the form of remittances from abroad.[15] Female emigrants were thought to be a good investment: they were able to secure jobs relatively quickly and were more likely than their male counterparts to send money home.[16] Some Irish migrants participated in emigration schemes from landed estates, charities, workhouses or other institutions.[17] Employers in North America also funded travel from Ireland. Margaret Haley, for instance, emigrated from Waterford to Lawrence, Massachusetts, one of seventy girls whose passage was paid by a Mr Chapire to work in his mill.[18]

Irish immigration in the nineteenth century permanently changed the population make-up of North America. In the 1850 United States census, the first to collect data on immigration, 2,244,600 individuals in a population of 23,191,876 were classified as immigrants. Of these, close to half were from Ireland.[19] The Irish-born population in the United States peaked at 1,871,509 in 1890, and an additional 2,924,172 US-born inhabitants had at least one Irish-born parent.[20] In Boston, the city where Delia Jones settled, around one third of immigrants were Irish-born by 1855.[21] In the same year, over a quarter of the entire population of New York City was Irish-born.[22] The Irish commonly congregated in neighbourhoods that, in the middle decades of the nineteenth century, were often seen as the worst slums. In one of these areas, New York's Sixth Ward, which included the notorious Five Points neighbourhood, 3,492 residents were recorded as living in just ninety-nine houses, an average of more than thirty-five residents per house.[23]

Irish emigration to Canada was well-established by the time of the Famine. These Irish migrants were often attracted by the availability of land and the cheaper passage fare in comparison to the United States.[24] The first Canadian census, in 1871, revealed that 24.3 per cent of the population was Irish-born.[25] As a British dominion, Canada was especially attractive to Irish Protestants and drew a disproportionate number of emigrants from Ulster. The Orange Order and other organizations provided important migratory links.[26] Two thirds of the Irish emigrants who settled in Toronto between 1825 and 1900 were Protestant.[27]

The dominant narrative of Irish emigration to North America focuses on those who came from humble beginnings in Ireland and made a better life for themselves. They or their children went on to become pillars of society. They became the Kennedys, a political dynasty, or the Eatons, who established Canada's largest department store chain and revolutionized shopping, or the Kellys, from whom Princess Grace descended. Less famous but equally prominent in the narrative of Irish immigration were the girls and women who became loyal domestic servants and nannies, the nuns and teachers, the good wives and mothers who raised a generation of successful Irish Americans. And, while many certainly did, this narrative is nowhere near the whole truth.

As the Irish became more upwardly mobile, establishing themselves within North American society, there was no appetite on either side of the Atlantic to face up to the reality that many Irish female emigrants did not succeed – and that many ended up on the wrong side of the law. At a time when Ireland, north and south, is beginning to re-examine its treatment of women who were considered to have defied societal norms, telling the story of these women is crucial to our understanding of the Irish past.

The Bad Bridget Project

The centrality of emigration to Ireland's history has resulted in much excellent research on Irish migration and the diaspora abroad.[28] But criminal and deviant Irish women have not been a major feature of that scholarship. We spent six years trawling archives and historical records, mainly in

New York, Boston and Toronto. We found huge numbers of Irish women who got jobs but were later fired, women who haunted the bars and drinking saloons, mothers who had their children taken away or who gave them up, and girls and women who were considered to be sexually immoral. These are the women we collectively dub Bad Bridget, and there were hundreds of thousands of them in the police stations, courthouses and prisons of North American cities.

Why did we decide to title our project Bad Bridget? By the mid-nineteenth century, the name Bridget or Biddy was widely used in North America to refer in a general way to Irish women. The Brooklyn-based Catholic newspaper *The Tablet* judged in 1914 that it was to St Brigid that 'the daughters of Erin owe their deathless legacy of virtue, which has made the name of Irish women the world over synonymous with purity and virtue'.[29] This myth of the pure and chaste Irish woman fitted with Christian ideals, as epitomized by St Brigid (or Bridget), the female patron saint of Ireland. On the other side of the dichotomy was the stereotype of the blundering, drunken, quick-tempered and uncivilized 'Bridget', a common object of ridicule in the theatre, newspapers and other Northern American mass culture of the nineteenth and early twentieth centuries.[30] This Bridget, depicted as 'Bridget McBruiser' in an 1875 book on the pseudoscience of physiognomy, was a sharp contrast to the virtuous saint she was named after (ill. 0.1). Mary McWhorter of the United States Ladies' Auxiliary Ancient Order of Hibernians lamented in 1915 that 'it is enough to make one shudder at times to hear thoughtless and ignorant people deride the name of Brigid'.[31]

Fig. 747. – FLORENCE NIGHTINGALE.   Fig. 748.—BRIDGET MCBRUISER.

o.1. 'Contrasted faces'.

Clearly neither St Brigid nor Bridget McBruiser is representative of Irish women in North America. Irish girls and women could be chaste and moral, but they were also sexually active and criminal. They could be drunken and quick-tempered, but they were also strategic and calculating in their illegal activity. And so it is between these two Bridgets that we explore the realities of Irish girls' and women's involvement in crime in North America. The stories we tell in this book show for the first time in detail the underbelly of Irish emigration to North America.

Counting Bad Bridget

After Delia Jones arrived in Boston, she worked as a domestic servant and a waitress, roles that were commonly taken up by Irish girls and women. But she never stayed long in any job. By the time she was thirty, she had been in court at least fourteen times, charged with offences including drunkenness and prostitution (ill. 0.2). Her sister Mary, who had paid for her passage, remarked that she had been 'nothing but a constant source of trouble'. 'My poor mother's heart would be broke if she knew', Mary added.[32]

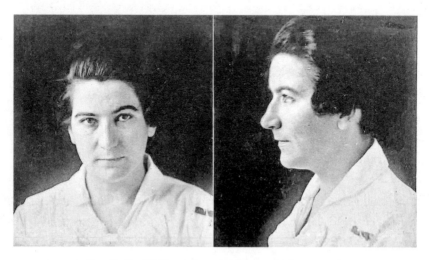

0.2. Delia (Bridget) Jones, prison mugshot 1918.

There was nothing unusual about Delia Jones's experiences. The numbers are stark. In Boston, 37.8 per cent of the girls and women admitted to the House of Correction between 1882 and 1905 were Irish, even though the Irish represented around 17 per cent of the city's population.[33] Between 1853 and 1863, 6,131 Irish women were admitted to Toronto Gaol, where they comprised about four fifths of the gaol's female population.[34] And in New York, where the Irish got into trouble with the law on a vast scale, Irish women were dramatically over-represented. In the early 1860s, when Irish men comprised about half the male prison

8

population there, Irish women made up 86 per cent of the female prison population.[35]

Irish women were not only over-represented in prison relative to women generally. They were also often more widely incarcerated than Irish males. Although women made up a higher proportion of the incarcerated population in these cities than is the case today, the numbers are remarkable. In Toronto Gaol, Irish females outnumbered Irish males every year between 1859 and 1868. In 1860, for instance, 529 of the 1,029 imprisoned males were Irish. In the same year, 820 of 1,027 incarcerated females were Irish.[36] At other Canadian correctional institutions, Irish girls and women were similarly imprisoned at higher rates than Irish boys and men.[37] The phenomenon is also evident in New York, where throughout the 1860s Irish females numerically outnumbered Irish males in prison.[38]

The frequent appearance of the Irish in police stations, courts, prisons and other institutions did not go unnoticed. The New York Association for Improving the Condition of the Poor (AICP) observed in 1860 that 'the excess of poverty and of crime also among the Irish as compared with the natives of other countries is a curious fact worthy the study of the political economist and ethnologist'.[39] Eight years later, AICP noted that 'the actual pauperism of the city mainly consisted of immigrants, and the accumulated refuse of about two and a half millions of that class who had landed in New York in the preceding 10 years. They were chiefly Irish, of the most thriftless habits'.[40] In 1867, a journalist from *The New York Times* compared Irish and German immigrants, the latter being said to arrive with around $100 each and then to go west. 'The Irish are different', the journalist wrote, 'They are mainly working people, coming over in search of an easy life and a lucky penny. The women vastly outnumber the men, and while there are exceptions, the great mass come without luggage and less money, but great expectations.'[41]

In some cases, such views of the Irish resulted in them being more heavily policed or incarcerated than other ethnic groups. But these attitudes, and the dramatic over-representation of the Irish in criminal statistics, changed with passing decades. One factor was that emigration from Ireland to the United States slowed. Between 1901 and 1910, for example, 173,656 female emigrants left Irish ports, compared to 557,634 between 1851 and 1860.[42] The socio-economic background of those who travelled had changed, and the new arrivals were likelier to be able to access decent employment and housing. By the twentieth century, the upwards socio-economic mobility of Irish and Irish American populations already in North America (which the mayor of Boston described in 1919 as 'One of the most remarkable chapters in the history of Boston') meant there was a stronger support network for new arrivals. These factors combined meant that the Irish were less likely to be driven to crime by poverty, and were less policed than their predecessors had been.[43] Immigrant populations from Eastern and Southern Europe took the place of the Irish at the bottom of the social hierarchy.[44]

In the ten chapters that follow, we tell the stories of Irish-born girls and women who were involved in diverse crimes in North America. Although there are some common threads to many of these stories – such as poverty, alcoholism and a lack of support networks – there is no singular Bad Bridget.

There were Bad Bridgets across the entire age spectrum, from girl offenders charged with being 'stubborn' or 'incorrigible' to career criminals active into their seventies and eighties. We look at Irish female immigrants who made careers of crime, and at others for whom the criminal case described in this book was their only appearance before the courts. Where we can, we have privileged the voices of the girls and women, even when it is mediated through prison or institution staff, or newspaper reports. The Irish-born girls and women who feature in the following chapters hailed from the thirty-two counties of Ireland, from urban and rural places, with a range of educational, religious and class backgrounds. They were married, unmarried, widowed and separated, mothers and without dependants. They all crossed the Atlantic Ocean at some point during the nineteenth or early twentieth centuries for a new life in North America and found themselves on the wrong side of the law.

1. Prostitution and the case of Marion Canning

On a warm summer's evening in July 1891, Marion Canning, who had migrated to New York City from County Leitrim around a year earlier, went 'up the Bowery', as she put it herself, 'to have some supper with a gentleman friend'.[1] The Bowery was a place of working-class entertainment, full of drinking establishments, theatres, dime museums and dance halls.[2] It was also a centre of commercial sex, with prostitutes soliciting on the streets or working from tenement brothels, cheap hotels and lodging houses.[3] Marion was a sex worker herself, and her 'gentleman friend' may well have been a client. She had turned nineteen only a few weeks earlier.

Later, as she made her way home alone in the early hours of the morning, she encountered Richard Bronkbank, a fireman recently arrived off the ship *Miranda* from South America. He approached her, asking, 'Do you want to go on a night's racket?' The pair walked on towards her house on Mulberry Street. When they got there, they disagreed about payment, and Richard accused Marion of stealing £5 sterling and his watch. At this point, their accounts differ. Richard claimed that he summoned a police officer to report the theft, but Marion insisted that it was she who called the policeman because she was being falsely accused. Marion was searched, and although neither the watch nor the money was discovered on her, she was charged with the crime, found guilty and sentenced to seven years in prison.

Before her arrest, Marion lived at 58 Mulberry Street in

New York, in the notorious Five Points neighbourhood (ill. 1.1). Jacob Riis, a social reformer and photographer who captured images of the area in the nineteenth century, described the Mulberry Bend, a curved part of Mulberry Street, as the 'foul core of New York's slums'.[4] By 1891, when Marion was living there, Mulberry Street was dominated by Italian immigrants, and it would later become part of Little Italy.[5] The 1880 census reveals seventy-four people living in the tenement house at number 58, all from Italian backgrounds; but the Irish immigrant presence was still felt, and a large number of Irish inhabited the tenement next door. When Marion was arrested, her bail was paid by an Italian man, Luigi Mega, who also lived at number 58.

1.1. Mulberry Street, New York City, c.1900.

Overcrowding in the tenements was one of Jacob Riis's main concerns as he photographed the area for his book *How the other half lives*, published a year before Marion Canning's arrest. Riis described the tenements, generally four to six storeys high with at least four families living on each floor, as:

nurseries of pauperism and crime that fill our jails and police courts; that throw off a scum of forty thousand human wrecks to the island asylums and workhouses year by year; that turned out in the last eight years a round half million beggars to prey upon our charities; that maintain a standing army of ten thousand tramps with all that that implies; because, above all, they touch the family life with deadly moral contagion.[6]

The dangers of the area were famously captured by Riis in the scene at 'Bandits' Roost', the alley at 59½ Mulberry Street (ill. 1.2). The image depicts members of one of the infamous gangs of the Lower East Side, one of them holding a club, while laundry dries above their heads.

1.2. Bandits' Roost, 59½ Mulberry Street, New York City.

Bandits' Roost was across the road from where Marion lived in 1891. The Leitrim teenager's tenement at number 58 was also home to a beer saloon, probably on the ground floor. A couple of weeks after Marion was arrested, a man called Michael Mayo, who lived in the same tenement and whose father kept the saloon, was accused of murder. Two years earlier, two Italian men were involved in a stabbing incident over money in the hallway of the saloon; and three years later Rosaio Marchiliano was stabbed to death in the saloon by his brother Gennario.[7]

A brothel or prostitution network also seems to have operated at number 58, which may explain how Marion ended up living there. A few months after Marion was sent to prison, Caroline Hayes, described by a journalist as 'a degraded looking creature' and a 'female bum', was brought before the court for drunkenness and was sentenced to two months in prison.[8] On her way out, she hissed at the arresting policeman, accusing him of being 'in the power of Italian Joe, who got you to do this. He's a murderer. I know he killed two women.' The presiding judge, overhearing this, questioned Caroline. She then revealed that Joe Rossa, who ran a 'headquarters for women' at number 58, had lived with her friend Kate Barry. He regularly assaulted Kate, Caroline claimed, which 'made poor Kate drink all the more; she wanted to die'. Caroline had been sent to prison the previous weekend for five days, and when she was released, she went to look for Kate and found out that she had died. She hadn't yet been buried, and when Caroline saw Kate's body in her coffin she noticed considerable bruising. Caroline also said that another woman, Annie Chambers, living in Joe Rossa's house, was 'almost dying from the beating' he'd given her and that he'd beaten a woman called Kate Reilly to death the previous August. 'It's justice that I want for them, sir', she told the judge. Caroline also claimed that she had refused Joe's invitations to live at his 'dive', and that because of that he 'put the cops on to her' any time she was even a little bit drunk.

The judge instructed the police to investigate Caroline's claims. But already biases were stacked against her. The detectives 'started out with the theory that Caroline Hayes had told a lying story'. After all, a journalist noted, 'What dependence could be placed on a statement of an outcast?' And although it was confirmed that Kate Barry had lived with Joe Rossa and had died, the coroner's ruling that Kate's death was caused by alcoholism meant that the police did not investigate further. While the truth of Caroline's statements cannot now be verified, it is clear that women with Irish-sounding names, who were part of or at least adjacent to Joe Rossa's prostitution network, resided in the same tenement building as Marion around the time that she lived there. Marion's life at 58 Mulberry Street is likely to have been a violent and dangerous one.

The prostitute life

The Five Points area was traditionally associated with Irish immigrants in the mid-nineteenth century. The notorious slum was built over a freshwater pond, causing sagging buildings and dampness.[9] In 1859, the New York Children's Aid Society described the area:

> At the windows, or on the door-steps, are the women of the class whose epithet, 'unfortunate,' only too feebly

pictures their wretched life, and more miserable death. In the basements . . . appears one of those filthy, bedraggled, blear-eyed, half-drunken Irish women, such alone as long habits of drinking, and the poverty of a city can produce. Every other shop is a drinking shop, and in some streets, each house seems a brothel.[10]

The hidden nature of prostitution can make it difficult to determine precisely how many Irish women like Marion Canning sold sex, but it was certainly far from unusual. A report on an inspection in Five Points in 1866 described the women in a brothel as 'brazen-faced, bloated, debauched young creatures; uncomely, unattractive and uneducated. They are mostly Irish. I saw but two faces that showed intellect.' The description of the next brothel inspected revealed even more of the author's feeling towards the Irish when he identified only one 'intelligent woman in the room . . . the rest of them were . . . unmistakably from the fatherland of the Fenians, every soul of them'.[11]

William Wallace Sanger, a renowned doctor and author, carried out a survey of prostitutes in New York in 1858 and found that 35 per cent of those questioned were from Ireland – double the Irish share of the city's population.[12] In Boston's House of Correction in the 1850s and 1860s, Irish women made up 37 per cent of all prostitutes.[13] And in Toronto, Irish women formed the majority of those convicted of offences relating to prostitution between 1855 and 1895.[14]

The charge against Marion Canning, of stealing Richard Bronkbank's watch, was not particularly unusual. Stealing from clients, and in particular the theft of watches, was a common charge against prostitutes.[15] It was an easy way for women to make extra money, especially given the likelihood that a client might not report it because of their embarrassment at having to say how the crime happened. In 1910, New York's *Democrat and Chronicle* provided a light-hearted account of such a theft. Prostitute Minnie Williams alias Kitty Williams allegedly 'nabbed $80 from Tootsie's pocket in a Syracuse resort last week', the newspaper reported. But 'Tootsie has a Mrs Tootsie and a couple of little Tootsies in a Syracuse suburb and it simply wouldn't do to bring the loss of the $80 into the public gaze.'[16] 'Tootsie' thus remained unnamed in the newspaper.

In New York, so-called panel houses developed, expressly designed to facilitate thefts from clients. When the client was in bed in the brothel, or suitably distracted, the woman's accomplice would sneak out from a hidden wall panel to steal his money or valuables.[17] Another tactic was revealed in the case of Mary Moran, also known as 'Irish Mary' or 'Honest Mary' (clearly an ironic moniker), described by *The New York Times* as an 'old time "panel" thief'. In January 1885, Moran was accused of stealing $50, a watch and chain, and a diamond stud from Ernest Washburne, a druggist in New York. This 'vulgar, frowsy-looking creature' had asked Ernest to go with her to a drinking saloon, where, when paying for the drinks, he 'exposed his money'. After they left the saloon, they came to the corner of West 3rd and Wooster streets, where Mary 'threw her arms about him and held him so tightly that he was helpless'. Her male accomplice stole his valuables. Mary had also supposedly stolen $34,000 in cash from a man who had returned from California and visited a brothel where she worked some years previously.[18]

Mary Ann Murphy appears in the Toronto Gaol records for a string of crimes in the 1870s, 1880s and 1890s, including drunkenness and assault, and four counts of stealing from clients.[19] In October 1870 she was accused of robbing a John Fahinbach of $3.75, but the case was dismissed when he was unable to identify her as a thief. Two years later she was back in court accused of stealing a silver watch and $80 from John Lithgow after going with him to a house to have sex. She was found not guilty. But Murphy was not as fortunate in January 1873, when she was found guilty of stealing a watch from George Watson, with whom she had gone to a laneway to have sex. She spent six months in prison. Over two decades later, in May 1896, she was again arrested for stealing a gold watch from a client.

For many women, especially streetwalkers with a largely working-class clientele, prostitution was not a lucrative business. Drogheda-born Mamie McGavisk admitted when arrested for being a common nightwalker in Boston in 1914 that she 'Has been with three men a night but has never made very much money.'[20] While most Irish women in New York and elsewhere tended to work at the poorer end of the industry, some catered for a more upmarket clientele. Galway-born Mary O'Malley made clear in 1914 that she specifically avoided picking up men on the streets of Lowell, Massachusetts:

> Went lots of times to one hotel – Merrimac – getting $2.00 and sometimes making $10.00 a night. . . . Some of them I used to stay all night with and get about $7.00. . . . The first one I ever went to a hotel with was a policeman, a man in plain clothes, who just took me to a drinking room. Just stayed and talked with him. There were three or four other fellows and girls there. I used to get introductions to the men by other girls – never picked up any one on the street.

The fellows would speak to me four or five times, but I wouldn't look at them.[21]

O'Malley stressed the difference, as she perceived it, between her work in hotels and selling sex on the street.

Some prostitutes lived and worked in luxurious surroundings.[22] Maud Merrill, who migrated aged eighteen from Cork to New York in 1870, left a job as a domestic servant to work in the sex industry. She ended up living in a high-class brothel with six other women at 10 Neilson Place in Greenwich Village. It was described as being 'gorgeously furnished' with velvet-carpeted floors and an abundance of paintings on the walls, 'many of them of rare merit and beauty'. Maud's 'large and richly appointed chamber' was on the third floor:

> A thick, soft carpet covered the floor, costly lace curtains and damask lambrequins shaded the windows, a lofty pier-glass, surmounted by broad gold-washed cornices, occupied one end of the room, and was reflected at the other end by an immense mirror set in the door of a rosewood wardrobe. On one side of the room was a high, carved bedstead.[23]

Maud also had invitations to high-class social events. On 9 December 1872, for instance, she attended a masquerade ball at the Argyle Rooms on Sixth Avenue. This was a far cry from the tenements of Mulberry Street where Marion Canning lived, and the streets of the Bowery where she worked.

Motivations to sell sex

Maud Merrill and Marion Canning both made a choice to work as prostitutes. A combination of factors could lead women into sex work, including the break-up of families, loss of support networks, or an inability to get or hold down an alternative job. Prostitution offered flexibility for those who could not, or did not want to, work regular hours, or who had children to mind. Ellen Cassidy appeared at the Toronto police court in June 1906 with her five-month-old baby in her arms, charged with being a 'frequenter of a house of ill fame'. Her plea to the judge, that she had no idea the house was a brothel and she had only been there for five minutes, was not believed. She was given a choice between paying a fine of $10 plus costs, or serving thirty days in prison. For financial reasons, she opted for the latter, presumably taking her baby to prison with her.[24] Dublin-born Georgiana Long, who had migrated to New York in February 1851, made a good living by tailoring. She married Richard Long, a first mate of the ship *Midwinter*, at Easter 1854. Only a few months later he was lost at sea along with the vessel and the rest of the crew on the way to Charleston, leaving behind a pregnant Georgiana. She gave birth to a son in December 1854 and supported herself for about three years after her husband's death until a Mr McIlwain offered to support her if she would become his mistress. She agreed and lived with him for a year before 'he turned her off and she gave herself to drink and a life of prostitution'. She later entered a Magdalene Asylum, but she was found to be suffering from a sexually transmitted infection and was sent to hospital.[25] Stella Weymouth began to sell sex in Boston following desertion by her US-born husband in December 1914. She insisted: 'I had to go some place to do something for myself'.[26]

Prostitution was also sometimes seen to offer a more attractive lifestyle, as in the case of Maud Merrill. Maud and her younger sister Charlotte were funded to emigrate by their maternal uncle, Robert Bleakley, who was already in New York. Charlotte emigrated first, and when Maud arrived in New York in 1870, she found her a job as a servant. Maud held several such positions over the next few months until her Uncle Robert helped her to get a job with the Rev. Mr Williams, an Episcopalian church minister. According to the *Brooklyn Daily Eagle*, Williams repeatedly asked Maud for character references before and after employing her, but she kept providing excuses as to why she did not have any references from previous employers. She then asked to get paid, but Williams refused because she had not yet worked a full month, and agreed to give her only a portion. That evening Maud's uncle, Robert Bleakley, called to the house. The Rev. Williams remembered that Robert, who seemed to have taken drink to steady his nerve, claimed that 'his niece had informed him that I had taken improper liberties with her'. Williams emphatically denied this, alleging that Robert was trying to blackmail him:

> I was willing that everyone should know all that happened
> while she was in my house; that my other servant was in the
> house all the time she was here, and further that if his object
> was to make money, he might spare himself the trouble, for
> I had none.

Unsurprisingly, given the accusation that had been made, Williams terminated Maud's employment.

In December 1871, a Mrs Hall hired Maud as a servant from New York's Female Employment Society. Hall would later recall that 'we all thought that she was a very nice girl and uncommon modest'. Around two months into this job, Maud's Uncle Robert visited her again. Shortly after he arrived, Maud 'came down the stairs looking very excited' and reported to a fellow servant that her uncle had slapped her across the face. He followed her downstairs, calling her a 'd[amned] w[hore]'. He asked Hall if she was aware that she was 'keeping an improper character in the house'. After he had left, Hall dismissed Maud for having 'misrepresented herself to me'. This dismissal from another job after questions were raised about her morals seems to have been the point at which Maud moved into prostitution on a full-time basis.

Charlotte later begged her older sister Maud to stop working in the sex industry. Maud agreed to stop after Christmas: 'she could not conveniently do it' straight away. Maud clearly equated sex work with economic stability, and without character references from her jobs in domestic service she knew that she would not easily secure other work. In addition to the necessity to provide for their own needs, Irish women were often under pressure to send money home to relatives in Ireland. For those in between jobs, who struggled to find work or who wanted to supplement a low income, sex work offered a financial opportunity.[27]

We don't know what led Marion Canning into sex work, but she had only been in New York a relatively short period of time and seemed to be without family or a support network. William Sanger believed that large numbers of prostitutes existed among immigrant populations because 'malign influences' imparted 'vicious ideas to young people' upon their arrival in port cities. Newly arrived girls and young women, Sanger wrote, would be 'exposed to the tender mercies of the emigrant boarding-house keepers, generally themselves natives of the "old country," who, having been swindled on their arrival, are both competent and willing to practice the same impositions on others'.[28] The Toronto Magdalene Asylum's annual report for 1859 expressed similar concerns about young immigrants arriving alone and without support: 'Ours is a land of strangers – and, as such, it presents many dangers to the young, the unprotected, and the friendless female. When she lands on the shores of our towns and cities, the tempter, and the seducer are not far distant'. Two years later, the annual report described how 'Some of the most affecting cases we have had to deal with, were those of young strangers arriving in this country, who having no friends to receive them, no emigrant's home to go to, were too easily entrapped in the snare of the soul hunter and soul destroyer.'[29]

Newspapers told tales of young Irish women being tricked or lured into brothels. In October 1856 a *New York Times* article recounted how Irish immigrant Eliza Thompson travelled to New York City to meet her sister, who was arriving from Dublin. She asked the conductor of the car in which she travelled to help her find a boarding house because she was unfamiliar with New York. He put her in the charge of a policeman, who took her 'to a house of prostitution'. Eliza had been 'neatly dressed' and had $15, but after the policeman left, the landlady confiscated the money and 'stripped the girl of all her apparel and put on her an old worn-out dress and soiled linen. She was then placed in a private room and a man was introduced, who attempted to commit an outrage on the person, but was foiled in his attempt.' Eliza remained at the house for a couple of days, trying to recover her money and clothing, 'until the brutality of the mistress of the house drove her into the street'.[30] Another newly arrived Irish woman was hired as a servant by a woman named Jackson at New York's emigration depot, Castle Garden in Manhattan, in 1869, but on reaching the house found herself 'basely entrapped' in a brothel.[31] A similar scandal struck an assisted-emigration scheme that facilitated the passage of around 1,250 Irish women to North America between 1850 and 1857.[32] In May 1857, twelve women sneaked off their boat with some sailors when it docked in New York. Two of them, Susan Smith and Ellen Neary, ended up in a brothel. Susan was later found wandering 'covered with bruises and her body with rags'.[33]

Rescue homes and missions told of the girls and women who had come to their institutions claiming to have been tricked or enticed into sex work. Dublin-born Ann Conway, orphaned at the age of nine and an immigrant in the United States by the age of eleven, boarded with a family in New York, where, according to the Five Points Mission, 'she was drugged so that she was unconscious of what she did and became a prostitute'. She had apparently since 'been very wretched [and] wishes to reform'. With the help of the Five Points Mission staff, she was looked after and then secured work as a servant in 1857.[34] The same year, the Toronto Magdalene Asylum told of an Irish woman 'with irreproachable character' who 'went to service in a tavern', where she 'learned to drink to excess, and had to leave her place' and couldn't find anywhere to stay. A couple who found the forlorn figure crying on the street brought her to a police station for shelter. In the morning, another woman engaged her as a servant and took her home. This employer 'seemed very kind and gave her whiskey freely; in the evening the house became filled with disreputable characters'. The woman fled into the street, where she was arrested by a policeman for drunkenness and sent to prison for a month. There 'she associated with the lost and abandoned, and when discharged she did not care what became of her'. She was saved from this life by the matron of the jail, who advised her to go to the Asylum.[35]

Terrifying stories of what could happen to young

vulnerable women seemed to justify the work of 'rescue' organizations, and strengthened claims that there was a need to better protect young Irish female migrants.[36] It was also often necessary for women to express remorse at being involved in the sex industry or to blame others if they wanted help from a charity or to receive a lighter prison sentence. And so the image of the helpless victim, a seduced innocent led astray through no fault of her own, or tricked or forced into prostitution, emerges from the records, even though for many women prostitution was an economic necessity and a choice, albeit from extremely limited options.[37] Ellen Katan, an Irish Protestant whose family lived in Boston, worked as a servant in New York until she 'was led from the path of virtue'. She lived as a prostitute until she was found in 1857 on the streets and helped by the Five Points Mission into the Magdalene Asylum.[38] Annie Bartlett, from County Tyrone, had, it was claimed, been imprisoned by a 'wicked landlady' in a beer saloon where she was trapped in 'disgusting slavery' and her 'ruin was accomplished by force'. But she 'rebelled' and was rescued and brought to the Five Points House of Industry in 1860.[39]

Concerns about 'white slavery' peaked in the first two decades of the twentieth century in North America and elsewhere.[40] It was feared that young women were being taken from the streets and forced into prostitution. In a police raid on a brothel in early twentieth-century Chicago, a 'big Irish girl was taken and held as a witness'. She was considered 'old enough, strong enough, and wise enough . . . to have overcome almost every kind of opposition, even physical violence. She could have put up a fight which few men, no matter how brutal, would care to meet.' She explained why she did not leave:

Get out! I can't. They make us buy the cheapest rags, and they are charged against us at fabulous prices; they make us change outfits at intervals of two or three weeks, until we are so deeply in debt that there is no hope of ever getting out from under. Then, to make such matters worse, we seldom get an accounting oftener than once in six months, and sometimes ten months or a year will pass between settlements, and when we do get an accounting it is always to find ourselves deeper in debt than before. We've simply got to stick, and that's all there is to it.[41]

Various institutions were set up to protect young women arriving in North American cities. The Mercy Sisters set up a House of Mercy in New York in 1848, which offered shelter and found jobs mostly for Irish women; and in 1883 the Mission of Our Lady of the Rosary for the Protection of Irish Immigrant Girls was established in the same city.[42] Staff of the latter met ships and offered accommodation to those without relatives or friends in New York and found them employment. Similar concerns in Boston led in 1883 to the suggestion that the Charitable Irish Society establish 'a home for the homeless respectable girls of our race cast upon our shores, many of whom are enticed into dens of infamy for the want of shelter on their arrival in the city'.[43]

In all three cities a variety of institutions to reform those who had entered a 'life of sin' were established by lay Protestant women and Catholic religious orders. But not all women who entered institutions were successfully 'reformed'. Twenty-year-old Mary Cotton, who had been 'living a bad life a long time', entered the home run by the New York Women's Prison Association (WPA) in June 1848, 'desirous of doing well now'. Although she 'behaved very well while in the house', it was recorded that she 'returned to evil courses' after leaving on an errand and failing to return.[44] Other women in the WPA Home showed little remorse for their actions and no desire to improve their behaviour. Honora Maxwell, a forty-year-old widow without children, had been in New York for twelve years when she entered the WPA Home in February 1848. Staff despaired of what to do with her, considering this was a case 'that there could be but little hope of, and one which we could never recommend, she was so rough in her manner and noisy about the house'. They admitted that she 'went out to see about getting a place for herself and did not return, which was a great relief to us as we had for a long time been thinking about getting her away but did not know how we were to accomplish it'.[45] Similarly, 22-year-old Bridget Scanlin had 'lived a bad life for a long time' when she entered the Home in March 1848. Staff considered that 'There seems but little to be said as we can say no good. We could not recommend her to anyone'.[46]

Marion Canning in her testimony in court admitted that she had 'lived a life of shame' since the previous January. But neither Marion nor Maud Merrill entered any of the reform or rescue institutions for sex workers in New York. Like many other women in similar situations, they may have had little interest in being 'reformed' or submitting to the strict conditions of life in a Magdalene Asylum or home.

The fates of Maud Merrill and Marion Canning

At around a quarter to four on 10 December 1872, Robert Bleakley rang the doorbell of 10 Neilson Place, the brothel where his niece, Maud Merrill, was living. Charlotte, Maud's sister, had been due to visit her that day, but Robert had insisted that he would go instead because 'he would not have any relative of his visit a house of prostitution'. A hairdresser in the house at 10 Neilson Place opened the door and directed Robert, whom she noticed was well dressed, up to Maud's room. The housekeeper, Mary Ann Allison, heard strange noises coming from the room and went to investigate. She encountered Robert on the stairs, 'cool and unconcerned'. When she asked him about the noise, he replied: 'I have just killed my niece, and I am going to give myself up.' Mary Ann rushed up to the room and found Maud lying face down.

A coroner's inquest later showed that Maud had been shot three times, in her chest, shoulder and right arm, and two other bullets were found lodged in the walls of her bedroom. Maud's body was described as:

> clad in a handsomely wrought flowing robe of fine, white linen, stained with blood from the wounds. With a neat little jacket of dark blue cloth, elaborately trimmed with gold braid, carelessly thrown about the shoulders, it lay with the right hand, ornamented with jewels, naturally reposing upon the chest, whilst the left was extended beside the body.

A journalist evoked Maud's funeral: 'At the head sat the sister of the deceased, an intelligent young girl of seventeen, while around the remains were twenty of the murdered girl's companions.' The pastor spoke to them, 'dwelling on the tragic death of their unfortunate friend, and implored them by the memory of their infant days, their affectionate parents and in the name of everything high and holy, to determine over the dead body of their companion to give up a life of sin and shame and seek to lead virtuous lives'.

In his confession to the police, Robert Bleakley claimed

that he had killed his niece 'to redeem her from her evil ways into which she had fallen'. His defence at his trial portrayed him as a 'religious fanatic' who killed his niece because 'she would not listen to his entreaties and reform, but insisted on leading a life of shame'. The killing, it was argued, was the 'aberration of a diseased mind', and his counsel made an insanity plea, using evidence of hereditary insanity among relatives in Ireland as well as his suicide attempt while in jail. But the jury decided that Robert was not insane, and he was found guilty of murder in the second degree and sentenced to life in prison.

While Maud Merrill's life ended tragically at the hands of a family member, Marion Canning's life was changed for the better by a relative. At the back of her case file in the New York Municipal Archives is a letter from her father, Thomas Canning, in Mohill, County Leitrim, to the judge who had tried her. The letter is dated 11 April 1892, eight months after Marion had been sentenced to seven years in prison. In the letter Thomas appealed to the judge's 'humane clemency' and asked if he would 'mitigate the sentence' or release her 'on the condition that I would take her home at once out of the country'. He pleaded with the judge to grant his request, which would 'give peace to her disconsolate and broken-hearted parents'. Marion had presumably written to her father about her situation, or perhaps the news found its way to Mohill through other immigrants who knew her in New York. But Thomas Canning didn't quite have all the details, and he admitted to the judge, 'I know not the cause of her misfortune.'

The judge replied that he was unable to do anything because the sentence had been passed, but advised Thomas Canning to write to the governor of New York State, who had the power to re-examine Marion's case. This Thomas did the following month. He pleaded with Governor Roswell P. Flower to 'accede to the prayers of the unfortunate child's parents, far separated as they are from her' and grant Marion's release from prison. The situation was, Thomas Canning insisted, 'heartrending . . . to an Irish parents heart'. He repeated his offer to travel to New York to collect Marion or to pay for her transport home. The district attorney who re-examined the case considered that Thomas's first letter was of 'such character' that he had enclosed a copy for the governor. He also felt that Thomas's offer to either collect Marion or pay for her passage home to Ireland and 'insure a proper life on the part of this wayward girl' strongly added to the 'merits of this application'.

The district attorney's investigation also revealed some troubling facts about Marion's prosecution. He spoke to James Downing, the police officer who had arrested Marion, himself an Irish immigrant. Downing explained that he had wondered at the time whether to even take Marion into custody because Richard Bronkbank behaved 'in such an unsatisfactory manner'. He decided to let his superior officer decide, and it was this superior who made the decision to arrest Marion. Downing patrolled the area where Marion was apprehended and knew that she was a prostitute, but he considered she was 'not of the low character of those who ordinarily frequent that neighbourhood'. He gave a further qualified compliment that 'so far as she could enjoy the same, following that nefarious calling, her character was good'; that she was of 'respectable parentage'; and that her course in life 'was more the fault of others than any evil tendency' on her part. This viewpoint had not been aired at the trial because, as the district attorney found out, Officer Downing had been on holiday when the case was heard.

The district attorney felt that the verdict would have been very different had the court had all the information that he now had, and so he recommended clemency and a pardon. The governor agreed and wrote to Thomas Canning in September 1892 to tell him the good news. Thomas was obviously delighted, but perhaps regretted his offer to travel to the United States now that it had been taken up. He replied saying that, 'having a large family to maintain', and given that 'times in Ireland at present is anything but good for making money', he 'would find it very hard to meet the double expense of traveling to and fro America'. Instead, he proposed to meet his daughter in Liverpool, 'and bring her home and will assure you she will never again visit that Country'. Thomas signed off his correspondence from 'her poor broken hearted mother and afflicted father'. He sent a £5 bank draft to the governor's office in January 1893 to pay for Marion's passage home.

She was released on 11 February 1893 after nineteen months in prison. Marion did return home and got married soon after. It's unlikely that anyone in Mohill ever knew the exact details of what had happened to her in New York. The disgrace attached to being in prison could have been enough to prevent a marriage taking place, never mind the additional shame of having been involved in sex work. Thomas not only saved Marion from a longer stay in prison, but also from a rough and dangerous life in New York afterwards. Perhaps he never found out the precise details of the charge against her, and perhaps he never asked.

2. Unmarried motherhood and the case of Rosie Quinn

2.1. The Fifth Avenue Hotel, undated.

The Fifth Avenue Hotel was a landmark in early twentieth-century Manhattan. The six-storey white marble building, which occupied an entire block at the corner of Fifth Avenue and Twenty-Third Street, was a venue for national and regional conferences, society events and political gatherings, and for several years it was the headquarters of the Republican State and National Committees. (ill. 2.1.)

The hotel was also home to the so-called Amen Corner, where wealthy and prominent New York men gathered nightly on four plush red sofas to talk and debate. It took its name from the practice of shouting 'amen' to indicate

34

agreement on an issue. Invitees to the annual Amen Corner dinner in 1904 in honour of New York City's mayor, George McClellan, included President Theodore Roosevelt, Governor Benjamin Barker Odell Jr, Senators Thomas C. Platt and Chauncey Depew, nine Supreme Court Justices, a number of Representatives and judges, as well as prominent businessmen and newspapermen.[1] One of the founding members and directors of the Amen Corner was General Charles Furlong, who had lived in the Fifth Avenue Hotel since the 1870s. He had been on General Ulysses S. Grant's staff in the Civil War and remained a close friend of Grant, who became the eighteenth president of the United States.[2] Journalists, too, often lingered around the hotel hoping for gossip or a whiff of scandal.

The hotel's illustrious guests would have noticed that many employees spoke with Irish accents. Of 153 live-in workers at the hotel on the night of 13 June 1900, 111 were Irish-born, according to that year's census.[3] By 1902, Rosie Quinn was among them.[4] The teenager, who was considered exceptionally beautiful, had secured a job at the hotel following her emigration from Ireland around 1900. The hotel's housekeeper, Bessie Dunbrack, would later describe Rosie Quinn as a very good worker, 'honest, faithful and attentive to her duties'. She had made a good impression in a short time.

At some point in the autumn of 1902, Rosie took leave from the hotel without telling anyone where she was going. A few weeks later, she returned to her work and lodgings at the hotel. And then, on 11 December, Rosie was arrested at the hotel and charged with the murder of her three-week-old daughter. The police had found a baby's body in a lake in Central Park and had traced the infant back to Rosie.

Upon her arrest, Rosie confessed that she had given birth during her absence from work. She had stayed in hospital with her baby to recuperate for three weeks following the birth, and when she left she wandered the streets of New York, unsure where to go. She asked a policeman for help and he directed her to the Foundling Hospital. She claimed that she followed his advice but that the Foundling Hospital wouldn't take her child, and that she received the same answer at the other charitable institutions she tried. In desperation, believing that she, an unmarried mother, and her baby born out of wedlock, had nothing to live for, she went to Central Park. Rosie described her despair to the policeman who arrested her: 'I went to the park, intending to throw myself and baby into the lake, I was so blue. I got to the stone bridge and was looking into the water thinking about it, when the baby slipped out of my arms into the lake. Then I got scared and ran away.'

Rosie Quinn was tried for murder in April 1903. After hearing the evidence across three days, the twelve men of the jury found her guilty of second-degree murder, and presiding Justice Francis Scott sentenced her to life in prison. The nineteen-year-old fainted on hearing the sentence and later cried as she was led out of the court. She was transferred to the state prison for women at Auburn, in upstate New York, later that month. (ill. 2.2.)

Rosie Quinn's story is shocking, but the circumstances that led to her crime were relatively common for Irish women. Some who became pregnant out of wedlock in North America married their boyfriends before or soon after childbirth. Others raised their infants alone or with new partners, or returned to Ireland, where they had family support. But Rosie Quinn was one of many who resorted to illegal abortions, child desertion or infanticide.

2.2. Rosie Quinn at her trial.

The shame

Rosie Quinn would have been only too aware of the stigma attached to pregnancies like hers. The jury who tried her considered her, as one juror later wrote, 'disgraced in the eyes of the world, friendless and deserted . . . as she wandered in the Park on that fateful Sunday afternoon'. They judged that the crime occurred because 'her disgrace overpowered her'. The foreman of the jury described how 'her hopelessness . . . and without any realization of the

37

awful nature of the deed, she took the life of her unfathered child'.

Of course, Rosie Quinn's baby did have a father. Bessie Dunbrack, the housekeeper at the Fifth Avenue Hotel where Rosie worked, considered her 'unfortunate . . . in meeting a man utterly without principle'. There appears to have been little discussion of the father of the baby or his whereabouts during the trial, likely because he was not directly involved in the crime. But he was identified in an article in the *Evening World* after the trial. The reporter, using some journalistic licence, described how 'one summer night on a trolley ride' a 'big lad in soldier blue' called John Warren first encountered Rosie. According to the article, a relationship developed and 'she dreamed of leaving service and becoming John Warren's wife'. But before that could happen, John was sent by the United States Army to Portland, Maine. He reportedly stopped writing back to Rosie on learning that she was pregnant, and so she gave birth alone in the Lying-in Hospital in New York. She left hospital with only fifty cents to her name, given to her by a kindly nurse.

Rosie Quinn became pregnant in the US, but for many Irish migrants an unwanted pregnancy was the incentive to leave Ireland. Commenting on the 'constant flood of immigration' to New York in the 1850s, William Wallace Sanger referred to women who 'become mothers almost as soon as they land on these shores; in fact the probability of such an event sometimes hastens their departure'.[5] Emigration to North America was a way to conceal an unwanted pregnancy at a time when an unmarried mother and her offspring were often ostracized in Ireland. Pregnant women feared rejection by their own families, who were worried about their social status and reputations, and about the impact of single motherhood on employment and marriage prospects.

Protestant and Catholic Irish women alike saw emigration as a way to escape the shame of an out-of-wedlock pregnancy. Maggie Tate, a Protestant, left Ireland for New York, according to an investigation by a charitable society, to 'cover her shame'. Described as a 'poor friendless girl with a babe', she expected the father of her child to join her in the United States and fulfil his promise to marry her, but he never arrived.[6] Some pregnant women were encouraged by relatives, friends or partners to leave home, while others kept their pregnancies entirely secret.

Irish women who emigrated hoping to avoid the stigma of a pregnancy outside marriage in their home country might have succeeded in getting away from a censorious family or community, but they encountered similar attitudes in the US. The Society for Helping Destitute Mothers and Infants in Boston wrote in 1878 of a young woman being 'turned out of her place by the employer who has discovered her situation'.[7] Bridget Mahoney was a 'young girl, yet in her teens', when she became pregnant in Ireland by 35-year-old Tim Dorgan, the brother of her employer. He persuaded her to emigrate and allegedly 'satisfied her heart with pictures of a speedy reunion, declared that he would follow soon to claim and care for his wife, and provided her with the money to pay for her journey across the ocean'. She landed in Quebec in 1883 and travelled onward to join friends in Boston. She seems to have worked for a while to support herself, but left her job as a domestic servant when her due date approached. She tried but, being obviously pregnant, failed to secure a place to live. In the end, Mahoney gave birth to her son in knee-deep snow on Waitt's Mountain, a hill in Malden, north of the city.[8] Another Irish migrant, Winifred Ruane, became pregnant after having sex with the son of her employer at a restaurant in Boston. She tried unsuccessfully to get another job after the birth of her baby but 'failed in the attempt [and] grew discouraged'. She was later arrested for leaving her son at a stranger's door.[9]

Even women with friends or relatives in the United States could not necessarily expect support. Sligo-born Elizabeth McGetterick was willing to assist her sister Ellen Kildunne, convicted of abandoning her infant son born outside marriage in Massachusetts in 1916, 'in any way possible', but she did 'not wish to have anything to do with Ellen's baby'.[10] In this climate, many women went to great lengths to prevent anyone from noticing that they were pregnant. In June 1870, Ellen McCarty told police in Toronto that she threw the dead body of her new-born baby into the water closet. Mary Healy, who lived with McCarty, said she had been completely unaware that the 27-year-old was pregnant: 'she never mentioned it to me, she complained of being swelled but attributed it to other causes.'[11] Mayo-born Elizabeth Preston laughed off her employer's comments on her increasing size, 'saying it was because she ate so much and did not walk off in the hot weather'.[12] In October 1915, 26-year-old Preston gave birth to a premature baby shortly after carrying rugs across a cellar floor. Only a few days before, she had carried two mattresses up the stairs. Following childbirth, according to her own account, she 'rolled the child up in cloths. Continued her work about the house.'[13]

But not all Irish unmarried mothers felt shame at their situations. Some raised their babies alone because they had the resources or support to do so, while others returned to Ireland with their American-born offspring in tow. Mary

McPater, who gave birth outside marriage in the 1870s, went from Flatbush Hospital to the New York Society for the Aid of Friendless Women and Children and stayed for one night. Her entry on the admission register recorded her as 'a bold impertinent girl' who 'said there was no harm about her if she were not married'.[14]

The fathers

Staff at The Haven, which supported unmarried mothers in Toronto, asked in 1891: 'Where are these fathers? . . . they are *never to be found*.'[15] The Haven's superintendent wrote to one putative father: 'We do not wish to be hard on you, but we think that any manly sort of man would be glad to help bear at least a part of the burden which presses so heavily on the unfortunate object of his passion.'[16]

In Ireland, men sometimes paid for pregnant women to emigrate. James Haley Brennan, a 'gentleman farmer' from Carlow, got Maria McGrath pregnant and then paid for her passage to the United States around 1868. She landed penniless: Brennan was interested only in distancing himself from her, not in providing for her welfare or that of their unborn child.[17] Sometimes, fathers in Ireland promised a subsequent reunion. In 1886, twenty-year-old unmarried Kate Sullivan, who had been in New York only a few months, was charged with infant murder.[18] A journalist in the city courtroom a few months later observed: 'Tears came to her eyes, and the words, tinged with an Irish brogue, came with effort.' She described having been duped by the son of a farmer for whom she worked in Ireland. He had allegedly 'shipped her over here, promising to follow on the next steamer' but did not.

Kate Sullivan seems to have concealed her pregnancy right to the end. Agnes Conners, the woman for whom she worked as a domestic servant, admitted: 'I saw nothing that would make me think that she was in a condition to have a child.' Sullivan was in fact pregnant with twins. She later admitted her guilt, claiming that the babies were born at her employer's house and lived for only around ten minutes. She took the bodies with her when she left this job a few days later. Other reports placed the birth at 98 Manhattan Street, where Sullivan had moved in with a relative after leaving Conners' house and where a janitor discovered the twins' bodies in the water closet. Rumours circulated that neighbours in adjoining apartments had heard a woman crying in pain and another woman directing 'Silence! Damn you! Lay down there! You will get over it.' Sullivan may have pretended that the birth occurred at her workplace to protect this other woman. But regardless of whether or not she had female assistance during the labour, it is certain that she received no help from the babies' father. Sullivan later pleaded guilty to manslaughter, and the sentence was suspended because of the sympathy that her case generated.

The stories of pregnant Irish women being abandoned by treacherous lovers are many. Kate McKinney killed herself by jumping from a ferry after her unnamed boyfriend left her. A journalist reporting on the case vehemently attested: 'May the brand of Cain be stamped upon the brow of the base seducer, and the ghost of his murdered victim haunt him to the grave!'[19] In 1844, John Jones, a button maker in New York, was brought before the courts for procuring an abortion for a teenager, Catherine Costello. She had worked for Jones for around four months, making buttons for $2 per week, and they had begun a sexual relationship after about two months. He then dismissed her, allegedly because she didn't get on with the other women who worked for him. She claimed that after she told him about her pregnancy he manhandled her into a room and forced her to take abortifacient medicine, resulting in a stillbirth.[20] A journalist in the courtroom reported that 'her plain, unvarnished story of seduction, and subsequent abortion, as detailed before the Grand Jurors, caused many a tear to trickle down the cheeks of the father and the brother, as she related it with heart-broken sighs and exhibitions of sorrow and distress'.[21] Whether Costello's story was entirely true or not – witnesses at the trial cast doubt on some of her claims – she clearly generated sympathy in court. The narrative of the seduced and abandoned damsel in distress was one that many could believe.

In both Ireland and North America, relatives, neighbours or clergy might encourage – or pressurize – a single man into marrying a woman he had impregnated.[22] But Irish female migrants on their own in America often lacked that support. One of the jurors at Rosie Quinn's trial later mused: 'Had she but one friend to whom she could have turned for consolation or advice, we are convinced, the crime would never have been committed.' Caroline Palmer, who was following Rosie's trial in the newspapers, also recognized how the lack of support might have motivated the crime. She wrote to New York's governor, Benjamin Barker Odell Jr, shortly after Rosie was convicted:

My heart is so burdened for that poor ignorant Irish girl (alone in a strange country, deserted by lover and friends) Rosie Quinn that I cannot rest . . . I have never seen the child [Rosie] but my heart aches for her and I would gladly help her to lead a new life if allowed – having two daughters of my own I cannot but feel that only 'by the grace of God' they were not in her place.

Rosie Quinn's pregnancy seems to have resulted from a consensual relationship, but other Irish girls and women were vulnerable to unwanted attention, sexual harassment, sexual abuse and rape. Catherine Kelly emigrated from County Leitrim to New York as a teenager in the early 1860s and travelled on to Lowell, Massachusetts, where she worked as an operative in a mill. She ended up in the poorhouse when she became pregnant after being raped. The rapist, a machinist in Lowell, was arrested but later escaped from police custody.[23]

Roscommon-born Margaret Murphy, who landed in New York in 1859 after her aunt paid her passage, claimed that she was raped by Michael Staunton in his mother's house in Lowell, Massachusetts. The nineteen-year-old domestic servant sought to have him arrested on the following day, but he fled. She later realized that she was pregnant.[24]

Some women may have felt unable to leave their jobs to escape work-based harassment or abuse because they had little support or money to fall back on, or may have been reluctant to press charges due to fear of reputational damage.[25] Domestic servants in North America were particularly at risk of sexual exploitation, because they typically lived in at their place of work. An unmarried mother could also find herself more vulnerable to sexual harassment than other women. Dorothy Eddis, who was involved with the Big Sister Association in Toronto, complained in 1918: 'When a girl has been in trouble of this kind and other men know of it, some of them think it gives them the privilege of abusing her also, she becomes "lawful prey" in other words.' Even the younger sister of an unwed mother, she noted, 'has had improper proposals made to her because of her sister'.[26] The tendency for Irish girls and women to travel alone and at a young age likely increased their chances of becoming pregnant outside marriage. The Boston Children's Aid Society acknowledged in 1904 that many of the unmarried mothers they dealt with 'are so young that they are properly counted upon our records as children, and require to be treated as children, and yet recognized as mothers'.[27]

While many Irish women had sex with men they thought they would marry, it is clear that others weren't thinking long term. Margaret Slattery, who migrated at the age of fourteen, was charged with the murder of her new-born son in Boston when she was twenty. The domestic servant admitted to the police that she didn't marry the father of her child 'because she did not like him', making clear that this was her decision.[28] George Bienvenue insisted that he had asked Ellen Kildunne to marry him several times after she became pregnant in 1915 but she refused, 'claiming that through [her] maternal grandmother in Ireland she would inherit some property which she would lose if married'. Kildunne abandoned their baby in a side street in Milton, Massachusetts, as she made her way from Boston to her sister's house. The baby was found face down and naked, but alive, by the police about half an hour after he was abandoned. Kildunne later told officials that she 'would not marry him [Bienvenue] because he was a Protestant'.[29]

Daisy Carey from Kilrush, County Clare, met George Whitman when she served him at Floyd's Cafeteria on Pearl Street in Boston. She spotted that George and his male companion had 'a pamphlet . . . on marriage written by a doctor'.

According to George, Daisy insisted that 'she c[oul]d show them something better than that, and the next night brought a very indecent photograph of herself'. This was the beginning of a relationship that resulted in a pregnancy. Daisy wanted to 'take some medicine' to abort the pregnancy, but George, she said, 'forbade her to do this, saying he w[oul]d stand by her and marry her'. True to his word, he provided her with an apartment, and paid her bills and a weekly allowance, but she consistently refused to marry him. On being questioned by a child protection agent, Daisy admitted that she liked a travelling salesman she was courting 'better than she does Mr Whitman'.[30]

Without supervision and community surveillance, many Irish women in North American cities had more freedom than at home to engage in sexual relationships. Catherine Conboy, imprisoned in 1914 on a charge of nightwalking, recounted her adolescence in County Galway in the 1890s: 'We had no fellows in the old country; my bro[ther]s would kill us.'[31] Eighteen-year-old Ellen O'Neil migrated from her parents' house in County Cork to South Boston, where her sister lived, and secured work in hotels. She admitted on imprisonment for the manslaughter of her new-born baby that she 'has been going with fast men, and got in trouble'.[32] Irish women's casual sexual relationships didn't go unnoticed by their self-appointed moral guardians. George Deshon, a Catholic priest, expressed concern in his 1871 *Guide for Catholic young women* living in the US that 'many a girl has no father or mother to look out for her and advise her' and 'far more discretion and prudence is required on the part of a young woman in this country than anywhere else'. He particularly warned against 'late visiting' of men to young women's houses, which 'has been the devil's means of ruining thousands on thousands of well disposed, good young women'.[33]

There were laws providing women with avenues to secure financial support from the fathers of their children, but they were limited. In Canada (as in Ireland at this time), a woman could sue the father of her child for breaking his promise to marry her if she had evidence to prove they had been engaged, was aware of the legislation, and had the desire and resources to bring a case.[34] Staff at institutions like New York's Almshouse used the courts to force fathers to pay child maintenance to women living in their care.[35] Massachusetts legislation in 1911 allowed for the imprisonment of a father who didn't pay child support, and the money earned from his work in prison would be handed over to his dependants.[36] The state's Mothers' Aid Act, which came into effect in September 1913, was praised for including not only widows but also 'fit and needy' deserted or separated wives, and mothers whose husbands were infirm or in prison. It was, however, restricted to mothers who had lived in Massachusetts for at least three years.[37] Newly arrived Irish migrants, therefore, were excluded, even if their babies were conceived in the state by a local man. The Children of Unmarried Parents Act, of 1921, finally allowed women in Ontario to secure maintenance from putative fathers.[38] In 1926, New York legislation allowed families to bring cases of paternity to court to compel fathers to pay child support until the child turned sixteen.[39] By the 1920s then, single mothers had avenues to secure financial support from the fathers of their children, and scientific advances meant paternity could also now be proven, if it were in doubt. But for women like Rosie Quinn these developments came too late.

Abortion

Women's understanding of pregnancy and abortion in the nineteenth century differed in some ways from how those things are understood today. For many, pregnancy was confirmed only after they felt the foetus move, known as quickening. Prior to quickening, inducing a miscarriage could be regarded as an attempt to restore menstruation rather than as an abortion. This distinction about the beginning of pregnancy had been recognized in statutory and common law, but legislation passed in Canada and the United States from the 1840s removed this distinction and criminalized those who carried out abortions as well as the women who sought them.[40]

Legislation was initially driven by medical professionals who were concerned about unqualified quack abortionists, but the focus then turned to the women themselves and the demographic implications of abortions. Historian Leslie J. Reagan argues that moves to criminalize abortions in the United States from the 1850s and 1860s were motivated by fears that the native-born, white, middle-class Protestant population would become outnumbered.[41] In Canada too, politicians and legislators feared the decline of births among native-born Protestant married couples and saw the prosecution of abortion as a solution.[42] Regardless of the legal situation, unmarried and married women whose periods had stopped and who didn't want to be pregnant used a variety of home-made concoctions, tried traditional remedies or took the pills regularly advertised in newspapers. If these did not work, then they may have accessed the services of abortionists.

It is impossible to determine how many unmarried Irish women in North America deliberately aborted pregnancies. Illegal abortion cases are not very numerous in the records, not because such abortions didn't happen but rather because they left little trace. Neither the abortionist nor the woman who had been pregnant would be inclined to report it. Most illegal abortions came to light because women died during the process or needed medical help, or because the abortion attempt failed and the mother later resorted to infanticide. Bridget Colman, who was around thirty-five years old, died in Springfield, Massachusetts, in 1858, after William O. Brown, an untrained doctor, injured her with a sharp implement in his attempt to cause a miscarriage.[43] Irish-born Ellen Frances McLoughlin, a seamstress, died at the age of twenty-five in her New York boarding house in 1856, having become pregnant by her cousin. He resisted relatives' attempts to coerce him into marriage, claiming that he would rather cut his own throat than marry her. McLoughlin then sought abortifacient drugs, which caused her agonizing death.[44] The following year, 23-year-old Annie Breen died in similar circumstances in Palmer, Massachusetts. Her boyfriend of two years, Samuel P. Davis, a clerk at Tockwotton House, had paid for the abortion drugs from which she later died.[45]

Irish-born Anna Clayton recalled in 1864 that her surgical abortion a couple of years earlier, at the request of her older lover, Orville Millard, left her in bed for months. She had needed two procedures because the first, for which Millard paid the very significant sum of $50, had no effect. Millard had employed the young Irish woman as his servant. 'He said he was deeply in love with me', she remembered, 'and although I was an Irish girl he liked me better than any girl he had seen for some time.' Initially Clayton wasn't keen on marriage: 'I said it would be better for me to continue a poor girl than to have my name exposed by marrying an old man'.[46] But eventually Millard won her over. When she became pregnant a second time, Millard revealed his hand: he had never planned to marry her, and instead managed to convince her to marry a man he had chosen for her.

It is difficult to determine from surviving evidence if abortion was more common among unmarried Irish women in North America than it was in Ireland.[47] What is certain is that women and men in cities on both sides of the Atlantic had greater access to abortionists and druggists than those in more rural areas. In the mid-1870s, Mrs Congdon, who lived in the rural village of Amityville on Long Island, failed three times to convince a doctor to abort her daughters' pregnancies. This evidence became public when the daughters, Lottie and Cassie Congdon, were each charged with infanticide following the discovery of the bodies of two babies in a swamp on the family property in 1876.[48] The case, which shocked locals, was dubbed the 'Amityville Horror' more than a century before the release of a book and films of the same name relating to an entirely different murder in the same village. The stocking and muslin tied in knots around the babies' necks showed that the family never intended them to survive. A few years earlier, the *New York Times* had estimated that 200 abortionists operated in the city, along with hundreds of doctors who might also carry out such procedures.[49] The Congdon family didn't have access to these resources.

Infant murder

Some women who could not or did not want to abort, or could not afford an abortion, or who had tried but failed to end a pregnancy, resorted to infanticide. The difficulty of determining whether a baby had been born alive or dead was often central to the trials of such women. Marks or bruises could be open to interpretation, especially if the woman gave birth alone. In many countries, including Britain and Ireland (from 1803) and Canada (1836), it was a crime for an unmarried woman to conceal a childbirth.[50] The laws arose from fears that women who gave birth alone were getting away with killing their babies.

Bridget Good emigrated from County Waterford in October 1894 and gave birth six months later in William Hammill's house in Dobbs Ferry, New York, where she was employed as a servant. She claimed that her new-born was dead when she put him into the lighted kitchen stove. Good was arrested on a charge of infanticide, but since it couldn't be determined from the partially burnt body if the baby was dead or alive when he was put in the stove, her case was dismissed.[51] Under New York law, a court had to accept the word of a mother who said that her baby had been born dead. This meant that many suspected cases of infanticide did not reach the courts, and those that did regularly resulted in a verdict of not guilty.[52] In Rosie Quinn's case, a variety of witnesses could prove that her baby had been born alive. In order to ensure a conviction, the prosecution needed to connect the baby girl found in Central Park to Rosie. The defence pointed out that the clothes the child was wearing were provided by the hospital, and at least six other babies left that hospital at the same time dressed the same way. But Rosie's own statement to police – in which she claimed she had gone to Central Park in a distressed state, and that the baby had slipped from her arms into the lake – was enough to establish that she was the mother of the dead baby. The jury did not believe her claim that the baby had entered the water accidentally, and convicted her of murder in the second degree.

Child murder was not confined to new-born babies. Close to midnight on 6 October 1913, 27-year-old Teresa Bernard walked into Police Station 12 in South Boston and confessed to having deliberately dropped her two-and-a-half-year-old son into the water.[53] Teresa was unmarried. Her father, Thomas Bernard, ran a successful photography studio in Limerick for decades, and many photographs still survive bearing the studio name. The family was also very musical. Her elder brother Paul, a member of the Incorporated Society of Musicians, directed many public musicals and performances, and later became proprietor of the Tivoli Cinema and Grand Central Cinema in Limerick. A few weeks after she turned twenty-two, Teresa migrated to New York from Queenstown, Cork. She disembarked at Ellis Island in September 1908, identifying herself on the passenger list as a musician. Reports in the local newspaper in the years before she left Limerick suggest that she was very accomplished.

Teresa moved to Boston, became pregnant and gave birth to a son in February 1911. The father of her child was described as an 'unscrupulous man in this city [Boston] who brought disgrace upon her'. After she struggled financially to raise her son alone for a couple of years, the Boston Children's Aid Society liaised with her brother to have her sent home to Ireland.

On the October evening before Teresa was due to sail,

Officer Daniel Conlan encountered her at a bridge leading to Castle Island in Boston Harbor. Conlan voiced aloud his concern at her presence there with a toddler and directed her to go home. As he watched Teresa walk away, it struck him that the child's white bonnet, grey jumper, pink suit and white shoes were insufficient for the October drizzle. It later transpired that Teresa did not in fact return home but instead went to the City Point Pier, where she deliberately dropped John into the water. The *Boston Globe* believed that she did not want to return to Ireland 'unless she could go back with a father to her child or a marriage certificate'. Her family's prominence in Limerick and the reputational damage she might cause on returning home with a child born outside marriage may have weighed heavily on her mind. The next day, when she should have been on board the ship back to Ireland, she was instead in prison, having confessed to the killing of her child.

Fears about so-called baby farms, a term used to describe childminders who looked after children for profit but often severely neglected them, prompted legal requirements for minders of multiple children to register their establishments. But many still existed. In 1898, for instance, Irish-born Elizabeth Malone brought a baby to the police in Toronto, explaining that she had found him in the snow on the corner of Perth Avenue and Bloor Street. The police investigation into the matter intensified when the baby died two days later from the effects of starvation. They realized then that Malone had supposedly discovered three babies in this manner in the previous nine months and that she had seven other children at home, six of whom she said were her own but whose ages seemed to bely that claim. Under the headline 'Slaughter of the Innocents', the Toronto

Evening Star outlined suspicions that more than sixty babies
had passed through her care at various addresses in the city:
'With each babe she received a sum of money and the
infants were lost to the view of their parents, and the police
suspect that some of them were lost to all human eyes.'[54] A
licensed childminder, Mrs Clifford, had heard Malone offer
'to take a baby for $5, and guaranteed that the mother would
never see it again'.[55]

Desertion and adoption

Women who wanted to distance themselves from their children born outside marriage had options less drastic than
infanticide. Irish mothers abandoned babies at private homes,
institutions and public sites in the hope that they would be
found and reared (temporarily or permanently) by someone
else, and charges of abandonment and desertion were much
more common than charges of infant murder or manslaughter. (Twenty-one Irish women served sentences at
the Massachusetts Reformatory Prison for Women for abandoning babies between its opening in 1877 and 1918, while
six served time for murder or manslaughter.) Theresa McNally,
a 22-year-old servant arrested in New York in 1886 for desert-
ing her child, admitted: 'I am guilty. I left my baby where I was
sure it would be found and knew it would be cared for. I had
no means to support the child.'[56] Catherine Wilson, who
migrated to the United States as a teenager, left her grand-
child on the steps of a convent in Boston in 1909.[57] Some
women tried to force the fathers to accept responsibility.
Mary Cunningham, a widow and mother of four, was struggling financially when she left her two-month-old son at

his father's house in Boston in 1901. She was sentenced to a year in prison for the crime.[58]

Temporary or permanent adoption was also an option. Ellen Mullin from Galway sought help from the Massachusetts Infant Asylum to have her son adopted. She claimed not to have seen the father of her child after around one month into her pregnancy and was unsure of his whereabouts by the time of their son's birth in June 1868. She struggled for several months to support her son, and decided to return to Ireland, but didn't want relatives at home to find out about the birth. Officials noted in the admission book that Mullin felt 'it would break her mother's heart'. They judged that she 'seems very fond of her child but cannot take it with her'. Mullin's son was instead adopted in Massachusetts.[59] Dublin-born domestic servant Helen Knowles placed her son up for adoption in the same way the following year. The admission register notes that James, 'a fine healthy boy – and a good subject for adoption', was 'born very soon after the mother came to the country. She has done what she could to take care of him but seems inefficient to take charge of him.'[60] Even when there was no good alternative, such decisions must have been exceptionally difficult for many women to make. The Society for Helping Destitute Mothers and Infants observed in 1874:

> It is frequently said that the mothers of illegitimate children do not feel the same love for their offspring that married mothers do. Such has not been our experience. We have known unmarried mothers whose infants had died, or who were compelled, by poverty, to give them away for adoption. We have seen with our own eyes the anguish of these unhappy women, and the recollection is one of the most painful that we have.[61]

Although attitudes towards unmarried mothers and children born outside marriage were not generally more liberal in North America than in Ireland, charitable resources were more plentiful. The Society for Helping Destitute Mothers and Infants in Boston aimed to give short-term care to mothers released from maternity hospitals, as well as unmarried mothers judged 'not yet depraved', and to find suitable foster homes for infants whose mothers had returned to work and were unable to care for them.[62] The New York Infant Asylum, which opened in 1865, received 'foundlings and infants abandoned by improvised or dissolute parents' and aimed to 'give guidance and protection to the unfortunate mothers, and thus aid in saving them from destruction'.[63] The Toronto Infants' Home, established in 1875 to combat desertion, neglect, baby-farming and infanticide, accepted babies who were orphaned, infants and their needy mothers who were poor, widowed or deserted, or babies of working mothers.[64]

Charitable bodies often had strict criteria as to who was deserving or not deserving of help. The Associated Charities, for instance, acted as gatekeeper to Boston's charitable societies and institutions from 1879. It sent staff to investigate an applicant's circumstances and eligibility, and ensured that the same family did not receive relief from more than one charitable source at a time.[65] Catherine O'Donnell, aged twenty-two, failed in her attempt to get help from multiple charitable and religious societies in Boston in April 1889. She was later found guilty of the manslaughter of her two-month-old baby and sentenced to one year in prison. O'Donnell, whose father had a large farm, hadn't realized she was pregnant when she left Ireland several months earlier. Officials at the Massachusetts Reformatory Prison for Women observed: 'She appears broken hearted. Thinks the man, by whom this trouble came upon her, will yet marry her. He is a book keeper in Ire[land].'[66] In sentencing O'Donnell, Judge Dewey claimed that he 'would not have believed that she could receive such inhuman treatment from the so-called religious and charitable societies and institutions of Boston were it not for the character of the evidence which had been produced at the trial'.[67] Other institutions in North America refused entry to African American women, or imposed a residency rule that discriminated against newly arrived immigrants.[68] Even those who managed to get into such institutions could find conditions quite difficult, and infant mortality remained high. Honora Manley, from Brooklodge, County Cork, admitted that she ran away from St Mary's Infant Asylum in Boston with her young son 'because they were so strict'.[69]

The later nineteenth century saw some institutions encourage and support unmarried mothers to keep their children. Staff at The Haven in Toronto insisted: 'The experience of years, during which many hundreds of maternity cases have been dealt with, is, that the future welfare of mother and child depends upon their *not being separated*'.[70] The 1918 report of the Talitha Cumi Maternity Home, run by the New England Moral Reform Society, shared this view: 'When a girl enters she usually feels that the baby must be disposed of in some other way than the natural one of having the mother provide for her little one.' Instead, women were encouraged to keep their babies, and 'when a girl finds that other girls, whom she likes and respects, disapprove of any plan which means the giving up of the baby she begins to consider ways and means of providing for the child herself.'[71] Efforts to keep mothers with their infants were not always entirely focused on their welfare, but also stemmed from a desire to make mothers accept responsibility for their offspring and to curtail the behaviour that had led to the pregnancy in the first place.[72] Despite such efforts, however, research on unwed mothers in Ontario in 1920 suggests that only 20 per cent of them remained with their children.[73] Other societies and institutions placed less importance on keeping mother and child together, due to the difficulties women faced in securing work and accommodation with a baby in tow, and because of the demand for adoption.[74] Middle-class officials also assumed that it was in many children's best interests to be taken away from an unmarried mother.

The fate of Rosie Quinn

After she was found guilty of murder in the second degree, Justice Francis Scott addressed Rosie Quinn at her trial in April 1903: 'I do not desire to add in any way to the disgrace you must be suffering . . . There are many persons interested in your case, and they will undoubtedly do something for you when the proper time arrives.' The judge was right. Many members of the public were moved by Rosie Quinn's pitiful story to write to the governor of New York State to ask for her pardon and a commutation of her life sentence. A doctor suggested that Rosie was suffering from puerperal insanity (what we might understand as postpartum depression) and wasn't mentally responsible for what she had done. Other writers emphasized her youth, naivety, lack of support and sense of shame.

Rosie Quinn's fellow workers at the Fifth Avenue Hotel also seem to have rallied almost immediately to her defence. They turned for assistance to the 'father' of the Amen Corner,

General Charles Furlong. Furlong would later say that the hotel staff 'would not give me any peace until I promised to take a hand in the case. I realized that it was an unusual thing to commute the sentence of a life prisoner, but I agreed to do what I could.' By this stage he had lived at the hotel for more than twenty years, although he doesn't seem to have directly encountered Rosie Quinn during that time. (ill. 2.3.)

GEN. CHARLES E. FURLONG.

2.3. Sketch of Charles E. Furlong.

Furlong's own investigation led him to view Rosie Quinn's case sympathetically. He was convinced that she was a 'poor creature' who had been 'sinned against more than she had sinned'. Like many of the women described in this chapter, she had, he considered, been 'betrayed by a faithless lover', and after she had given birth to her child she was 'driven out into the cold world'. Furlong believed that her 'rash act' was understandable because she had no relatives or money and was all alone in the city. He spent a month tracking down the jurors who had convicted her, and presented them with a petition to commute her sentence, which they all, he later recalled, 'cheerfully signed'. Justice Scott, who had sentenced Rosie Quinn to life in prison, also signed the petition (and according to Furlong 'commended my efforts'), along with other key politicians in the city, many of whom Furlong knew personally. Furlong presented this petition to the state governor, Benjamin Barker Odell Jr, a fellow member of the Amen Corner.

Although Furlong described his involvement as 'only an act of charity', there may have been more to his willingness to assist Rosie Quinn than he admitted. Furlong was generally silent on his upbringing and his personal life. But after his death it was determined that he was probably Irish-born and he included as beneficiaries in his will Furlongs in County Limerick. Although he left most of his fortune to charities in New York and Mississippi, he also left bequests to four staff members at the Fifth Avenue Hotel, including Irish-born chambermaids Eliza Murray and Jennie McLaughlin.[75] Perhaps Rosie Quinn's Irish background was part of what inspired Furlong to get involved.

Or perhaps Furlong could appreciate how Rosie had found herself pregnant and unmarried. Twenty years before Rosie Quinn gave birth, he had been sued by his fiancée, Sophia Allen, for breaking off their engagement after they consummated their relationship. Allen claimed that, only weeks before, he had taken her to Tiffany's, where she had selected an engagement ring, later engraved with their initials.[76] During their courtship they spent time reading in Central Park, where Furlong walked daily when he lived at the Fifth Avenue Hotel, and where Rosie Quinn dropped her baby in the water.

At 6.30 on the evening of 15 December 1904, Rosie Quinn walked out of Auburn Prison, her sentence commuted by special order of Governor Odell. 'Thank God, I'm free', she exclaimed on leaving prison after one year, seven months and sixteen days. Rosie's early release was labelled a 'Christmas gift', along with the pardon at the same time of Sarah Silvermeister, a Russian-born married mother of five who had been convicted in January 1895 of arson.[77] Silvermeister had served nine years of a twenty-five-year sentence and was released early as a reward for her bravery in saving a staff member who was being attacked by another inmate. Rosie was taken for the night to Osborne House, a hotel close to the prison, before returning to New York City early the next morning with General Furlong. A reporter for the *Post Standard* who was waiting for them at the station observed that Furlong, in his high silk hat, 'looked the part of an aristocrat'. Rosie Quinn struck a romantic figure by his side in her flat felt orange and brown hat and warm winter coat, a bunch of holly in her hand. She was also accompanied by Jane Dolan, a fellow servant at the Fifth Avenue Hotel, whom Bessie Dunbrack, the hotel's housekeeper, had sent as a chaperone.

It was rumoured that Furlong had found work for Rosie out west. At that point she disappears from the records. Less than three years later, in early September 1907, newspapers reported that General Charles Furlong was gravely ill in Portland, Maine, where he had holidayed annually for years (and where Rosie Quinn's boyfriend, John Warren, was said to have been stationed). Furlong died later that month and in accordance with his wishes his body was returned to the

Fifth Avenue Hotel. Members of the Amen Corner agreed to pay the costs of his funeral and to have his body placed in a receiving vault at Woodlawn Cemetery. He was later buried in Green-Wood Cemetery.[78] In April 1908, the Fifth Avenue Hotel closed. The red plush sofas of the Amen Corner were moved to the nearby Hoffman House hotel.[79]

3. Child neglect and the case of Annie Young

On 10 October 1908, a clerk from Boston's juvenile court telephoned the Massachusetts Society for the Prevention of Cruelty to Children (MSPCC). Boston resident Annie Young, the clerk revealed, had been arrested the day before and fined $25 for keeping a disorderly house. The charge of keeping a disorderly house usually involved allowing unmarried couples to live together, prostitution, gambling, or alcohol or opium use. In Annie's case, she seems to have permitted lodgers to engage in selling or buying sex. Annie had not yet paid the fine so would likely go to prison, and this was a concern because she had a one-year-old daughter. A lodger in the house was looking after baby Marie in Annie's absence but would not be able to do so for much longer.[1]

The call was not in itself particularly unusual. The courts, and neighbours, relatives, policemen, schoolteachers or staff at institutions, regularly alerted the MSPCC, and other child protection agencies, to parents who were thought unfit or unable to take care of their children.

After they received a tip-off, MSPCC caseworkers – or 'agents', as they were called in the records – visited families, generally unannounced, to judge for themselves if they needed to get involved. By the late nineteenth century, social work had become more professionalized and, as historian Linda Gordon notes, 'a new group of middle-class "experts" replaced upper-class charity workers as those who set standards for family life'.[2] Many parents needed support, and an

MSPCC agent could put them in touch with relevant groups or individuals in the city, or provide child-rearing advice or instructions. Irish-born Mary Pond wrote to one agency in 1908: 'I am very thankful to you for your kindness. You are indeed very good and kind and I will never forget what you have done for me and the advice you have given me and aid. I haven't got no mother hear and my sister nor cousins don't come near me.'[3]

Other parents were thought to require a warning to ensure that they attended better to the needs of their children. Irish mother Elizabeth Martinelli and her Italian-born husband were advised to 'have no more rum in the house or there would be trouble for them'.[4] Mary Lynskey was warned in 1912 that 'it was not enough that she and fa[ther] kept sober, but that she must keep out of their house, people who drink and become intoxicated; that otherwise she was in as much danger of having her ch[ildre]n taken away from her as if she became intoxicated herself'.[5] Some parents were ultimately deemed entirely unfit or unsuited to parenthood. Their children were removed from them and placed in an institution, at their expense if they wanted to maintain their parental rights, or fostered or adopted by parents who were considered more suited to the role.

When the MSPCC social worker, Katherine O'Rourke, called to Annie Young's home at 248 Shawmut Avenue following the phone call from the Boston court, it was Annie who answered the door. She had paid the fine, she said, and returned home to take care of her young daughter. O'Rourke was invited inside – or perhaps invited herself. She needed to determine if Annie was fit to take care of Marie, and had a list of probing questions to ask. Over the course of the next few minutes, the MSPCC agent listened to what Annie said, as well as what she did not say. O'Rourke's private notes (later typed up by an assistant) offer a glimpse of Annie's life with her young daughter, as well as O'Rourke's assessment of what good motherhood looked like.

Annie had a tendency, according to O'Rourke, to talk 'volubly' but to be 'very vague in her statements, and often contradictory'. O'Rourke listened as Annie spoke of her upbringing on a farm in rural Sligo. As the daughter of Irish-born immigrant parents, O'Rourke likely had some understanding of the background Annie described.[6] She heard of Annie's migration six years earlier, when she was around twenty years old, and her marriage a couple of years later to Scottish-born William Young. Their first child, William, born in the lying-in hospital, died soon after birth. (This was in no way unusual: a study published a few years later revealed an infant mortality rate of 60 per cent for children born to immigrant mothers in New York, as compared to 30 per cent for children born to native-born mothers.)[7] The *New York Times*, commenting on infant mortality among the Irish in 1874, noted:

> the living children of the Irish class . . . present an appearance which makes this excess of mortality among them not surprising. It is from no casual observation, but from a careful examination of them by thousands, that we are able to say with confidence that a more unhealthy, feeble, pithless class of people (if we may call such little children people) than these cannot be found in the country. They are pale and spare, but not with that paleness and spareness that is often accompanied by health, strength, and tenacious vitality. Their skins look sodden, their eyes dull, and their flesh has no firmness.[8]

O'Rourke also heard about the disintegration of Annie's marriage while she was pregnant with her daughter, Marie.

She recorded in her notes that Annie left her husband because of his 'immoral habits', a phrase that probably signified infidelity. By the time of Marie's birth at the Massachusetts Homeopathic Hospital in June 1907, William Young was no longer on the scene. If Annie knew where he was, she did not tell O'Rourke.

Annie probably did not realize that the woman in front of her already knew some of this history. Four months earlier, Miss E. M. Locke at the Destitute Mothers and Infants Home in Boston had contacted Dr Carl Christian Carstens, head of the MSPCC. Locke had heard from a resident in the Home that Annie, who then lived at 37 Fayette Street (just a few doors away from the Home at number 20), had been seen close to midnight a few days earlier wandering the street, with her baby in her arms. A doctor who examined Annie at Locke's request agreed that the Irish mother was irresponsible, but he did not consider that her situation was desperate enough to justify admission to the Destitute Mothers and Infants Home, and so Locke wanted the MSPCC to investigate the case instead. Annie, she judged, was caring for her infant daughter 'after a fashion', but was 'incapable'. A week after she contacted Carstens, Locke got in touch with the MSPCC again, this time to tell them that Annie had now moved from number 37 without saying where she was going. The landlady of Annie's house had promised to alert Locke if she were seen again in the neighbourhood, but when O'Rourke called to the Home on 1 October she was told that Annie had not since returned. In fact, until Annie's arrest for keeping a disorderly house, which prompted the court to ring the MSPCC, she had evaded the child protection agencies. Now, her arrest brought her back to the attention of the MSPCC.

Child protection workers encountered all sorts of characters on their home visits. In the same year that Annie was visited, the agent who called to Irishwoman Catherine Lane and her family was 'greeted by mother, who opened the door, with the question, "what in hell do you want?"' He recalled that she 'cooled down immediately' when he explained why he was on her doorstep.[9] In another case, at almost ten o'clock on an October night, agent William R. Critcherson, who had joined the staff of the MSPCC from the Boston Police Department that year,[10] went with a police officer to the Hennessy family at Athens Street in South Boston, evidently anticipating an arrest. They found the Irish-born mother drunk in a small bed, nursing a baby. She was, according to the agent, 'very boisterous and perfectly willing to fight the officer'.[11] In 1919, Irish-born Catherine Hickey 'went into a perfect rage at ag[en]t's visit; refused to give ag[en]t any information; stated that her h[usband] was dead, all her ch[ildre]n were dead and there was no point in ag[en]t pestering the life out of her. Flew at ag[en]t several times.'[12]

It is not clear how Annie Young felt about O'Rourke's unannounced visit, or the questions about her love life, background and living arrangements. But it is unlikely that she foresaw that this interview was the start of a series of interactions with the MSPCC that would continue for years and lead to her child being taken from her.

Living conditions

Katherine O'Rourke was on the lookout for indicators that Annie was an unfit mother. 'The house is a typical, filthy S[outh] E[nd] lodging house of the poorer class', her report on the house began. By the early twentieth century, Boston's South End had become a lodging-house district where tenants rented rooms in elegant buildings originally constructed for the wealthy, white, native-born Protestants.[13] Businesses sprung up around the lodging houses, including dining rooms and cafes, licensed and unlicensed bars and saloons, brothels, pool rooms, dance halls, laundries, tailors and drug-stores.[14] O'Rourke paid particular attention to hygiene and cleanliness in the home, describing the scene she encountered:

> The interview was in mother's room on the second floor, which contained a bed, small range, rather large desk and small table. The remains of her luncheon were on the table; she cleared up, putting the eatables in the desk. The room was filthy and unsanitary; shades were drawn; windows closed.

O'Rourke wrote her observations of Annie's daughter, Marie: 'Baby, without shoes or stockings, was filthy and poorly dressed; had some sort of skin disease.'

The things O'Rourke observed were mild compared to the desperate conditions child protection workers sometimes encountered during home visits. In 1888, an agent found Mary Kilty, who had migrated from Ireland seven months earlier, in her home in Hudson Street, Charlestown, on the north side of Boston, with her three-year-old daughter, Margaret, and one-year-old son, Charles, 'nearly naked'. Their home comprised 'two rooms, one broken bedstead, one broken table, one stove and three chairs'. They were entirely without food. Mary's husband had gone to Colorado, presumably in search of work.[15] When an MSPCC agent visited Irish-born Annie Black and her six children at

Belmont Street in Charlestown in February 1908, a few months before Annie Young was visited, she:

> found the home filthy, not a decent chair to sit on, – in fact it would have been dangerous for Ag[en]t to sit on anything in that room. The furniture consisted of three partially broken chairs, a table with a cloth black and stiff with filth, and [sic] old couch covered with dirty clothes, a washtub full of partially washed clothing. Mother and children were stiff with dirt; mother wore an old sweater fastened with a nail.[16]

The following month, an anonymous note alerted the MSPCC to the O'Brien family at Stone Street in Charlestown, where an Irish-born mother, Mary, resided with her English-born husband and three children. The agent who visited had to 'wade through filth and rubbish which was piled up to the first step of the door way'. Nobody was at home but the agent found a means of access at the back and entered the house anyway. She wrote in her notes: 'There were two rooms and the bed room was *indescribably filthy*: 3 beds in this room where the entire family sleep; a bucket of filth was in the middle of the floor, and the stench to say the least was sickening.'[17] In 1914, MSPCC agent Critcherson found Mary Lynskey at her two-roomed home in Silver Street in Boston, 'with a black eye, very very dirty in appearance'. He described the tenement where she had lived with her three sons and husband for the previous four months:

> House has been condemned by the B[oard] of H[ealth], no water in the house for 7 wks., pipes frozen and burst and flooded the house and all the floors were covered with ice as well as the stairs and hallway. Only one door in the tenement, no hinges. Found one old dirty bed and a cot. Very

little clothing, only 3 dishes in the house and one knife and fork.

The baby was described as 'very dirty, eyes matterated and neck sore', and was taken into state care along with his two half-brothers.[18]

Irish women tended to have more mouths to feed than native-born mothers, which exacerbated poverty and poor living conditions, and in turn increased the likelihood that they would come into contact with child protection agents for neglect. According to the 1910 US census, married Irish female immigrants had an average of five or six children, whereas native-born married women had two or three.[19] A writer in 1840 commented on the high birth rate in Irish families: 'Did wealth consist in children, it is well known, that the Irish would be rich people'.[20] Bridget Donnelly, who was born in Tyrone in 1856 and migrated to the United States aged twenty, claimed that if 'she had known anything about married life she would have remained single. Nine children are too many for any woman to bear. Six are too many to keep clothed and fed.'[21]

The mother's lifestyle

Irish women not only tended to have more children than others. They were also more likely to be raising them by themselves. In New York at this time, more than twice as many Irish women headed families than either German or US-born women.[22] And in Boston 27 per cent of Irish families had a female head of household by 1880.[23] Bereavement, desertion, divorce and separation left many Irish women on their own with their children. As Annie Young's case shows, women also left their husbands.

A Miss Watson, who previously lived at Annie Young's lodging house, told Katherine O'Rourke that she had seen baby Marie 'left in a go-cart in the front hall practically all day while mother was out'. This was an extreme example of a fairly common practice. Cornelius Desmoran, interviewed as part of an investigation by social worker Elsa G. Herzfeld into the New York of the early twentieth century, recalled that his Irish mother supported her five children 'by going out to wash by the day' after the death of his father in 1868. While doing this laundry work, she 'left the children to shift for themselves'.[24]

Lack of parental supervision might partly explain high infant mortality among immigrant families. Mary Elizabeth O'Flaherty was born in King's County in 1859 and travelled alone to New York aged seven to join her parents, who had sold their pub and emigrated two years earlier. She married Fermanagh-born Adam Kelly in 1880. Two years later, she gave birth to a daughter, Loretta. A son, Joseph Alexander, was born in February 1884 but lived only a few minutes. Another son was born in 1886 and died fifteen months later from sunstroke while playing on the roof. A baby was still-born in 1887. In October 1888, O'Flaherty gave birth to a daughter, who later fell out of her sister's arms and was paralysed. Annie was born in 1890 and died of burns aged five after her clothes caught fire. Cecelia was born in 1891, Adelaide in 1895 and Frances in 1897. Frances fell down the stairs as a baby and suffered permanent physical impairments. Another son, William James, was born in 1900. When he was around a year and a half, he ingested lye that O'Flaherty had left on the kitchen table to make soap. It would be more than a year before he recovered.[25]

Annie Young claimed that she had left her husband because of his bad behaviour. Seeking to verify this, Katherine O'Rourke followed her interview with Annie with a visit to a Mrs Lynch, at 52 Malden Street, where Annie had lived before marriage and, she claimed, took her new husband afterwards. Lynch's version of events did little to ease O'Rourke's suspicions that there was more to Annie's marriage story than she had revealed. Lynch claimed that William had never lived there, and even cast doubt on whether the couple had ever been legally married. Two days later, O'Rourke called at the registrar's office in Boston in search of a marriage certificate. Annie said the couple had wed three or four years earlier at the Cathedral of the Holy Cross in the South End. O'Rourke noted that 'no record could be found of the marriage of William Young and Annie Fahey or Vahey in '04–5 or 6.' The questions over Annie's marriage fed into suspicion that she was immoral, at a time when single motherhood was viewed as deviant. O'Rourke probably thought she had caught Annie out on a lie. It wasn't until some months later that O'Rourke realized that she'd overlooked the record. Irish-born Annie Furey, listed as a waitress, had married William Young, an oiler from Scotland, at the cathedral on 7 December 1905.

Childcare and work

Like many Irish women, Annie Young worked as a domestic servant or housekeeper. Before Marie's birth, she told O'Rourke, she earned 'good wages', amounting to $5 or $6 per week. But Marie's birth in June 1907 complicated these arrangements. Annie needed to earn a living but she had few childcare options and she clearly struggled, as shown by her requests to various organizations in the city for charity. A few days after Marie's birth, Annie asked the Society of St Vincent de Paul (SVP) for help. She had contacted the Society a few weeks before Marie's birth as well, but when a staff member called to her home at McLean Court, they found that Annie had been evicted. When Annie got in touch with the SVP after the birth of her daughter, staff organized her admission to the Temporary Home for Women and Children at Chardon Street. She and Marie entered the Home on 5 July. They remained there for four nights and then left. Annie also sought help from other charitable societies in the locality, including the Society for Helping Destitute Mothers and Infants.

Such charities and homes provided needy parents with a temporary solution. The records of the Temporary Home for the Destitute, known as the Gwynne Home, are full of examples of Irish parents struggling with childcare demands. Irish-born widow Margaret Scarlett left two children at the Home on 16 October 1858, 'till she can decide what to do with them'. She collected the children a week later, evidently having found some solution and 'expressed much gratitude for the care her children had rec[eive]d at the home'.[26] Bridget Halloran left her two children, aged six and two years, in the Gwynne Home on 10 June 1898. Her husband was then in the Worcester Insane Asylum and she was looking for work to support the family. Her one-year-old son was with a friend, and another daughter was in a home. Bridget collected the two children just under four months later in October 1898.[27]

Annie Young's case file in the MSPCC collections notes that she 'boarded Marie', meaning she paid for her care and accommodation in an institution or a private home. But

Annie found that Marie 'did not thrive'. Childcare could be patchy in its quality and it was not unusual for childminders – typically women – to end up in court blamed for the deaths of children in their care. Institutional care could also pose a risk to young children. Mary R. Martin of the Associated Charities of Newton admitted in 1908, the year that Annie was first investigated by the MSPCC, that she was reluctant to send young children to a large Catholic asylum in Boston because 'In every instance that we have done so, one or more of the children have died'.[28] Not satisfied with the care Marie was getting, Annie removed her and took up a position as housekeeper in the town of Gloucester, north of Boston. She also seems to have applied to the Children's Mission for a place for Marie to board, but when someone from the Mission followed up on the case, Annie had moved from 78 Oak Street, the address she had given.

In the summer of 1908, Annie paid a deposit of $100 to 'buy out' the lodging house at 248 Shawmut Avenue, where tenants rented by the room. Albert Benedict Wolfe, a professor of economics and sociology, described the practice in his 1913 study of South End lodging houses:

> The buying of a lodging-house is substantially the same as buying a grocery-store, or a physician's practice. You buy the equipment or stock on hand, and the custom or good-will of the business. The good-will of the lodging-house is its lodgers, and its reputation, if it has any.[29]

In 1902–4, the average cost of buying out a lodging house in the area was $800.[30] Annie likely bought from a real estate agent, paying over her savings of $100 as a deposit and committing herself to paying the remainder in weekly instalments. Wolfe noted that lodging-house keepers were vulnerable to exploitation by real estate agents and 'the prey of all sorts of sharpers, and if they survive and finally establish their house on a paying basis, it may be at the cost of their tempers, their health, and their moral sensibilities'.[31]

It was at Shawmut Avenue that Katherine O'Rourke first met Annie. O'Rourke judged her to be 'irrational and irresponsible, and it seemed incredible that she could be running a lodging house'. Miss Watson, a former resident, told O'Rourke that when Annie took on the house she evicted 'the old lodgers', and Watson left two weeks later because she feared the house was 'running down so rapidly'. Watson confirmed O'Rourke's view that Annie was 'a bit unbalanced'.

Separation

On 4 June 1909, a few days before Marie Young turned two, the police raided Annie Young's South End lodging house and again found that she was running a disorderly house. This time there was no uncertainty about what was going on behind the closed doors: three women were arrested for engaging in prostitution. The police planned to evict all the residents. The next day, Miss Maynard, the municipal court probation officer, informed the MSPCC, and staff there sprang into action. Judge Harvey H. Baker, who presided at the Boston Juvenile Court from its establishment in 1906 until his death in 1915,[32] ordered a warrant for Marie's transfer into state care under the Neglect Act, 1903, and by nine o'clock that night she was in police custody. She had been found wearing a new white dress and coat, over a filthy vest, and had a bonnet on her head. She was barefoot and her face was caked in dirt. The police removed four other women from the house as well, 'with dishevelled hair, some without shoes or stockings, and all in a most shameful state of undress'. An agent from the MSPCC collected Marie from the South End police station and brought her to the Home for Destitute Catholic Children (HDCC), established by Bishop John B. Fitzpatrick in 1864.[33] Marie was now physically separated from her mother. She was one of 638 children that Baker sent to the HDCC while he presided over the Boston Juvenile Court.[34]

A couple of days later, Annie appeared in court with her attorney, Mr Fairbanks, protesting her separation from Marie. She claimed to be breastfeeding the toddler, but her pleas to be reunited with her daughter fell on deaf ears. In the same year, another Irish mother, Winifred Murphy, pleaded in vain with the MSPCC for contact with her eight-year-old daughter, who had been taken into care following the mother's arrest for drunkenness:

> if they are Sisters of Charity I canot see where their Charity comes in . . . I wish if it is not asking too much you would ask them to let her write to me my heart is broken I try not to feel bad but I wake in the morning it seames as if I could not stand it Oh don't think I am a bad woman will you if I could only see you I could tell you better my feelings . . .[35]

Mary Mahoney expressed similar feelings after her children were taken away to the Harrison Street Home in Boston in 1914:

> 'I cant forget them one minute night or day I cry myself to sleep every night thinking of them', she wrote, 'you dont know how heart broken I am when I think of how happy I was with my children one time and to think I had to come to this it seems as if I would go insane . . .'[36]

In 1891, Frank Fay, the General Agent of the MSPCC, insisted that 'parents' rights are forfeited by their misconduct'.[37] A judge in a child protection case also made clear that he 'was unwilling to reform parents at the expense of their ch[ildre]n'.[38] Records of the Children's Friend Society in Boston describe five-year-old Irish-born James Scranger as a 'fine boy; much to be pitied on account of his miserable parents'. A note beside this entry reads: 'How distressing that *parents* should be so strongly opposed to the best interests of their children!!'[39] By 1918, Massachusetts had approximately 12,000 children whose relatives were perceived to be incapable of minding them, 10,000 of whom were with foster families.[40]

A nurse who called to Annie's house at the request of the MSPCC on the day after her court appearance found Annie 'in an intoxicated condition, which may have been the result of a drug as well as of liquor'. An unnamed companion 'was "weeping" drunk; the house too disorderly for description'. Annie was arrested that night for drunkenness and thus missed the sitting in the juvenile court on the following day. On 2 July, Attorney Fairbanks revealed to the juvenile court that Annie had been sentenced to serve one year at the State Farm in Bridgewater. She appealed her sentence, but the Superior Criminal Court confirmed the decision of the lower court a few days later. Katherine O'Rourke swore before Judge Baker as to Marie Young's neglect, and Marie remained in care. A review of the case in October 1909 resulted in a continuance for one year.

In September 1910, her sentence at the State Farm now complete, Annie called at the MSPCC office. She was due to sail home to Ireland at noon that day and wanted to take her daughter with her. MSPCC records note that Annie was 'informed that this was impossible'. And so Annie travelled alone to Queenstown, Cork, on the White Star Line SS *Cymric*, leaving behind her young daughter, whom she probably hadn't seen in fifteen months. From there she made her way back to her parents in Sligo. Annie was one of at least ten children born to James and Winifred Furey in the mountainous Geevagh region. She grew up in the family's two-roomed thatched cottage, the fifth-born, and it was there that she returned following her few years in Boston.

A couple of months later, Dr Carl Christian Carstens, the head of the MSPCC, wrote to Annie's father in Sligo, at the request of the judge at the juvenile court, to find out if Annie had reached home. Annie responded:

> In Reply to your letter I would have rote to you Bee fore now but I was not feeling well and the Truble of the death of My mother also that I heard when I came home it Surprised me greatly as I landed in my Fathers house nearly exausted out when I herd about my mother.

Clearly, Annie had been unaware of her mother's death, in July 1907, until she reached Sligo in September 1910. Her transient lifestyle as she moved from one house to the other in Boston's South End would have thwarted any attempt her family made to communicate this news to her. She continued:

> My father and two brothers in the house and all around Coming to see me and My Friends inviting me and all very glad to see me and I felt lonsome I had not my child with me as I went through a lot of trouble as I would like to know my little girl as I do not know yet as I think it would be wild in the winter to go on sea and I do be very much uneasy about her.

She added a postscript: 'Good By. Remembering my child', and signed off as Annie Young.

Almost two years later, in October 1912, Marie Young's case was back before Judge Baker. A Massachusetts couple, Mary and John Gilmore, had been fostering Marie, by arrangement with the HDCC, and were now keen to adopt her. The couple had by this stage been married sixteen years and had no children of their own. John, a stonemason engaged in seasonal work, was now in his early fifties and his wife, who had worked as a domestic servant before marriage, was in her mid-forties.[41]

Massachusetts had been the first US state to introduce legislation for adoption, in 1851.[42] It would be more than a century before adoption was legalized in Ireland. Research on the Temporary Home for the Destitute in Boston shows that between 1851 and 1893 children from an Irish background were the most common ethnic group to be adopted.[43] 'Send us a smart, stout, saucy boy of six. Irish parents', one correspondent directed the New York Foundling Hospital.[44] Marie Young's ethnicity may have been attractive to the Gilmores: Mary Gilmore had immigrated from rural County Cavan.

It is not clear how much the Gilmores knew about Marie's background. A petition for custody that the Gilmores filed in October 1912 misnamed the biological parents and claimed that they had abandoned their daughter two years earlier. Mary Gilmore might not have been privy to Katherine O'Rourke's notes, but she had much in common with the biological mother of the child she wanted to adopt. Both women were the daughters of farmers (although Mary's father was wealthier), and both married Scottish men around three years after migrating to the US.[45] The Gilmores may well have appealed to those involved in the case because they, like Marie Young, were Catholic. An Irish mother of three, Catherine Harrigan, had told O'Rourke only a couple of years earlier that she had been chastised by the local parish priest for putting her children in a Protestant home: 'He didn't like it at all, he wants to know why I didn't put them in a Catholic Home'.[46] Fears were commonly voiced that Irish children were being removed from Catholic parents and handed over to Protestant institutions, societies or families. In 1859, the *Irish-American* publication claimed that in this manner 'at least five hundred children the off-spring of Irish Catholic parents, are proselytised, corrupted and morally speaking, debauched, yearly in New York'.[47] Staff at the Five Points House of Industry in New York in 1865 complained that Mrs K., an Irish-born widow with two children who 'lodges with a woman in a room as clean as a pigpen . . . fears we will ruin the children because we are Protestants'.[48] To quell similar fears, the Canadian Juvenile Delinquents Act of 1908 banned the placement of Catholic children in Protestant homes and vice versa.[49]

In 1883, the MSPCC, defending its decisions to remove children from parents, insisted that parents 'still have the opportunity, after a reasonable period, to recover their children, if they can show they have a proper home and character to justify their restoration'.[50] But it could prove difficult for parents to demonstrate enough improvement or reform to get their children back. They had to overcome all the factors that had led to the removal of their children in the first instance, with the added difficulty that judges might compare their circumstances to those of the potentially wealthier foster families currently raising their offspring.

The case files of the MSPCC make for heart-breaking

reading as parent after parent sought to be reunited with their children. In June 1908, James Kelly called at the MSPCC office to ask for the return of his five eldest children, who had been taken into care three months earlier. Agent Critcherson told him: 'we were glad to hear that his wife was doing better and that his home was fixed up, but we could not return the children yet, as his wife had only stopped drinking 3 weeks and he himself admitted that he was taking an occasional glass.' The mother, Nora Kelly, called with the same request twice the following month. On the second occasion, Critcherson assured her that he would visit her at her home 'at some future time'. An MSPCC agent called to the Kelly family's home weeks later, and found 'a tenement of 4 rooms, 3 beds; tenement in fair condition; beds in fair condition. No evidence of drink on the part of the mother, very little on the part of the father. They had bought furniture worth nearly $40 on the instalment plan, which they had paid for with the exception of $5 or $6.' The parents were told to let the agency know when the furniture was paid off. Critcherson confirmed in his notes: 'We feel that this may be a case where the children should be returned.' But when the mother called at the end of October to ask again about the children's return, she was informed that MSPCC agents 'did not feel they should be returned at the present time as she is soon to become a mother but at some future time we would call on her'. The file notes suggest that that call never came.[51] Galway-born Catherine Conboy, whose children had been placed in a home following her arrest for being a common nightwalker in 1914, wrote to the superintendent of the Massachusetts Reformatory for Women months after her release: 'the children I expect them home next week it is easy to take them but it is a hard time to get them back'[52] (ill. 3.1).

3.1. Catherine Conboy, prison mugshot and admission details, 1914.

The Gilmores' petition for custody of Marie Young in October 1912 was refused because the directors of the HDCC, which had guardianship of Marie, 'could not recommend the Gilmore home'. But the Gilmores persisted and on 9 January 1913 they adopted Marie, now aged five and a half, and changed her name. An MSPCC agent who visited the family over a year later, noted that the couple 'are devoted to the ch[ild] . . . Rooms clean and well kept. House an old frame one.' When Mary Gilmore visited the MSPCC office a couple of days later, Marie was noted to be 'an attractive, happy looking ch[ild]'. The case was closed.

The fates of Annie Young and Marie Young

In the Irish censuses of both 1901 and 1911, Annie Furey is listed as living at home in Geevagh, County Sligo, with her father as head of household. The census gives no indication of the life she lived in between: her migration to the US, her marriage to William Young, the birth of her two children, William and Marie, her management of lodging houses in Boston's South End, her heartbreak at her son's death and her enforced separation from her daughter. It is not clear what Annie's family at home in Sligo knew of her life in the US. In 1911, she was listed in the census as unmarried, as she had been in 1901. But tucked away in the MSPCC files at the University of Massachusetts in Boston is the astonishing account of her life in the intervening years.

Annie's daughter grew up in Massachusetts, thousands of miles from her Sligo relatives. Marie's adoptive father died in 1918, and she became a sixteen-year-old orphan in November 1923 upon the death of her adoptive mother. In September 1930, the woman formerly known as Marie Young published in the *Boston Globe* a plea headed 'Seeks mother after 21 years' separation'. By that stage, she was aware of some details from her early life: she had her birth parents' marriage certificate and knew that she had been taken from her mother in 1909. She knew she had been born at the Massachusetts Homeopathic Hospital, but she had her day and year of birth wrong and was actually almost a year older than she thought. She must surely have recognized that her attempt to find her birth mother through the newspaper was a long shot. It is unlikely that Annie Young ever saw or heard her plea.

4. Rebel girls and the case of Ellen Nagle

On 6 April 1902, the *Boston Post* carried the headline 'Ellen Nagle found'. Police officers and the public who had been on the lookout for the seventeen-year-old must have breathed a collective sigh of relief. Irish-born Ellen, described as 'Handsome, petite and a dashing little blonde', had run away from her family home at 99 Warwick Street in Boston's South End almost a week earlier.[1]

Ellen blamed 'bad girls' for coaxing her onto the streets. Her father, William Nagle, clearly vexed by her behaviour, had her arrested and placed on probation, which meant she risked a custodial sentence if she was again charged. A little over a year later, on 13 May 1903, he had Ellen arrested again, and this time she was imprisoned for twelve months in the Massachusetts Reformatory Prison for Women in Sherborn (ill. 4.1). Her crime, as William Nagle and the courts saw it, was being a 'stubborn child': an offence recognized in Massachusetts legislation as far back as 1641 and still prosecuted in the twentieth century.[2]

Ellen Nagle's parents, William and Ellen, had emigrated from Fermoy, County Cork, to Massachusetts in 1887. Their three children, all under five years old, had remained behind in Ireland with relatives. William was a baker by trade, and he and his wife likely wanted to secure work and a place to live before bringing their children over. (Ellen Senior was pregnant at the time with their fourth child, which may also have been a factor in the decision to travel without the children.)

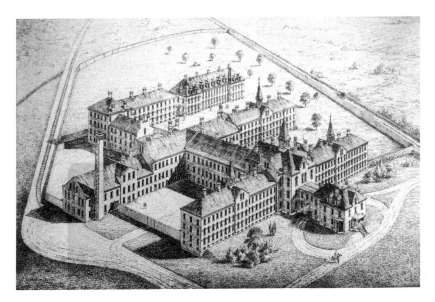

4.1. Massachusetts Reformatory Prison for Women.

The Nagle children followed their parents to America in 1888, and there met their new baby brother, George, who had been born in Massachusetts in January of that year. Subsequent siblings followed. By 1900, Ellen Senior had given birth to ten children, seven of whom were then living. The environment in which William and Ellen Senior raised their Irish- and Massachusetts-born children, with its department stores, dance halls, cafes and restaurants, saloons, and indoor and outdoor amusement venues, meant an upbringing that was very different to their own.

Ellen Nagle was one of fourteen girls and women, ranging in age from seventeen to twenty, who entered the Massachusetts Reformatory Prison for Women for the offence of stubbornness in that year.[3] The offence could encompass a multitude of behaviours, but for girls especially it was often connected to perceived or threatened sexual immorality. In New York and Toronto, girls and women were similarly punished for being 'wayward', 'incorrigible' or 'out of control'.[4] From 1886, New York City legislation allowed for the incarceration of girls aged twelve or more who were found in brothels or who were 'wilfully disobedient' to their parents or 'in danger of becoming morally depraved'.[5] Such legislation covered a very broad spectrum of behaviour and allowed the courts (and parents) a flexibility to charge girls who were known to be frequenting brothels, as well as those who defied their parents' orders, associated with particular companions, or went to dances or other social venues at night. Parents could thus resort to the courts in an attempt to induce obedience. In the same year in Toronto, a Morality Department was established to focus police attention on girls and women whose sexual behaviour was seen as a threat to themselves and others.[6]

Controlling rebel girls

Long before Ellen Nagle was locked up for the crime of stubbornness, Irish-born juveniles frequently found themselves on the wrong side of the law. In the twelve months preceding 30 September 1873, 2,009 male and female juvenile suspects were brought before the courts in Massachusetts. Of these, over 70 per cent were Irish-born.[7] And Ellen's father was far from unusual in having initiated his daughter's incarceration. Of those who entered the State Industrial School for Girls in Lancaster, Massachusetts, in its first year in 1856, 41 per cent were committed by parents, 32 per cent by the state, 6 per cent by concerned citizens, and 21 per cent by other agents (some of whom would have been acting on behalf of parents).[8]

A variety of institutions attempted both to punish and to

reform young women and girls. The Massachusetts Reformatory Prison for Women, where Ellen Nagle was sent following her conviction for stubbornness, had opened in Sherborn, around twenty miles from Boston, on 7 November 1877. Its establishment was influenced by contemporary nineteenth-century views across Europe and North America that women offenders were best served in distinctly female prisons with a largely female staff.[9] The institution was the result of several years of campaigning by philanthropic individuals and societies in Massachusetts.[10] It was based on fears that without a prison structure tailored to their gender, girls and women would be unable to reform and would leave prison more criminal than when they entered. Male wardens were also a concern. In 1874, Massachusetts lawyer and politician Emory Washburn argued: 'There is something positively revolting in the idea of shutting up women, few or many, under the care and control of a body of rough, coarse men, and practically without the pale of any outside influences in their favor.'[11] Women's prisons, on the other hand, would ideally have a female staff to ensure the reformation of erring girls and women through an orderly system of discipline, work, education and religious instruction specifically tailored to their sex.[12]

Prisoner number 1 at Sherborn was thirty-year-old Irish-born Hannah Sullivan, sentenced to a year for vagrancy.[13] She was one of 247 Irish girls and women admitted to the prison in its first eleven months. They made up 57.8 per cent of all 'foreign-birth and parentage' admissions and 31.1 per cent of the entire prison population during that period.[14] Sullivan and the other new arrivals to the institution were told of the hope that their admission 'would be a new starting-point in their existence for all eternity, a pause in this earthly life, a time for reflection, an opportunity for new principles to be formed, holy resolutions to be made, in the strength that God alone can give'.[15] By 1 October 1918, the Massachusetts Reformatory for Women had admitted 11,320 girls and women.[16] Our calculations indicate that at least 2,186, including Ellen Nagle, were Irish-born.

In addition to considerations of gender, penal reformers and philanthropists were also concerned about the mixing of offenders of diverse ages behind bars. The New York House of Refuge, the first juvenile reformatory in the United States, opened in 1825 for boys and girls. Irish children made up 63 per cent of all admissions between 1850 and 1855.[17] There girls worked in the laundry or were assigned other domestic tasks. Until the 1880s, girls who were considered reformed could be discharged as indentured servants, usually to families living in the country away from urban temptations.[18] But some came back to the institution. Irish-born Bridget Meuldary, who was admitted to the House of Refuge in January 1858 for stealing a coat, having previously spent ten days in jail for disobeying her mother's orders not to go to a fair, was returned by her master in July 1859 after three months. Bridget was indentured again in October but left that employment in April to live with her brother in Brooklyn.[19] The Ontario Industrial Refuge for Girls, which was attached to Andrew Mercer Ontario Reformatory for Females in Toronto, accepted girls as young as five years of age for petty offences.[20] Among the residents was Irish-born Mary Dean, sentenced in October 1882, aged thirteen, to five years in the institution for stealing, and eight-year-old Maria Thornton, admitted in April 1889 for a year for vagrancy. Thornton's return to the Refuge shortly after her release, this time for theft, shows that many girls who spent time in institutions were ill-prepared for the reality of life on the outside.[21]

In 1893, the Refuge was replaced by the Alexandra Industrial School for Girls.[22]

The State Industrial School for Girls in Lancaster, thirty miles outside Boston, admitted girls aged seven to fourteen. It was the first public reformatory in the United States designed more as a family unit than a prison, and had eight female staff members (known as matrons) assigned across four cottages.[23] Inhabitants' days were regimented, with chores, religious services, limited schooling, sewing or other domestic work deemed appropriate to their sex, and mealtimes, with only around one hour for free recreation.[24] Margaret O'Brien ended up in Lancaster in the 1870s at the request of her widowed mother, Kate. The death of Margaret's father in Ireland had left Kate a single mother and she had migrated alone to Boston to earn her living. When Margaret was around ten years old, Kate had sent money home to enable her daughter to join her in the United States and the two lived together while Kate worked as a servant in a boarding house. Margaret later became a waitress, but her misbehaviour vexed her mother and she ended up at Lancaster for three years.[25] Later Lancaster became a juvenile prison, taking girls who were too young for other penal institutions.[26]

From the 1850s, Catholic religious orders developed a range of institutions for the protection and reformation of children.[27] A number specifically catered for girls and young women and offered an alternative to the reformatory or prison. In Boston and New York, the Good Shepherd Sisters established institutions, as they did in Ireland, initially for the reformation of girls and women involved in the sex industry. By the turn of the twentieth century these institutions also accepted women and girls convicted of other crimes. Between 1857 and 1907, 13,018 females were admitted to the

New York House of the Good Shepherd, two thirds of whom were committed by the courts and one third of whom entered of their 'own will'.[28] In 1897, 52 per cent of girls in the Boston House of the Good Shepherd had been placed there by the courts.[29]

Large numbers of Irish girls were among the early admissions. According to the Good Shepherd Sisters in New York, these new immigrants were ignorant, duped into having accepted 'unawares their first night's shelter in abodes of sin, – to the ruin, alas! of their virtue!' Not all was lost though, because, the Sisters considered, 'the lively faith characteristic of the Irish soon awakens remorse, and they come to our door to be restored'.[30] Girls were generally admitted between the ages of eleven and sixteen and could remain until they were twenty-one.

Across this period, adolescence became increasingly seen as a distinct phase in the life cycle. Teenagers were not quite children, but they were not adults either and, as historian Barbara Brenzel points out, there was a perception that 'the onset of sexual maturity was a particularly vulnerable time for young girls already in some sort of trouble'.[31] Into the twentieth century, courts became more specialized in their treatment of juveniles, and legislation expanded the scope of prosecutions.[32] The first juvenile court was established in 1899 in Chicago, with New York following in 1902. Similar thinking about the nature of childhood was behind a national campaign in 1885 to raise the legal age of sexual consent, which in most states was either ten or twelve years.[33] The age of sexual consent in Boston increased to fourteen in the 1880s and sixteen in 1900,[34] and in New York it rose from ten to sixteen in 1887.[35] Boston's juvenile court opened in 1906, in a separate part of the Suffolk County Court House to the criminal courts, and in 1907 1,140 children were tried there.[36] In Canada, the Juvenile Delinquents Act, 1908, legislated for a juvenile court, which began hearing cases from 1910.[37] This was part of an international trend to distinguish between child and adult suspects and to ensure that a juvenile offender's presence in court didn't damage their future prospects. In the place of court reporters and the public were often judges, social workers and charity or state agents who wanted to offer protection and salvation and guide the young offender onto the right path. But if there was change in the treatment of children, there was no change in the highly gendered conception of many juvenile offences. A study in 1912 showed that 80 per cent of girls brought before the juvenile court in Chicago were charged with offences relating to sexual immorality, compared to just 2 per cent of boys.[38] The development of a women's night court in New York City in 1910 (which was a day court by 1918) and a women's court in Toronto in 1913 was similarly motivated. Among the defendants were hundreds of Irish-born teenagers, like nineteen-year-old Sarah Cooney, summoned to the New York court by Margaret Cooney (presumably her mother) in January 1911 and sent to the House of the Good Shepherd.[39] As historian Amanda Glasbeek points out, the establishment of such courts 'simultaneously legitimated and authorized a moral code that penalized women more than men for offences against morality'.[40]

The threat of city life

By 1900, Ellen Nagle was fifteen years old. She lived at home with her parents and siblings on Tremont Street in Boston's South End and worked as a cashier in a dry-goods store. She had attended school when she was younger, and it is likely that she left because the family valued her income more than her education. Legislation sought to restrict child labour, but the law in Massachusetts allowed children aged 10–14 to work up to eight hours a day if they attended school for six months of the year, and placed no restrictions on labour for children older than fourteen.[41] And the law could not reach the many Irish girls who worked in their own homes. Towards the end of the nineteenth century, truancy officers were appointed to monitor school attendance, but many poor families continued to depend on child labour either inside or outside the home.

Ellen Nagle grew up in Boston's South End, a district that was the subject of a study by Albert Benedict Wolfe around the time she lived there. In his book *The lodging house problem in Boston*, Wolfe singled out three streets that had a particular problem with 'social parasites': Shawmut Avenue (where Annie Young, from Chapter 3, lived in 1908), Washington Street, and Tremont Street, where Ellen lived at the time of her conviction for stubbornness. Wolfe mused: 'Just why so many palmists, card-readers, business mediums, trance-artists, astrologers, and the like should congregate in the South End, would be hard to say, but they are there and constitute an unpleasant feature of the district.' He added: 'Some are no doubt conducting places of prostitution in disguise.'[42]

Social reformers in North America also frowned upon girls' paid employment in particular venues. An official from the New York Children's Aid Society described a visit to an Irish mother in 1855. Her daughter was supposed to attend one of their industrial schools but was instead at work:

> We climbed again one of these rookeries. It is a back garret.
> A dark-eyed, passionate looking woman is sitting over the

little stove – and one of our little scholars is standing by – one of the prettiest and brightest children in the school. One of those faces you see in the West of Ireland, perhaps with some Spanish blood in them. A little, oval face, soft brown complexion, quick, dark eyes, and harsh, dark black hair.

The mother, on the other hand, 'looked like a woman who had seen much of the worst of life'. 'No, sir, I never did send them to school', she replied to the visitor, 'my husband, sir – he drinks, then he beats me. Look at that bruise!' she exclaimed, pointing to her cheek. The mother also described her young daughter's work: 'There's Peggy, goes selling fruit every night to those cellars in Water street – and they're *hells* sir. She's learning all sorts of bad words there, and don't get back till 11 or 12 o'clock.' The visitor asked why she allowed her to go there, clearly anxious about the 'sweet, dark-eyed little thing, getting her education unconsciously, every night in those vile cellars of dancing prostitutes'. 'I must sir', the mother insisted, noting that her husband 'makes nothing for me'. The official directed her to call to the Children's Aid Society offices to arrange a move to the country.[43]

In the latter decades of the nineteenth century, economic growth brought new employment opportunities for girls and women in restaurants and cafes, factories, shops, offices and the entertainment industry. The number of women earning a wage in the United States increased from 1.72 million in 1870 to 4.83 million by 1900. By 1920, this had increased again to 8.28 million, and women comprised a fifth of the total waged workforce.[44] These female workers had money to spend – and they sometimes spent it in the amusement parks, restaurants, dance halls and cinemas of urban America.

But these venues were also perceived as a threat to girls'

well-being. Sixteen-year-old Irish-born Mary Sheridan, who lived in New York, was 'in the habit of staying out nights and going to dances and refused to obey her mother or brother', so they had her admitted to the House of Refuge in February 1859.[45] Twenty years later, Irish teenager Ellen Morrissey's father 'sternly forbade' her to go to places of amusement and threatened arrest if she disobeyed him. When Ellen continued to go, her father kept his word and had her admitted to the same institution.[46] In the year preceding her arrest for being a stubborn child in 1882, Bridget Burns 'has been going to dances and living an immoral life'.[47] The content of theatrical and cinematic performances was thought to instil unrealistic fantasies, and along with saloons, restaurants and amusements facilitated youthful interaction between the sexes beyond parental surveillance. Organizations like the Young Women's Christian Association (YWCA) tried to provide alternative entertainments, as did homes like the Working Girls' Home off Harrison Avenue in Boston's South End.[48] But such efforts were not always successful. After Ellen Nagle ran away from home in 1902, she was said to have 'a passion for the stage' and to idolize theatre actors. When caught by the police she had been on her way to a theatre in the South End. Her pockets bulged with theatrical souvenir postcards and pictures.

Sex and the city

The Toronto Big Sister Association commented on unruly girls in the twentieth century: 'Often the whole root of the trouble is the absolutely loveless homes some of these girls appearing in the Juvenile Court come from. They get no encouragement, sympathy, or happiness in their home life, so who can blame them for going elsewhere to try to find these things?'[49]

Surviving records do not typically provide much insight on the realities of the home environment, but scraps of evidence point to the neglect and abuse of Irish daughters by family members, which might have influenced their running away. Seventeen-year-old Irish-born Maggie Miskelley acknowledged that she vexed her father by 'attending dances and shows which he disapproved', but she also said that he was 'very severe, and abusive'.[50] Mary Scott revealed that her widowed mother's drinking motivated her to run away from home.[51]

Nineteen-year-old Elizabeth Fingliss's prison case file, compiled after she was charged with stubbornness in April 1915, offers an unusual level of detail on family dynamics (ill. 4.2). She had emigrated with her parents, seven younger siblings (including four-month-old twins), paternal aunt and grandmother, from Drogheda to Fall River, Massachusetts, in 1907.[52] Their uncle, who was already in Fall River, had provided the passage fare.[53]

At her trial in 1915, Elizabeth Fingliss's mother described Elizabeth as keeping 'very unreasonable hours' before she ran away to New York with a travelling salesman. By Elizabeth's own admission, she 'had no special liking for him, but wanted to see NY'. When Elizabeth was asked if she had anything to say in response to her mother's claims, she replied: 'No, what's the use? She has said it all.' The probation officer pleaded with Elizabeth to show some remorse for her behaviour, but she 'emphatically declared that she would never again set foot in her home'. Judge Hanify hoped that another night in the police station 'would break the girl's spirit some', but on the following morning Elizabeth remained steadfast. The matron who admitted her to the

4.2. Elizabeth Fingliss, prison mugshot and admission details, 1915.

Massachusetts Reformatory Prison for Women, on a sentence of two years, described her as a 'girl who certainly shows a defiant, stubborn nature' and as 'bitter towards parents and everyone in general except fellows'.

Elizabeth's later conversations with prison staff, and their interviews with some of her relatives, revealed another side to the story. Before the family left Ireland, Elizabeth seems to have been reared by an aunt and a grandmother. When she was around twelve, her parents requested her to return to them so that she could help in the home. Following the family's immigration to Fall River, Elizabeth attended public school and cared for her siblings in the afternoons. When she was fourteen she left school to work in a mill. Elizabeth's mother was bewildered by her adolescent misbehaviour, because as 'a child Elizabeth was quiet and obedient'. She said that Elizabeth had always handed over her earnings, 'and if she earned any extra money which she could easily have kept [she] gave that to mother also'. Following an injury at the mill, Elizabeth took up work at a hotel. Her mother, though aware that hotel work was not necessarily considered appropriate for teenage girls, 'thought that as she had always been such a good girl that it was perfectly all right for her to go there'.

Elizabeth's Aunt Mary, who had cared for her in Ireland, revealed that Elizabeth had not wanted to return to her parents' care when she was twelve, and that she complained following the move that 'she would never be happy again'. In prison, Elizabeth reported that her father was 'a hard drinker' who 'frequently struck Eliz[abeth] or her mother'. He deserted the family before the birth of Elizabeth's youngest sibling and remained away for about six weeks. Elizabeth remembered his violent abuse when her mother was pregnant: 'He licked my moth[er] awful just before the last baby was born.' Elizabeth's Aunt Mary, her grandmother and her uncle (who 'bought her very pretty clothes') had anticipated sending Elizabeth to high school and judged 'it to have been a serious mistake that Elizabeth was not permitted to finish her schooling'. Mary also accused Elizabeth's mother of being 'a very queer mother not to know where her daughter was' and 'very negligent' in allowing Elizabeth to work in a hotel. She blamed Elizabeth's parents 'wholly' for her behaviour.

A prison official, S. L. Shea, who interviewed Elizabeth's Aunt Mary and her mother while Elizabeth was incarcerated in the Massachusetts Reformatory Prison for Women, viewed Mary as a reliable informant and described her as 'A thin, worried looking person who feels the responsibility of all that happens in the family . . . undoubtedly would be a splendid companion in all ways for Elizabeth.' Elizabeth's mother, on the other hand, was described as 'the type who feeds her family but beyond this has no plan for their future; not capable of controlling a girl with wayward tendencies'. Her house was a 'five room tenement in a large frame house. A cheap desolate neighbourhood. Furnished comfortably but everything was cluttered and untidy. The smell of boiling cabbage filled the house and had attracted many flies.' Shea concluded that it was a 'most unattractive home for a young girl'.

After having run away from home, Elizabeth Fingliss explained that she and her female friend 'went around with men "of their own kind"', likely a reference to race. She admitted that during this time she sometimes 'had only one meal a day. What she did have, was given her by men.' As historian Mary Odem has observed: 'Young women discovered early on that their sexuality was a valued commodity that they could trade for things they wanted or needed.'[54] 'Treating' was the name given to the practice whereby girls provided favours 'ranging from flirtatious companionships to sexual intercourse in exchange for men's treats'.[55] Girls who did not have their own income, or who were compelled to hand earnings to their parents, could enjoy leisure venues like the cinema, theatre, restaurants and cafes through this practice. While Elizabeth allowed the men to buy her meals, she insisted that 'she did not take money' on these occasions.

The idea that money was not directly exchanged seems to have differentiated, in the girls' minds at least, treating and prostitution.[56] Officials, of course, had other views of the activity of so-called 'good-time girls'.[57]

In January 1916, after eight months in prison, Elizabeth Fingliss was interviewed by members of the parole board. The questions show the board's concern with Elizabeth's sexual history, while her answers reveal the blurred lines between 'treating' practices and prostitution. With probing, the board determined that Elizabeth had been sexually active for around three years:

Q[uestion] How many different men had you been going with during that 3 years?
A[nswer] About 4 men. . . .
Q. What was the longest period you were with any man?
A. Just for an evening, I think, I don't remember.
Q. Come, you must remember that. Every girl remembers when they do wrong. You want us to help you, and your past history is such that you need some treatment. Where had you been living with those men?
A. I never lived with any man.
Q. Where did they take you, to a hotel?
A. Yes.
Q. How much did the men pay you?
A. There was only two of those men I ever got any money from, they were Fall River men.
Q. How much would they pay you? By the night, or how?
A. When I didn't have any money I would ask them to give me some.
Q. You would always feel when they wanted you you would go?

A. Yes.

Q. Were they men of standing, or men who worked in the mill?

A. One was a business man. They were well-respected men in Fall River.

Q. Did you know other girls who went with these two men?

A. Yes.

Q. They made a business of it?

A. Yes.

Q. Would you meet these men in the cafes? Or where did you meet them first?

A. On the street.

Q. Did somebody else point them out to you as men you might earn money from?

A. No, I got acquainted with them.

Q. Would those other girls get money?

A. I don't know.

'The error of her way' and the fate of Ellen Nagle

There was a strong cultural desire to see the criminalization of stubbornness, disobedience and sexual waywardness in girls and young women as serving a reforming purpose. Those who fell foul of this system learned to speak its language.

Elizabeth Fingliss was released on parole in January 1916 to the care of her Aunt Mary. Elizabeth, who had been adamant at her trial in Massachusetts that she would not return to her family home, struck a different note while on parole. She wrote to the superintendent of the prison: 'I intend to be a good girl and lead a good life because it pays to be good in the long run.' Eighteen-year-old Catherine Holmes, who emigrated from Ireland with her parents when she was around six, ended up in the same prison in 1901 because she 'Kept company with bad girls and did not go home nights.' Her mother had threatened her 'for a long time past that she would have her sent away but she did not think she meant it'. Holmes's prison record notes that she 'is sorry she did not mind her mother'.[58] A few years earlier, Bridget Kennedy similarly recalled that she did 'not obey her mother who disapproved of her staying out nights and thought she knew what was best for herself. Now thinks she sees the error of her way. And can appreciate her mother.'[59]

Ellen Nagle was released from the Massachusetts Reformatory Prison for Women on 9 March 1904 after almost ten months behind bars. Her father, who had had her put away, lived long enough to see her marry Greek-born Michael Cazis in February 1906, when she was twenty and Cazis was twenty-two. He would also have known about Ellen's subsequent pregnancy, but he died six weeks before the birth of her daughter. The 1910 census listed Ellen as living in the same tenement building on Tremont Street as her now widowed mother, widowed aunt, brother, and niece and nephew. Perhaps this was the sort of case the secretary of the Board of State Charities was thinking of when he observed in 1873 that 'A bad girl who has become a good woman will bless the firm hand that saved her.'[60]

5. Drink and the case of the Toronto drunks

'Sin and whiskey were written in the faces of every one of them', a journalist wrote on observing a group of women in the Toronto police court in May 1865. A 'harder, more uncivilized and depraved looking set of abandoned women never appeared before the Court' than this group of eleven women who had been arrested on Garrison Common. Seven of them were Irish and they were all arrested for being drunk. The women were described as 'stargazers', a term used for sex workers who worked outside. They had been drinking and probably soliciting for trade from the soldiers in Fort York beside the Common.[1]

Margaret McCormack was the eldest of the group at eighty years of age. She may not have been an active sex worker, but had been caught drinking and was arrested with the others. She found her situation in court hilarious and 'with spasmodic fits of laughter enjoyed her elevation in the dock'. Julia Tracy, who was twenty years old, kept elbowing Margaret to get her to stop laughing, but her efforts had little effect and Margaret repeatedly dissolved into giggles. Twenty-year-old Maria Lee was apparently someone to whom 'temperance, honesty and industry were a thing of the past', and Elizabeth Stamford, who 'with a red comforter around her head' repeatedly shouted to the other women what was on the menu in jail that day, added to the confusion and chaos. Catherine Glinn was 'a frail one', dressed in tattered rags, and 21-year-old Margaret Howard promised the magistrate that she would behave herself in future. This group of women were sent to prison together for sixty days.

That May Saturday night in Toronto was clearly a busy one for Irish women. Charged alongside the seven Irish women who had been arrested at Fort York were another four Irish women who had been picked up in the city. Among them was Margaret Sherlock, another court regular, who went 'astray with a glass of whiskey' and was so drunk that she could not find her way home. The journalist joked that 'She will have a free ride to the gaol – her proper home – and lodging for two months.' Sarah King, another eighty-year-old suspect with a bad reputation, was ill and requested that the judge sentence her to a few months in prison, evidently seeing it not as a punishment but as a chance to get well again.

George Denison, writing about his experiences as a magistrate in the Toronto police court from 1877, described how the Irish 'added very much to the humour of the proceedings in the Court'.[2] During his time as a magistrate, he likely encountered individuals like these eleven Irish women, or like Letitia Dixon, an 'old offender', who had been in the court only a few days before. She was considered by the court reporter to be 'one of the drunkest looking citizens who could be picked up'. Alongside her was 24-year-old Ellen Price, who cut a striking figure with a red feather in her hat. As Price left court to begin her sixty-day sentence, she burst into a rendition of 'The Rocky Road to Dublin', suggesting that she might still have been feeling the effects of her night's spree.[3] Singing was also part of Eleanor David's conviction. This so-called 'virago' had been drunkenly singing in front of one of Toronto's music halls when stopped by a policeman a few months before Ellen Price's arrest. She refused to move and he was compelled to drag her along the street until reinforcements arrived to carry her to the police station. Eleanor David told the policeman that she loved whiskey and 'as long as there was a drop of Irish blood left in her body she would drink it'. She declared that 'she wouldn't stop until the sods of the valley covered her'.[4]

When the *Toronto Globe* began to include the nationalities of offenders in reports of court proceedings in the spring of 1865, it became apparent that many of the women in the courtroom were Irish-born, and most of them had been charged with offences relating to alcohol.[5] For the Irish in North America, both male and female, alcohol-related offences were the most common cause of conviction. In 1859, 58.8 per cent of all Irish convictions in the New York Courts of Special Sessions were for being drunk or for disorderly conduct.[6] By 1876, the Irish were no longer the largest ethnic group arrested and prosecuted for most offences, but they continued to top the table for intoxication and disorderly conduct offences.[7] In Boston too the rapid increase in arrests for drunkenness in the 1840s was blamed on the influx of Irish immigrants and the 'Irishman's appreciation of spirituous drink'.[8]

Did the Irish really drink much more than everyone else? The Catholic Archbishop of Toronto, John Joseph Lynch, considered that they were just unusually susceptible to the effects of alcohol. He noted in 1875: 'the Irish people do not drink more than others; but their blood is so hot, and their nature so fervid and exuberant, that adding to it the fire of alcohol the Irishman becomes more unreasonable than men of other and more plodding temperaments'.[9] Irish drinking practices were also thought to contribute to their high arrest rate. A *New York Times* journalist considered that Irish men's fondness for drinking in bars and saloons resulted in their drunkenness; German immigrants also consumed considerable amounts of alcohol, but typically drank in more family-friendly social settings with their wives and children.[10] According to historian Kevin Kenny, Italian immigrants' tendency to consume food alongside alcohol rendered them less susceptible to charges of drunkenness than Irish men drinking in bars and saloons.[11]

Irish women also dominated the statistics for drunken public order offences. In Boston, New York and Toronto these were the most common crimes for which Irish women were arrested or prosecuted. In the Boston House of Correction, for example, 81.6 per cent of the charges against 6,481 Irish women sentenced between 1882 and 1915 were alcohol related.[12] In a sample of 3,032 Irish women who entered Toronto Gaol between 1853 and 1908, 2,007 (66.2 per cent) were convicted of drunkenness.[13] In New York, 63.4 per cent of a sample of 1,124 Irish-born women convicted at the Women's Night Court between 1911 and 1918 were there for intoxication.[14] These figures do not include charges of disorderly conduct without an explicit reference to alcohol, but it seems certain that alcohol was a leading factor in many such disorderly conduct charges as well.

Contemporary accounts often revealed negative associations between the Irish and alcohol. The New York Association for the Improvement of the Condition of the Poor (AICP) described the Irish in 1860 as having 'little thrift, economy, or forecast, and are often addicted to intemperance'.[15] Elsa Herzfeld, in her 1905 ethnographic study of families living in New York tenements, found that 'Often the Irish do not wish to be called Irish because that implies a term of contempt' and that they were commonly viewed by other nationalities as drinking and fighting 'continually'.[16] Even Irish writers commented on the problem of alcohol and the Irish in America. Thomas Colley Grattan devoted the first chapter of the second volume of his 1859 book *Civilized America* to the Irish in America. He believed that it was in response to discrimination that the Irish became 'the mass of ignorance and intemperance which disgraces the Atlantic cities'.[17] In 1868, Irish writer and politician John Francis Maguire took the view that alcohol was 'the most serious obstacle to the advancement of the Irish in America'. On his travels around North America he found that 'invariably the lowest class of groggery [liquor shop] . . . is planted right in the centre of the densely crowded Irish quarter of a great city'.[18]

The Irish hard drinker, criminal yet often comical, became a stock character in North American culture from the mid-nineteenth century. Historian Richard Strivers argues that Irish hard drinking was about creating an Irish identity in America and the more the Irish drank the more they conformed to the stereotype of the Irish drinker.[19] Irish women were also perceived to drink more abroad than at home. Some contemporaries argued that Irish women were moral and sober before emigrating but were corrupted by American city life, where wages were higher and alcohol was cheaper and more freely available than in Ireland.[20] In his advice book for Irish Catholic domestic servants, George Deshon warned of the 'sin of drunkenness'. He cautioned that it could turn a 'pretty, modest girl' into a 'bloated, coarse looking woman, who has not, apparently, combed her hair for a week', living in a 'miserable, dirty hovel'.[21] But regardless of the stereotype, what is clear is that the association between the Irish and problematic drinking was based on a reality whereby Irish women and men dominated the criminal statistics for drunk and disorderly offences, and Irish immigrants suffered the highest rates of alcoholism and alcohol-related deaths of any ethnic population in the United States in the late nineteenth century.[22]

The evidence from courtrooms often points to sad or tragic circumstances in the lives of women who found themselves in the dock for drunkenness. In other cases, defendants cheerfully played up to their attentive audience. This chapter tells the stories of the drunken escapades, alcoholism and poverty of Irish women abroad, against a background of the stereotype of the drunken Irish.

Drunken Irish women

Drunkenness among the Irish in America was closely interwoven with poverty. The 'disorganizing effects' of being poor could lead a woman to drink, while her addiction to alcohol could in turn render her unable to escape poverty.[23] The New York Five Points *Monthly Record* described in 1865 the living conditions of an Irish Catholic family with a small baby:

> If dirt engenders disease we certainly need not be surprised at the poor little moaning specimen of humanity in that rough cradle, for never was foot set in a dirtier den, and here live her mother and father – whose features tell a sad tale of intemperance and vice.[24]

Staff of the Five Points Mission who visited another Irish Catholic family in the same month similarly observed that they lived in a 'miserable dark room', 'yet the husband is a strong healthy man, and the wife a powerful woman in the prime of life. But intemperance has opened the door, and let in poverty and misery'.[25] New York philanthropist and author Helen Campbell described the Irish living in New York tenements in the 1890s:

To many of them the saloon is heaven compared to the hell of their miserable homes. A few cents often obtained by pawning the last decent rag that covers their shivering children will buy enough drink to make a father or mother insensible to the wretchedness that awaits them at home. With these people to be drunk is to be happy.[26]

But drinking could render charity workers less sympathetic towards those in poverty, as a member of the AICP in New York revealed when he visited an Irish woman's home in 1879. She was in tears because her landlord was going to evict her, and her husband had been injured at work. The AICP worker admitted that his 'sympathies for her were not so strong when I saw a pitcher half full of beer on her cupboard shelf'.[27]

The Irish were not merely consumers of alcohol. An 1851 survey in Boston found that most groggeries were in Irish hands;[28] and in New York by 1860 between a third and a half of the liquor trade was run by the Irish.[29] In Toronto, Irish drinking revolved around shebeens that sold poteen and became dens of gambling, prostitution and violence.[30] In the Boston area, grog shops or illicit drinking places were 'likely to be little more than a table and a few chairs set up in the kitchen or bedroom of a tenement'.[31] Massachusetts legislation from 1875 required licences to sell alcohol in public spaces, but many of the Irish who ran these kitchen barrooms didn't take out licences because they couldn't afford the fee required. Instead, they took the risk of getting a small fine as punishment.[32]

Likewise, in Toronto, selling liquor without a licence was not treated particularly severely. Thirty-four Irish-born women were identified in the Toronto police registers for this offence between 1861 and 1893. Of these, eighteen were fined between $20 and $40, fourteen had their cases dismissed and two cases were adjourned. Where an occupation was given, nine of the women were identified as grocers and were presumably selling alcohol illegally out of their shops. Others were tavern keepers, ran boarding houses or were listed as prostitutes. Thirteen of the women were domestic servants or had no occupation recorded so were most likely selling alcohol from their homes.[33] Of a sample of 3,032 Irish-born women in Toronto Gaol from 1858 to 1908, only three were charged with illegally selling alcohol, for which they were punished with a relatively light sentence of 30–40 days in prison. Among them was Mary Downey. She appeared before the Toronto police court in December 1877, charged with selling liquor without a licence and had her case adjourned. She wasn't so fortunate several months later when she was up before the court again for the same offence. This time the magistrate was less sympathetic and sentenced her to thirty days in prison. The 75-year-old was listed as a boarding-house keeper, although a newspaper report two years later in 1880 telling of her arrest for keeping a disorderly house suggests that she was involved in a range of illegal activities.[34] Another Irish offender was fifty-year-old Annie Sexton, who was undone in July 1878 by James Macdonald, one of Toronto's 'whiskey detectives', whose job it was to detect illegal alcohol sales. He told the court how he had gone to Sexton's house with two companions and they each had a glass of whiskey, which Macdonald had paid for. Sexton pleaded not guilty but was found guilty and was sentenced to thirty days in prison.[35]

As in Ireland, pubs and saloons were generally for men, and women who frequented them were considered of dubious moral character.[36] Women typically had to drink elsewhere and, given the poor living conditions in many urban areas, this was often outside, on the streets. Outdoor drinking made women publicly visible, like the Toronto 'stargazers' who opened this chapter. They were thus easy targets for the police. In May 1865, Bridget Burns was found drunk by the police on Portland Street in Toronto and arrested, as were Bridget McDonald and Mary Taylor, who were drunk and fighting on Bathurst Street.[37] In Boston, Mary Fitzpatrick, who 'always drank beer; never drank whiskey till a year ago', was sitting on her doorstep, drunk, when she was arrested in 1896.[38] Writer Robert Ernst observed that in the Irish-dominated First Ward in New York 'immigrants were easy prey for policemen'. Fearful of the consequences of raiding 'gambling dens, brothels, and criminal hideouts', police instead 'kept a sharp eye for slight misdemeanours committed by persons of no political influence'.[39] Arrests for intoxication occurred when there was a violation of public decency, and women drinking on the streets and causing a public nuisance fell into this category.

Specific streets and areas with bad reputations attracted more police attention. In his memoirs, Toronto magistrate George Denison described Stanley Street, inhabited by Irish immigrants, as 'one of the slums of the city' that had 'acquired a very unsavoury reputation'.[40] The police had an easy arrest on Stanley Street in May 1865 when Bridget McDonnell was found 'lying comfortable', clearly drunk, in an empty yard. She was sentenced to sixty days in prison, alongside the other Irish women who opened this chapter.[41]

In the 1870s and early 1880s in New York, women were convicted at a higher rate than men for drunk and disorderly conduct, while making up a smaller proportion of arrests. The Board of Police Justices in 1874 reasoned that this was because women were 'more frequent and persistent' than men in coming back again and again to court, and also that 'public exhibitions of drunkenness in females indicate a depraved and abandoned condition'.[42] This view of women involved in public drinking motivated the New York police to remove these 'public exhibitions' from the streets to the prison. In Toronto, from 1913 the women's rate of conviction for drunkenness was higher than their overall conviction rate for all other crimes.[43] Women, then, were more likely to be convicted when charged with drunken and disorderly behaviour than for other crimes. When Mary Gleason was brought to the Toronto police court on a charge of drunkenness in 1881, she insisted that she was innocent. She argued that she couldn't have been drunk because she had been working all day. But Gleason wasn't believed and she was sentenced to a $1 fine or thirty days in prison.[44] The combination of the 'cultural stereotypes of Irish drinking', along with the public visibility of women on the streets, undoubtedly contributed to the high number of arrests of Irish women for drinking offences.[45]

Unsurprisingly, therefore, many Irish female drinkers became caught up in a constant cycle through the courts and jails. In New York, arrested prisoners were often detained until trial in the Hall of Detention, commonly known as the Tombs. If found guilty they would usually be transferred to other penal institutions. The police court, where minor offences such as drunkenness were heard, was located in the Tombs and those found guilty in this court were regularly sent to the penitentiary or workhouse, which were on Blackwell's Island in the East River. Many women arrested for drunkenness didn't even reach Blackwell's Island because their offences were considered so minor that they were released after spending five days in the Tombs. But they were often arrested again in the days or weeks thereafter to repeat the

cycle. Flora Foster, the matron of the female prison department at the Tombs, considered these repeat offenders the
'saddest feature' of her work. She described the 'five days'
corridor', where 'the scum of the city, its moral filth, is turned
in daily to remain in masses of indescribable wretchedness and drunkenness for five days, and then to be sent to
Blackwell's Island or discharged to return again and again'.[46]
Many women, known as 'rounders', spent years 'alternating
between the prison and liquor saloons'.[47]

The Women's Prison Association (WPA) in New York
condemned the short sentences given to women, which kept
them 'incessantly fluctuating between the street and District
Prisons and workhouses', where they 'do not recover from
the effects of one spree before they are turned adrift to
become victims of another'.[48] Hundreds of examples of
'rounders' can be seen in prison registers in Boston, New
York and Toronto. Ann Burns, who was in her twenties, was
admitted to Toronto Gaol nine times between January and
November 1868 for being drunk and disorderly. Ann Healy
entered the same prison on at least thirty-four different occasions in our sample of cases between 1873 and 1898. She was
eighty-four years old at her last known prosecution for being
drunk, in September 1898. Mary Benson, a 34-year-old char-
woman, was convicted five times for being drunk in 1903
and seven times in 1908, and undoubtedly had many more
convictions in the intervening years.[49]

The WPA believed that if women spent time in a halfway
house, such as the one it ran in New York, it would break the
cycle of drink and imprisonment. There the 'victims of
intemperance', who had been 'led astray at first by the social
element of the Irish, and by an inherited appetite' for alcohol, could be watched to make sure they didn't 'fall back

under the despotism of old habits'.[50] Increasing calls were made for longer sentences for 'habitual rounders'. By the turn of the twentieth century, the WPA argued that a more prolonged, forced abstinence from alcohol would allow convicted women to receive medical treatment and recover from 'the effects of dissipation', before they could be given training in particular industries.[51] In the early twentieth century, the Toronto press referred to the short sentences given for drunkenness as a 'rest cure', and this was about as much reformation as habitually drunk women received.[52]

Temperance activists grew more vocal into the twentieth century, leading to a prohibition on the production and sale of alcohol in Toronto between 1916 and 1927, and in the United States from 1920 to 1933. It was only in the 1930s, following the ending of prohibition, that there were any real changes in how alcohol abuse was treated. Alcoholics Anonymous was founded in 1935 and extended to Canada in 1940. It offered a radical new approach to managing alcoholism – much too late for most of the Irish women who feature in this chapter.[53]

Bad company and lonely women

Groups of drunken Irish women, like the motley band who appeared before the Toronto police court in May 1865, were a common sight in North American cities. Drunkenness was, in other words, a very social phenomenon, and 'bad company' was often blamed for introducing women to the demon drink and leading them astray. Ellen McGuire migrated to New York in 1844 when she was eighteen. Four years later, while housed in the WPA Home after being released from prison, she explained that she arrived alone to the city and 'happened to see an old woman that she had seen in Ireland' who was kind to her and took her in. But this associate 'was in the habit of drinking' and McGuire 'very soon learned' the same habit.[54] A similar tale was told by 24-year-old Ellen O'Neil when she entered the WPA Home a month after McGuire. She had become lonely when looking after her sick mother, she explained, and spent time with a neighbour who 'was in the habit of drinking and they would insist on her drinking with them'.[55] An Irish woman in Toronto, identified only as E. J., had not been in Canada very long when, according to a mission worker at Toronto Gaol in 1869, she 'picked up the acquaintance of some evil disposed persons'. She had 'one of those amiable and easily led dispositions who cannot say "no"' and this led to her transformation from a 'sober, respectable, useful girl' to a 'total wreck, fallen so low in so short a time, as to become a confirmed drunkard, and leading a life of shame'.[56]

Of course, many women saw the need to present themselves as innocent victims who had been led astray, in order to secure charity or sympathy from the authorities. But it should not be assumed that such claims were entirely false. For those who had migrated by themselves or at a young age, loneliness, homesickness and a desire for any kind of company are unsurprising. Such dynamics often led exceptionally young girls into trouble with alcohol. When ten-year-old Mary Watson was admitted to Toronto Gaol in 1868 for being drunk, it was her tenth arrest. Another ten-year-old Irish girl, Bridget Golding, was sent to the same prison in the same year for being drunk and disorderly.[57]

Other Irish women's explanations for drinking point to heart-breaking experiences of separation, bereavement and personal tragedy. Minnie O'Connor migrated to the US at the age of fifteen. Three years later she married Billy Scannell, who was described as 'the greatest comedian of his class in an age, the gem of the cluster among the singers of Irish melodies and the Irish comedians'.[58] Following his death in 1894, the grief-stricken Minnie 'altered her manner of living'.[59] She was charged with drunkenness in March 1905 and sentenced to the Massachusetts Reformatory Prison for Women. Once 'envied and admired from one end of the land to the other', she there, according to a journalist, 'joins the others who have fallen by the wayside of the drink demon's thoroughfare'.[60]

Historian Gunja SenGupta observes that 'some variation of the phrase "Trouble drove her to the first glass" ran like a refrain through New York WPA case records'.[61] Margaret Wilson reportedly resorted to drinking after her husband of five years left her and took their children to his aunt in Springfield, Massachusetts. The 23-year-old explained that 'she was always a good woman until she discovered her Husband was supporting another woman. This is the cause of her intemperance.'[62] Julia Murphy, aged thirty-two, was similarly 'not happy with husband, felt melancholy and took a little to cheer her up once in a while'.[63] Irish-born 24-year-old Elizabeth Pierce said her husband 'did not treat her kindly' and had taken her child away and she then got 'so discouraged she drank too much'. Her parents and friends were in Ireland and she had no friends in America.[64] Mary Sweeney explained, following her imprisonment in the Massachusetts Reformatory for Women, that after the death of her first husband she 'became entirely discouraged, started drinking and has kept this up for the past 24 years'.[65]

Infant mortality rates were unimaginably high by present-day standards – 52 per cent in New York in 1850, for example – and this meant that motherhood for the poor was often 'a wrenching experience of loss and despair'.[66] For many Irish women, the death of children drove them to drink. By 1848, 24-year-old Catherine Ryan was already a widow and had lost two children. Her mother was in Ireland and, according to her own account, she had 'no friends in this country'. She was in the Emigrant Hospital in New York for six months, but even in the hospital there was 'so much liquor she was induced to drink'.[67] By 1892, Annie Proud in Boston had 'buried several children and drank to drown her sorrow'.[68] Another Irish woman, 28-year-old Mary Connor, 'lost her little daughter' a week before her incarceration on a charge of drunkenness. She explained that she 'was lonely and discouraged[,] took a drink to drown her sorrow[,] says she never indulged in intemperance before'.[69]

Mary Mountjoy's father died in Ireland when she was thirteen. She worked as a domestic servant until her marriage aged seventeen but was a widow by the age of thirty. She buried seven children in Ireland before migrating to Massachusetts around the turn of the century with her two surviving sons. She married again. On arrest for drunkenness in 1910, she explained that she was 'intemperate a good many years' and that 'her husband also drinks'.[70] When her second husband died, she remarried, this time to a man whom she described as 'crazy as the devil himself when drunk'. Prison officials observed that Mary was 'more than good-natured' when she returned to the prison on another charge of drunkenness. 'I'll have a bed to sleep in and a bite to eat', she said.[71]

The drunken mother

On both sides of the Atlantic, it was feared that women's drinking caused the degeneration of society through the breakdown of domestic order.[72] Mothers who drank were particularly condemned by religious and charitable authorities. The 1856 annual report of the New York Children's Aid Society described the 'ghastly wounds and diseases of society' that saw 'women, mad with liquor, abandoning their children'. In the Irish-dominated area of 'Dutch Hill' in New York, the report went on, 'the women all drink' and the children are 'ragged and unprotected'.[73]

With the establishment of child protection organizations in the 1870s, children were increasingly taken from drunken parents. The possibility that taking children away from their mothers might encourage, rather than discourage, alcohol consumption was not often considered. Child protection agents, law enforcement officers and charitable society staff often made judgements about a mother's drinking based on living conditions or appearances. In March 1908, Miss Early from the Cambridge Associated Charities in Massachusetts reported an Irish mother, Mary Kelley, who supposedly 'drinks hard', to the MSPCC. Early had never seen Kelley drunk, nor spoken to any witnesses who had, but believed 'she had every evidence in the woman's appearance and conditions in the home'.[74] The agent of the New York Society for the Prevention of Cruelty to Children (NYSPCC) who visited Mary Rooney in November 1880 came to a similar conclusion, and while Rooney insisted that 'she never drank', the agent judged that 'her dissipated face and unsteady gait told a different tale'.[75]

Alcoholism could, of course, lead to parental neglect. In Boston, in 1841, Mary Byrnes was found drunk on a bottle of rum less than twenty-four hours after starting a new job as a servant. She absented herself a few days later but left behind her five-year-old daughter, saying she would return for her when she found a place to stay in Boston. After two weeks, Byrnes's former mistress still had not heard from her and feared she would not return for her daughter.[76] In 1899, Mary O'Connor's husband, Thomas, had her arrested for drunkenness in Boston. A local newspaper described the case as a 'sad one' whereby Thomas, 'a hard working mechanic, has the sympathy of all who are acquainted with the struggle he has made during recent years to keep his wife away from liquor'. Thomas revealed that his wife had pawned their children's clothes, sold the family's groceries, and pretended that her children were sick in order to get money to fund her addiction.[77]

Child protection agency records are full of descriptions of drunken Irish mothers. In Brooklyn, an NYSPCC officer directed Maggie Kearns's arrest in August 1891 after neighbours found her two young infants alone and crying for food. The father was discovered in a police station, where he had been imprisoned for intoxication, while Maggie was found 'hilariously drunk' at a picnic. They were accused of 'unnatural conduct towards their children' and sent to jail to await trial. Their children were placed in an institution in the interim.[78] Frank Lennon reported to the MSPCC in 1908 that his Irish-born ex-wife was using his child support payments to fund her alcoholism and he felt their seven-month-old baby would be better off with him instead.[79] Another Irish woman was investigated by the MSPCC over several years following her arrest for drunkenness in May 1908. An agent described her as 'intemperate and immoral', while neighbours considered her a 'hard drinker'. The agent described the mother thus: 'Irish, has vicious, dissipated looking face'. But before her marriage she had been a model and had been known as the 'belle of the North End' for her beauty. Her husband, described as 'a large fat Italian', was supposed to have spent more than $4,000 in fines following her fifty-three arrests.[80]

James Greene filed for divorce from his Irish-born wife, Mary, in 1906, while she was being held in the Massachusetts Reformatory Prison for Women on a charge of drunkenness. The Boston tailor argued that 'if his wife left Sherborn and he was denied a divorce he would be compelled to leave Boston to escape her annoyances'. Their twenty-year-old daughter testified that she 'had been compelled to leave one place of employment on account of her mother's visiting her store for money while intoxicated' and on other occasions had had to hide underneath the shop counter to evade her mother. She 'had no memory of ever having seen her mother sober'.[81]

Drunk and dangerous

The majority of women who were arrested for drunken behaviour were habitual criminals who were found drunk on the street, making noise, fighting or generally behaving in a way that was considered disorderly. But in some cases women's extreme drinking landed them in dangerous situations or fuelled criminal or violent behaviour. Mary Duffy had a narrow escape in July 1858 when a police officer found her hanging from the windowsill of a fourth-storey window of a house on Seventh Avenue in New York. Mary was described as 'an Irish woman, of intemperate habits' who had 'recently been suffering from *delirium tremens*'. The police advised her friends 'to keep a sharper eye on her, and not to allow her in future to sleep at such an elevated height from the ground'.[82] A year earlier, Mary Brown had been arrested at three o'clock in the morning running down Queen Street in Toronto in the nude while suffering from delirium caused by 'excessive use of ardent spirits'. She was sentenced to a month in prison.[83] Ellen O'Brien was released from Toronto Gaol on 27 July 1900 having served thirty days for drunkenness. About 11.30 that morning she went to King Street East, where she began to drink with two associates. The three women drank around four litres of beer to celebrate O'Brien's release. Later in the afternoon the police were called to the house following a report that a woman had died. They found O'Brien dead and the other two women almost unconscious. The inquest into her death determined that she died from asphyxiation, having rolled over on her face on the floor.[84]

Some women's extreme drinking caused them to harm others as well as themselves. Catherine Duffy, known as 'Drunken Kitty', was suffering from delirium tremens when she came home from a night of drinking in New York and assaulted her husband, Patrick. The patrolman who attended the scene described hearing loud screams. He entered the couple's apartment to find the bed on fire. Patrick, who was also in flames, was 'dancing around the room', while Catherine was 'standing in the middle of the room, with the kerosene oil can in her hand, shrieking like a demon'.[85]

Certain areas of cities, particularly Irish ghettoes, were closely associated with alcohol and drinking. It was said that men and women could be seen hurrying home to the Boston tenements on Saturday nights with 'well-filled cans' in their hands or 'protruding from the folds of a carelessly arranged shawl'. Women were apparently 'more conspicuous' than men at these tenement parties that 'began in a private glass between friends' but could assume 'public and painful proportions'.[86] This was the case at number 20 Rochester Street in Boston's South End in September 1885. Bridget Hennessy and her husband were drinking together, and by ten o'clock they had become 'highly intoxicated' and began to quarrel.[87] Their landlady, Nora O'Brien, a seventy-year-old Irish widow, was in the apartment next door with her guest, Mary O'Leary. Mary had been working all week and, after drinking a pint of whiskey, she 'extended her weary limbs' alongside Nora in the bed. But just as they were going to sleep, they heard the Hennesseys arguing. Mary 'yelled out to them to shut up and go to bed like decent people'. This enraged Bridget, who 'came to the door and had some words with Mary' and then threw a tin can at her head. A little while later Nora O'Brien rose from the bed to get some water at the shared sink and again encountered Bridget. Mary recalled: 'the next thing I knew was that Mrs O'Brien had gone down the stairs with a crash that startled everyone'. Mary was sure that Bridget had pushed Nora but admitted that she 'could not swear to it'. The neighbours summoned the police, but by the time an ambulance arrived Nora was dead.

Bridget Hennessy went on the run following the incident, leaving her husband asleep in a chair. A description of Bridget was circulated to all police stations. She was five feet tall, 'rather stout', with dark hair and dark eyes. When last seen she was wearing an old calico dress and a faded patterned shawl, which she used to cover her head. She was caught a few hours after the incident, whereupon she gave her account of events. She claimed that they were all drinking together that evening. Later she enraged Mary O'Leary by refusing to stop singing after Mary and Nora retired to bed. Mary grabbed Bridget by the hair, pulling out several handfuls, and hit her. Bridget tried to go upstairs to her room but, she claimed, Nora O'Brien refused her permission to do so. Bridget admitted that she was 'mad, and had liquor in, and without meaning to harm her gave her a little tip and she fell downstairs'. Bridget said her husband had given her shawl to her and directed her to run away, which she did. When the case went to trial Bridget initially pleaded not guilty to manslaughter but later changed her plea and was sentenced to five years in Boston's House of Correction.

Four years later, Irish-born Sarah Ann Ward and Ann Hennessy, no relation to Bridget, got into an argument following an afternoon drinking spree.[88] Sarah Ann accused Ann of having 'undue intimacy' with her husband. They started to fight, and Sarah Ann grabbed a flat iron and hit Ann on the head with it. When Ann was found, she was lying unconscious in a pool of blood on Sarah Ann's floor. When she regained consciousness, she also revealed that Sarah Ann had kicked her while she lay on the ground and had thrown her shoes into the street.

Sarah Ann recounted a different story as to how Ann ended up with a four-inch gash on her head. She said that a man had come into the house with a 'pint of liquor', which they all consumed. When Sarah Ann directed the man to leave, Ann threw a cup at her, so Sarah Ann ordered Ann out of the house as well. As Ann was leaving, Sarah Ann recalled, she fell and hit her head. In this version of events, Sarah Ann made Ann entirely responsible for her injury.

Although the truth of what happened is not clear, it is obvious that alcohol permeated these women's lives. Ann had been released from prison only the day before the incident, following a three-month sentence for drunkenness. She was also pregnant at the time. Both the women's husbands were in Dedham Prison on charges of drunkenness. Sarah Ann joined them behind bars following the assault on Ann. When the case was initially discovered, Ann's injuries were so severe that it was thought they would prove fatal. But she lived to tell the tale, and reappears in the records a few months later, charged again with drunkenness. She was imprisoned again, alongside her husband.

Defiance, deviance and drink

Charges of drunkenness offer a glimpse of women's lives that would otherwise remain hidden to the historian. Many cases reveal women's diverse personalities, their refusal to take their punishments meekly, their creative excuses for their behaviour, or their fearlessness in engaging with legal officials. Some women sought leniency by promising to stop drinking. Irish-born Bridget Dwan, who came before the Toronto police court in June 1881, 'had been drinking for some time, she said, but thought that she could keep sober now if let go'. The judge clearly believed her and 'the experiment was tried'.[89] But two months later Dwan was back in court. She wasn't drunk, she insisted to those present, but the constable who arrested her refuted this, claiming that she was in fact 'very drunk', and she was found guilty.[90] In April 1882 she was back in court again. This time a policeman had found her in the street 'disrobing herself for the purpose of selling her garments to buy whiskey'.[91]

Jane Little offered different explanations for her drunken escapades each time she appeared before the Toronto police court. She pleaded for mercy on 23 December 1879, because 'it was Christmas time, and she had two little children at home'. Her pleas fell on deaf ears – perhaps because she was a repeat offender – and she was sentenced to twenty days in prison.[92] In November 1880, she denied the charge of drunkenness levelled against her and explained that people assumed she was drunk because she '"stammered" when walking in consequence of having no power in her right leg'. Once again, her excuses were ignored.[93] When she returned again in January 1881, she insisted that she wasn't drunk but had slipped and fallen, and was then arrested for it. The magistrate observed that it was 'a common thing for people to slip, especially when they were drunk'.[94]

The *New York Times* in 1860 reported how Officer Studley of the Fourth Precinct arrested on Cherry Street a drunken prisoner, who 'presented the appearance of a rather handsome young sailor, being dressed in gray pants, red shirt, monkey jacket and Kossuth hat, and had within his cheek the inevitable "quid"' (chewing tobacco). But on reaching the police station 'the supposed mariner, much to the astonishment of the officers, gave her name as Ellen Smith, and demonstrated beyond question that she had a right to a feminine appellation'. Smith explained that 'she was out on a "lark," and had paraded the streets a hundred times before in the same dress'. Had Smith not been arrested, 'she may have continued her exploits for an indefinite period without fear of detection'.[95] Instead, Smith ended up being imprisoned for six months as a vagrant for this activity, although she could have been prosecuted under legislation that prohibited cross-dressing in New York, as well as in most US cities in the second half of the nineteenth century.[96]

Ellen Smith's story provides a very brief glimpse of gender nonconformity. Women sometimes dressed as men to join the army or navy in the late eighteenth and nineteenth centuries, and US newspapers regularly reported stories of 'female husbands' or 'sexual inverts'.[97] In Smith's case, it is not clear if cross-dressing was indeed just a 'lark', as Smith said, or if this was how she lived, identifying and passing as a man. It is likely that Smith was not the only Irish woman to act in this manner, but this story survives in the records only because Smith was found drunk.

'Thank you, your honour'

When Maggie Smith appeared before the judge at the Washington Place police court in New York in June 1876, the interaction was recorded in *The New York Times* under the title 'An amusing female inebriate'. Maggie was a familiar character to the court officers. The judge recognized her: 'You here again?' he asked and Maggie replied: 'Yes, your Honor' in a 'trembling tone'. The court reporter was unconvinced by this performance, observing that Maggie also 'unsuccessfully endeavored to shed a few repentant tears'. When the judge asked her if she would sign an abstinence pledge, Maggie answered 'with a remarkable effort of pathos: "I can't, your Honor . . . I've got the asthma, and must drink".' In reply to the accusation 'you're a dissolute woman, Maggie', she responded with 'some spirit': 'No, your Honor . . . I'm an Irish woman.' The judge was clearly amused and concluded: 'you're a woman, anyway', to which 'with increased emphasis', Maggie replied: 'No I aint . . . I'm a girl twenty-seven years old.' Maggie's response was met with laughter from those in the courtroom, and she was 'removed to an institution where she will be afforded ten days of seclusion to make up her mind whether to profit by the Justice's suggestion and sign the pledge, or continue to relieve her asthma with strong drink, rendering herself liable to repeated imprisonment by imbibing too much of the alcoholic medicine'.[98]

In her quick-witted retorts, Maggie Smith referred to her Irishness in connection with her drinking. In doing so she echoed Eleanor David, who, as noted at the beginning of the chapter, wanted to keep drinking whiskey 'as long as there was a drop of Irish blood left in her body'.[99] Kathryn Ryan, who appeared in court in Brooklyn in 1903 for being drunk, said that she drank whiskey because she came from 'a long line of historic drunken Irish'. Her father and stepmother had summoned her to court, she having 'annoyed' them by demanding money. Her father accused her of being both a whiskey drinker and a 'morphine fiend', and while Kathryn denied the latter, she accepted the former. 'May God forgive you, father', Kathryn said, bursting out crying, 'There is not a drop of blood in my veins that has not come through a line of drunkards.'[100] These women saw a clear connection between their drinking and their Irish identity.

Some of the drunken women mentioned in this chapter were defiant in court about their actions. For others, the court and jail had become part of their lives and a means of surviving in a tough world, like Elizabeth Stamford, who knew what was on the menu in prison, or elderly Margaret McCormack and Sarah King, who expressed their relief at having somewhere to stay.[101] Ann Jane Fox blessed the magistrate when he convicted her for drunkenness in Toronto in 1890.[102] Ann Kelly, when appearing before the court in New York for intoxication in July 1885, smiled at the judge and said: 'Thank you, your Honor' when she was given a twenty-nine-day sentence. Ann had only been out of prison a few weeks after her last sentence of ten days, but was clearly not sad about returning, and 'with a smile on her face she marched back to the pen'.[103]

6. The hired help and the case of Carrie Jones

At around 10.45 on the morning of Sunday, 21 May 1899, Carrie Jones took twenty-month-old Marion Clarke to Central Park for a walk. Carrie was a childminder for the Clarke family, who lived on New York's Upper East Side. Following the birth of their second child, a son, in February of that year, Marion's parents had responded to an ad that Carrie had placed in the *New York Herald*, and had hired her in mid-May after an interview. Carrie moved into the family's apartment in a four-storey brownstone at 159 East 65th Street that same week. Margaret was delighted with Carrie, describing her as 'so modest, so self-effacing, so quiet'.[1] And Marion adored her.

Carrie took Marion out in her pram for fresh air for a few hours each day, usually while Margaret was looking after her infant son. That Sunday, Margaret watched from the window as her husband, Arthur, helped Carrie and Marion to cross Lexington Avenue. The day was unusually cool for the time of year, but the park was in bloom and there was plenty to entertain the toddler. A short while later, Arthur too strolled to Central Park where, to his surprise, he happened upon his daughter's empty pram. A nearby park attendant reassured him that Carrie had taken Marion out of the pram to show her the bears at the nearby menagerie and had asked her to keep an eye on it. After looking around for a while, Arthur concluded that Carrie had probably just forgotten where she had left the pram, and he returned home for Sunday lunch at one o'clock.

But Marion and Carrie were not at home either, and Arthur began to grow increasingly concerned. He gulped down his food and went back to the park, but neither he nor the park attendants could find the childminder and her charge. Word was sent to Captain England at the Central Park Police Station. England thought that Carrie might be lost or else 'gossiping somewhere', but he sent a policeman to help Arthur locate his missing toddler. Thus began what a newspaper reporter would later describe as 'one of the most remarkable cases of police investigation ever known in this city'.

Around three o'clock, a messenger boy called at the Clarke house with a note. Marion's parents must have felt the panic rise as they read:

> Do not look for your nurse and baby, they are safe in our possession, where they will remain for the present. If the matter is kept out of the hands of the police and the newspapers you will get your baby back safe and sound. If instead you make a big time about it and publish it all over, we will see to it that you never see her alive again. We are driven to this by the fact that we can not get work, and one of us has a child dying through want of proper treatment and nourishment. Your baby is safe and in good hands. The nurse girl is still with her. If everything is quiet, you will hear from us Monday or Tuesday.

The note, handwritten in ink, concluded with a puzzling signature: 'Three'. The police quizzed the thirteen-year-old messenger boy, Frederick Lang, who told them that a woman, who seemed 'very much excited', had handed him the note to deliver. He knew nothing else about Marion's well-being or whereabouts. It was at that point that Arthur and Margaret Clarke began to wonder if their new childminder was implicated in Marion's disappearance.

Captain George W. McClusky, Chief of the police department's Detective Bureau, headed the investigation into Marion's abduction, reporting to the Chief of Police, William S. Devery. Descriptions and sketches of Carrie and Marion were issued across the country. Marion was described as fair-skinned with long blonde curly hair and blue eyes (ills. 6.1 and 6.2). By this stage she had twelve teeth, with a gap in the front. When last seen she was wearing a 'frock of old rose colored cloth, white silk cape, with cap to match; buttoned shoes of soft black leather and black stockings'. The toddler also had a noticeable red birthmark on her hip, which would become key in attempts by strangers to identify her.

 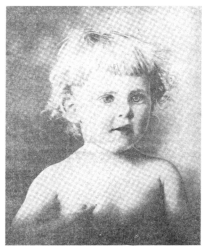

6.1 and 6.2. Portraits of Marion Clarke.

The missing childminder, Carrie Jones, was described as 'twenty-one years old, 5 feet 2 inches, slender, weight 115 pounds, pale, high cheek bones, upper teeth prominent, American born' (ills. 6.3 and 6.4). Her clothing was detailed

This is a portrait of Carrie _____, as she called herself, the nurse who disappeared with little Marion Clarke last Sunday. It is drawn from

6.3 and 6.4. Sketches of Carrie Jones.

in the hope that it might prompt witness recollections; she wore 'a white straw sailor hat, with black band and military pin on side; blue check shirt waist, black skirt, black laced bicycle boots, white collar, and black tie'. But there was at least one mistake in this description. Unknown to the Clarke family, Carrie Jones was not American-born. She was, in fact, from Hollymount, County Mayo. And her real name was not Carrie Jones.

The hired help

Carrie Jones concealed her Irish origins, but the truth would have been no great surprise to her employers: Irish immigrants were synonymous with paid labour in New York homes in the nineteenth and early twentieth centuries.[2] The *New York Times* observed in 1867: 'The men come to dig. The women to work as servants.'[3] In 1825, Irish women comprised 60 per cent of the 2,000 job applications to the New York Society for the Encouragement of Faithful Domestic Servants.[4] By the 1850s, 80 per cent of females employed in New York City homes were Irish-born.[5] In Boston, similarly, 72 per cent of domestic servants in 1870 were Irish.[6] By 1900, across the US, 61 per cent of Irish female immigrants were employed in homes, compared to 28 per cent of Scottish, 22 per cent of English and Welsh, and 9 per cent of Italian female immigrants.[7]

In North America, as in Ireland, work in domestic service typically included room and board. It was regarded (sometimes mistakenly) as a safe environment, and the work was considered good experience for a woman who might manage her own home and family in the future. Without bills to pay, live-in servants could save their earnings. The *New York Herald* noted in 1860 that Irish female workers in American homes 'who do not let their love of finery turn their heads send what money they can spare to their relatives, either to relieve their poverty and comfort their old age, or, if they are young, to bring them to this land of promise'. The 'amount of money sent to their parents, brothers and sisters, and other relatives, by the Irish servant girls in this country', the editorial observed, 'may well astonish the public'.[8] Remittances to Ireland were estimated at £1.7 million in 1845 alone (the equivalent of around £102 million in 2017).[9] Between 1848 and 1900, Irish immigrants are estimated to have sent $260 million to Ireland, $104 million in the form of passage tickets.[10]

Irish women came to dominate domestic service despite prejudice against them. Historian Sarah Deutsch writes that Boston employers did not 'easily accept the plentiful Irish

Catholic immigrants who came to dominate the trade. They persisted in advertising for white Yankee Protestant workers, the very sort most likely to head for factories and shops.'[11] In Canada, similarly, the *Irish Canadian* warned intending Irish immigrants in 1869 to:

> be prepared to be frowned down upon, and insulted, should they happen to possess those religious feelings, which are almost indigenous to the soil of Ireland – the religion of St. Patrick. They will find out through bitter experience, that whether as a day laborer, an artizan, or parlor-maid, their prospects are damped, their chances are curtailed, and the openings of employment lessened, because of their religion . . .[12]

In 1829, even before the Great Famine led to mass emigration from Ireland, a family on Broadway, New York, advertised for a childminder, adding: 'No Irish need offer.'[13] Another family advertised in 1851 for 'a young Protestant Woman, to do the general housework of a small private family in South Brooklyn. . . . No Irish Catholics need apply.'[14] In August 1899, three months after Carrie Jones advertised her childminding services, a prospective employer at Fifth Street requested 'to do general housework in a family of adults, a young girl: can sleep home if preferred: no Irish need apply'.[15] The blanket exclusion of Irish immigrants was not a feature of the majority of advertisements for jobs within the home, and it did at times attract criticism, but it was nonetheless evident across the period.

In 1873, Louisa May Alcott, author of *Little Women*, recounted how she dismissed her Irish servant Biddy: 'an unusually intelligent person, but the faults of her race seemed to be unconquerable, and the winter had been a most trying one all round'.[16] A series in the *Daily Evening Transcript* in 1852 laid out perceived problems with Irish female domestic employees. They were, the paper said, ignorant of the ways and expectations of American middle-class families, 'not in any way prepared for what they undertake; they have acquired absurd ideas that they can do as they please in America, and more – they are naturally improvident'. They were also wasteful: 'The mistress of the house must be continually exerting an irksome (or, as she sometimes thinks to herself) an almost *contemptible* watchfulness, if she does not wish to find bread enough thrown into the refuse barrel to feed a colony of starving emigrants'.[17] And they were lazy:

> Young Irish girls, who have worked hard in the open air at home – who have aided in many of the coarser operations of the husbandman and of the outdoor mechanic, complain of being 'tired out' in this country by the simple building of one fire, the making of a couple of beds, the sweeping of one or more rooms, and the occasional 'minding' (to use their own expression) of one or two children.

The author, 'Veritas', asked: 'Would her labors have been less onerous if she had been employed at home [in Ireland] in bringing water from the river side, or, would she have been less weary with "digging round" if she had been occupied at home in disinterring the "murphies?" '[18]

Although it was highly unusual for an Irish immigrant to steal a child in her care, property theft by the hired help was not all that uncommon. Irish-born Mary Hamilton had a string of aliases and disgruntled former employers when she was charged with stealing in New York in 1860. Her practice was to remain as a servant only a few days, departing with valuables such as clothes, jewellery and homeware, which she then pawned.[19] Another Irish servant, Mary Leyden, used a similar tactic on several families in Massachusetts around 1900, accumulating women's clothing worth an estimated $4,000.[20] Mary Hennessey, described in the *Toronto Globe* as being 'from the Emerald Isle . . . although not one of the Three Graces', stole a carpet bag, six or eight dresses, a jacket and some silver spoons, as well as $130 and left in the night for the boat to the United States.[21] Another Irish servant, Delia Warren, a 'stylishly dressed woman of 20', stole clothing, jewellery, cutlery and home accessories worth $98.15 from her Massachusetts employer a couple of days before her departure home to Ireland.[22] Evidently Warren wanted to bring home more than she could afford, either as presents for relatives or for herself. Historian Maureen Fitzgerald has highlighted that thefts like these might have been regarded as compensation – or revenge – for being mistreated and underpaid.[23] The employer of Irish-born Jane Mills hid her bonnet and shawl to prevent her leaving. The sixteen-year-old, who by that stage had worked as a servant in various households for around six years, retaliated by stealing her mistress's expensive hat and shawl.[24]

Employers attempted to protect themselves from unscrupulous new hires by requiring character references. Margaret Clarke recalled a conversation with Carrie Jones on the subject:

> 'Have you no letters?' I asked. 'Something, perhaps, from your clergyman or from some lady where you worked in the country?' 'I never worked out before,' she answered, 'but I can get letters, of course.' . . . She was so nice to Marion and to baby Arthur, so attentive to their wants, that I let her stay on, and, God forgive me, I neglected to demand her letters of recommendation.

As one employer pointed out, good references were no guarantee of anything: 'People have not a sufficient sense of honor to tell the truth about their servants. Very often it is because it is the easiest way to get rid of them without trouble, and again they are afraid of them.'[25] Many Irish women did cause trouble for former employers. After being let go from her position in Boston in November 1875, Catherine Nolan returned to the house later that night and stole provisions, including jam, butter and sugar. She was sentenced to two years in prison.[26] Irish servant Kate Goley was so incensed at having been dismissed in New York in 1882 that she returned to the house on the following day, grabbed an oil painting valued at $1,600 on loan from an art dealer, and pierced it with the heel of her shoe and her umbrella.[27] But the idea that a child could be stolen by the hired help shook middle-class America. One reporter considered it particularly alarming for every mother who employed staff within the home because it 'appallingly suggests the possibility of a form of domestic treason of which she has never dreamed and against which she has never thought of even trying to guard herself'.

The investigation

The kidnap of twenty-month-old Marion Clarke generated huge public interest, described by one reporter, more than a week after her disappearance, as 'a little hysterical'. Journalists gathered outside the Clarke house, as did a steady stream of curious New Yorkers and children from the nearby school, desperate for updates on Marion's disappearance. Detectives were pulled off other criminal cases and one of them slept in the Clarke home in the immediate aftermath of the kidnapping. They went undercover in the neighbourhood, listening to local gossip and rumours. The case must have reminded the public of the kidnapping of Charlie and Walter Ross, aged four and six respectively, sons of a wealthy Philadelphia merchant who had been lured into a carriage almost twenty-five years earlier.[28] While Walter was later discovered having been abandoned, Charlie was never found.

As part of their investigation, the police considered if one or both of Marion's parents, Arthur and Margaret, could have been involved in her disappearance (ills. 6.5 and 6.6). The couple had by then been married less than

6.5 and 6.6. Sketches of Margaret and Arthur Clarke.

three years. Arthur had migrated to New York from England around two decades earlier. Census records place Margaret's birth in New York, to English and Irish parents. Her Irish-born mother, Mary Betts, initially objected to the union because Margaret was Catholic and Arthur was Protestant. She may also have been concerned about the not insignificant age gap between Arthur and Margaret. He was thirty-nine years old and a widower, while Margaret, who lived with her mother at 534 Fifth Avenue in New York City, was only twenty. Later Mrs Betts consented to the marriage but the couple wed in haste, the small wedding party arriving unannounced at Alderman Fred Ware's house one July evening. Neighbours told the police and the press that the couple were happily married and devoted to their children. A few days after the kidnapping, Captain McClusky declared publicly that the police did not suspect the parents of criminal activity. He said: 'it was only necessary to witness the distress of the bereaved father and mother at once to be convinced that their grief was genuine, and that they knew nothing of the plot that had robbed them of their baby.'

The police turned to the evidence at hand. The note sent a few hours after Marion disappeared implied that the kidnapping had been financially motivated. Arthur earned a good income working as a travelling salesman for the publisher Knight and Brown, but the police didn't consider the Clarke family rich enough to be 'a tempting bait for the kidnapper or blackmailer'. Nor could the family think of anyone with a personal vendetta against them.

The format and presentation of the note seemed to suggest that its author might have some knowledge of typesetting (ill. 6.7). The underlining of 'Three' could simply have been the author's embellishment, but in a typesetting context it

6.7. Reproduction of the ransom note.

signified that the word should be printed in capital letters. The caret symbol, indicating a missing letter in the word 'nurse', was more common in typesetting than in everyday letter writing. The paper on which the note was written was also of a sort frequently used in the newspaper industry. The police and press considered that these details offered a potential lead, pointing to the author's identity as a typesetter, editor, reporter or someone associated in some way with these occupations. In the days immediately following the kidnap, some newspaper reporters claimed that the abduction was a ploy by their rivals to sell copies, or an attempt to demonstrate superior investigative journalistic skills when its reporters 'solved' the case and found missing Marion.

A man who had previously worked as a reporter was placed under police surveillance but proved to be unconnected to the case. A woman named Sarah Johnson was arrested after pieces of paper similar to that used for the ransom note were found in her possession. Another suspect, Lizzie Poole, who looked like Carrie Jones and was 'the only newspaper woman in New York', was also pulled into the case (ill. 6.8). She worked for a periodical, the *Catholic Union*

6.8. Portrait of Lizzie Poole.

and Times, and, it was said, 'thoroughly understands the preparation of copy or manuscript for the press'. Poole denied involvement and, although 'very much disturbed' when questioned, 'expressed her readiness to help the police to capture the kidnappers'.

The detectives also investigated the background of Carrie Jones. Margaret's younger sister, who had accompanied Carrie on a walk earlier that week, reflected that Carrie seemed very familiar with the winding paths of Central Park, casting doubt on her claim to be new to the city. Margaret Clarke remembered that Carrie had claimed to come from the small town of Deposit in upstate New York. This detail, reported in the press, prompted Mrs Jerome Foster of Mount Vernon, the wife of a wealthy cigar manufacturer, to come forward. She suspected that her former servant Mary Carlson might be Carrie Jones. While in Foster's employment, Carlson, whom many in the locality considered to match the description of Carrie, mentioned the town of Deposit. Carlson also 'made much of Mrs Foster's two-year-old child, and asked in vain to take the child for walks'. After being in Foster's employment for four days, and having again been refused permission to take the child out by herself, Carlson disappeared with jewellery worth $2,000, some of which was later found in pawn shops in New York. Carlson was eliminated from enquiries when it was determined that she was missing her front teeth, whereas Carrie's were considered prominent. Detectives also visited other women from Deposit now living in New York City, but they had no information about the case.

Without any obvious leads, the police turned to the public. They heard about a Carrie Jones who had worked in a dry-goods store up to three weeks before the abduction. She had told colleagues that she planned to go to Sweden to meet a paramour who had deserted her a couple of years earlier when she became pregnant. This man had now inherited a fortune, but for Carrie to have a claim to that money she needed to be able to produce their child, who had since died. This theory offered a motive for the kidnap of Marion Clarke. Detectives monitored ships to Europe and plain-clothes officers mingled with passengers, but they failed to identify anyone fitting the descriptions of Carrie Jones or Marion Clarke. Another lead brought the police to the Haas Brothers' clothing factory in New York, where Samuel Haas had employed a young woman, Carrie Aruborg, in mid-April 1899. Aruborg could not handle the work and stayed for only three days. Several employees at the factory now believed that Carrie Jones and Carrie Aruborg were one and the same. Carrie Aruborg had also been seen wearing clothing and a straw hat similar to Carrie Jones's, but she was later eliminated because she was a few inches taller than the missing childminder.

On 27 May, six days after the abduction, the *New York Times* headlined a story 'A clue to the Clark baby', with a subtitle, 'Woman known as Carrie Jones crazed by loss of her child'. The reporter claimed that Carrie Jones was Carrie Wilkinson, a childminder who had been treated at Vanderbilt Clinic in New York for mental health problems following the death of her two-month-old daughter. A journalist approached the doctors who had cared for the grieving mother. One could not remember the patient and the other refused to give any details. A third recalled Carrie Wilkinson, particularly 'the prominence of her cheek bones, and the fine evenness of her teeth'. She was, the medic considered, 'much saddened by her trouble and worry'. The reporter also seems to have accessed institutional admission records, secured Wilkinson's last-known address and interviewed neighbours, some of whom talked and others of whom refused to comment. Miss Underhill, who worked at the

Florence Night Mission on Bleecker Street, read the *New York Times* article. She recognized immediately that Carrie Wilkinson was currently a resident in her institution, and had been since March. Carrie Wilkinson was thus ruled out of enquiries.

In Brooklyn, a woman who had ordered a baby's locket found herself under suspicion when she failed to pick it up from the shop. She was forced to admit that the locket was for a baby born of a secret marriage. Louis Kasper, a barber from Brooklyn, told the police that Carrie Jones was Kate O'Neill, a friend of his sister's. He suggested that O'Neill had fled to his sister in Massachusetts, taking Marion with her. O'Neill, having got wind of the story, confronted Kasper, likely furious that he had dragged her name into the newspapers in connection with the case. When another suspect, Belle Green, was told that the police wanted her photograph for identification purposes, she collapsed in tears, fearing that it would be published in the newspapers: 'I would not cry if I was guilty of anything, but to be charged with a thing like this is awful.'

Captain McClusky claimed to have received around a hundred letters within a week of Marion's disappearance, written by 'cranks or sensation seekers'. Among them was a promise from a clairvoyant that by 'the exercise of the mystical powers possessed by her she could discover where the baby was hidden'. She was very annoyed when the police would not give her name to the newspapers, evidently having hoped to drum up business. Another letter writer claimed to have 'exterminated' Marion Clarke 'in a most novel and unique mode', gruesomely described, because her parents reported the crime to the police.

An element of religious intrigue was added when a letter sent to the *New York Journal* and signed 'One of the Three' alleged that Marion was in a Catholic institution in Three Rivers, Quebec. Another letter claimed that Fr Hartigan, a priest at

Lexington Avenue, where Margaret Clarke was a parishioner, had kidnapped Marion and hidden her in the Catholic Foundling Hospital. The same author wrote to the Rev. James A. O'Connor, leader of the Reformed Catholics in New York, accusing Captain McClusky of bowing to the power of the Catholic Church. O'Connor described it as 'a remarkably intelligent letter for a crank' and pointed out that Margaret Clarke's marriage by an alderman should have resulted in her excommunication from the Catholic Church. When a reporter put that to Fr Hartigan, he laughed, asserting 'We don't do such things as that. . . . This is the nineteenth century.' The mother superior at the Foundling Hospital, Sister Theresa Vincent, insisted that she had not admitted a child as old as Marion in months, and Fr Hartigan likewise confirmed that 'anyone is welcome to visit and inspect it at any time'. In fact, detectives had already visited the Foundling Hospital in search of Marion, as they had similar institutions in the city.

Eventually, the post office redirected all letters addressed to the Clarke family to Captain McClusky, so that Margaret and Arthur would not have to read the 'many incredible, disgusting, and atrocious communications'. Detectives read each letter carefully, wary of missing a ransom note. They identified two potentially significant letters. The first, an unsigned note addressed to Margaret Clarke, was received the day after Marion's disappearance. It was written on the same kind of paper as the original note and read: 'Be patient. O.K. Further notice.' The second letter, received a few days later, was signed 'Mephisto Secundo, King of the American Mafia'. It explained that the wrong baby had been taken and if the family kept the information from the police and reporters, Marion would be returned home unharmed and without the need to pay ransom. The author insisted:

Your maid, notwithstanding the esteemed World, Journal, and so forth, is as green as the proverbial grass and swallowed a good story readily, and has been in hysterics half the time since we have had her detained in our place. Your baby is well and a perfect little gem, and you will get her back as soon as it is safe for my henchmen. That is, when these crazy, erratic, dope-hitting reporters get through frothing at the mouth.

The reason the police considered this bizarre letter to be from the kidnappers was that it included a small religious St Anne's medal, a cross and a satin heart identical to those that Margaret Clarke had tied around her daughter's neck on the day she went missing, and which had not been described in the press.

Hundreds of suspected sightings of Carrie Jones were reported in the days following the kidnap. Frederick Lang thought that the woman who had given him the letter to deliver to the Clarke household had a bandaged finger. A newspaper stand owner knew that one of his customers, Kate Long, wore a similar bandage. She was interrogated but proved to be unrelated to the case. A Danish man, Charles Johnson, claimed that he had seen two women arguing over a baby in Central Park, and his descriptions of one of the women and the child seemed to match Carrie and Marion. Later he identified the elder woman as Minnie Smith, but Smith adamantly denied that she knew Carrie Jones. Johnson subsequently admitted that his descriptions may have been influenced by what he had read in the newspapers.

On the same day that the *New York Times* featured the story of Carrie Wilkinson, the *Democrat and Chronicle* offered a different lead: Marion Clarke and a woman had supposedly been seen boarding a train at Poughkeepsie, about eighty miles up the Hudson from New York. A passenger who recognized them from newspaper images called Marion's name and the girl responded. Others noticed that the toddler looked to be sedated, and that the supposed mother told conflicting stories about herself. Two men on board telegraphed the Rochester police, so that when the train stopped at Rochester, a policeman was there to question the woman. The policeman did not detain her, which seems to have disappointed the passengers on board. They tried again, and when the train pulled into Buffalo just before 1 a.m., the woman was stopped by two policemen. She explained that she was Mrs Sharkey, a resident of Buffalo. Friends meeting her at the train station confirmed her identity. The little girl, named Marie (which likely explains why she responded to 'Marion'), identified Sharkey as her mother, could name her older sister, and was able to say where she lived. An exasperated Sharkey explained that the rumour she had kidnapped Marion Clarke 'was started on the train by a man who was half drunk'.

The police hoped that the intense press scrutiny might force the kidnappers to abandon the child, and staff at the city's various institutions were on high alert. Bellevue Hospital staff became convinced that they had found Marion when a multiracial woman who identified herself as Sarah Mitchell Gibbs walked into the hospital on the evening of 27 May, accompanied by a blonde-haired, blue-eyed toddler. When an attendant approached the little girl and called 'Marion', the child 'turned its head and held out its hand'. The mother said that the baby's name was Alice, but this did not settle the matter. With a child on her hands showing symptoms of diphtheria, and incessant questions from staff about her daughter's parentage, skin colour and recent movements, Gibbs understandably became very anxious. She insisted on accompanying Alice in the ambulance to Willard Parker

Hospital, where she was questioned by the police. So convinced were staff and policemen that they had located Marion Clarke that Arthur Clarke, Marion's father, was brought in to identify the baby at the hospital. To the shock of those present, it proved another false alarm.

Newspapers continued to give widespread coverage to the case, lamenting the lack of tangible leads (ill. 6.9). Just over a

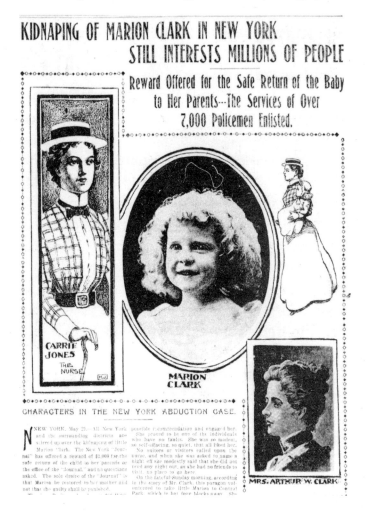

6.9. The kidnapping of Marion Clarke made newspaper headlines.

week after the kidnap, police issued another 50,000 circulars with a portrait of Marion and descriptions of her clothing and that of Carrie Jones. Detectives admitted that even after all their efforts they were 'just where they were when they received the first word that the child had been carried off by her nurse'.

Margaret Clarke was in a state of shock following her daughter's disappearance. She was attended daily by a doctor and permitted visits only from close friends and relatives. The stress had reportedly caused paralysis on one side of her face. On 27 May, a massive headline jumped off the front page of the *New York Journal*: 'Baby Clark *must* be returned or her mother *will lose her reason*'. Another newspaper reported that Margaret 'borders on delirium. Fears for her little daughter's safety wring her like thumbscrews.' Margaret would later recall that while she was holed up in her house, awaiting news of her daughter, 'Everything, from the pictures on the walls to a certain nick in the door, where one day for sport I had measured her, recalled the memory of my lost child.' McClusky advised Arthur Clarke to 'keep up a brave heart and not to be worried', and Arthur admitted that for his broken-hearted wife he 'endeavored to put on a bold front and an air of confidence that he was far from feeling'. A week after her daughter's disappearance, Margaret was said to have 'given up hope that her child will be returned to her alive'.

On 30 May, John H. Watts walked into the Central Park Police Station, accompanied by a blonde-haired, blue-eyed girl. 'This may be Marion Clarke', he declared, and the pair were immediately taken to Captain England's office. Watts had found the girl unaccompanied in the park. A short while later, a frantic woman rushed into the police station, 'in great excitement, and when she spied the little stranger ran up to it crying:

"Oh, Jennie, where have you been?"' Captain England, who must have been disappointed not to have found Marion Clarke, surmised that 'all blonde-haired babies look alike'.

At around 2 p.m. on the following day, Wednesday, 31 May, ten days after Margaret and Arthur had last seen their daughter, a woman and young child walked into Austin Conklin's general store in St John's, a small rural settlement in the Ramapo mountains between Sloatsburg and Haverstraw in Rockland County. Austin Conklin's daughter, Mamie, noticed that the child bore a striking resemblance to a photograph of Marion she had seen in a newspaper. She rushed to get the newspaper to compare, but the woman and child had left the store by the time that she came back. The woman and child had gone to the post office. After they left, the postmistress similarly consulted a photograph of Marion Clarke. So certain was she that she had just seen the missing toddler that she closed the post office, harnessed her horse and hurried to the local police.

There are conflicting accounts of what happened next. Deputy Sheriff William Charleston seems to have presented the postmistress, Ada Bessie Carey, with all the images of Marion he had in his possession. She remained adamant that the girl she had seen was Marion Clarke. She had also recognized the woman who had been with the child as a former schoolteacher in the locality, and not one she had rated particularly highly. Charleston was convinced. He considered the postmistress a reliable witness. She was originally from Guernsey, became a missionary and later worked as a teacher at the House of the Good Shepherd orphanage in Tomkins Cove in Rockland County. She had settled in St John's when she realized that the children in the locality had no teacher, and she set up a classroom in the forest. It was because of Carey's philanthropic endeavours that a wealthy widow,

Margaret Zimmerman, had funded a church at St John's in the 1870s, which could also be used as a classroom.[29]

In the early hours of Thursday morning, Charleston set off with Carey on the twelve-mile journey to Garnerville to secure a warrant from a Justice of the Peace, Isaac Herbert, for the arrest of the woman, whose name was Jennie Wilson. On the same morning, Mamie Conklin convinced her father to telegraph the Chief of Police in New York about the child seen in their store. Detective Herlihy was dispatched to investigate. But the local police deputy sheriff had had a head start. With his arrest warrant in hand, Charleston located Jennie Wilson with a man who identified himself as her husband, James Arthur Wilson. He arrested her, and took her and the child to Justice Herbert's house, while James, who was not under arrest, explained that he would go to New York City to make arrangements to assist his wife.

Those gathered at the Herbert household excitedly compared pictures of missing Marion Clarke with the girl now in their care, noting a striking resemblance. Someone remembered the red birthmark, and anxiously scanned the toddler's body: 'We've found the baby! We've found the baby!' Herbert cried when the red mark was spotted, 'with tears running down his cheeks'. Two hours later, Arthur Clarke was making the forty-mile trip to Garnerville in the company of a detective. He arrived around 6.30 p.m. His hopes of finding his kidnapped daughter had been raised and dashed many times, and this wasn't the first blonde-haired girl he had been asked to meet. But this time things would be different. 'Where is she, where is she?' Arthur cried, as he burst into Justice Herbert's house at Garnerville. He grabbed the girl from a woman and, according to a reporter present, 'smothered it with kisses and caresses. "This is my child," he cried. "This is my little

Marion. This is my baby!"' After eleven days, Marion Clarke had been found alive. Jennie Wilson, who was sitting nearby, 'sobbed wildly for a moment, and then swooned away'.

The arrest

After being reunited, Arthur and Marion left Haverstraw at 8.50 p.m. on a single-car train chartered by the *New York Journal* (ill. 6.10). A crowd had gathered, and the local police were said to have had 'the fight of their lives to keep the women from mobbing the little girl'. It was, one reporter deduced, 'the most exciting day that neighborhood has known for years'.

MR. CLARK AND BABY MARION COMING HOME ON THE JOURNAL'S SPECIAL TRAIN.

The Journal placed its special train at Mr. Clark's disposal that the nearly crazed mother might have her child again without delay. The happy father accepted the invitation gladly. On the way he kept the baby in his arm, refusing both to part with her, even for a moment.

6.10. The *New York Journal*, having paid for the train for Arthur and Marion Clarke, had exclusive access to them and the detectives on the journey home.

The New York City police were keen to insert themselves in the celebrations. The Chief of Police, William Devery, and the Chief of the Detective Bureau, George McClusky, greeted Arthur and Marion when they reached the city and helped them into a carriage. When the carriage reached the Clarke family's Upper East Side home at 10.20 p.m., it met 'a roar of cheers that demonstrated as nothing else could have done how deep has been the public interest and sympathy aroused by the case'. Margaret Clarke, waiting at home with her baby son, heard the cheers of the thousands-strong crowd that heralded the carriage's arrival. Arthur later told the reporters: 'My wife is, of course, crazy with joy . . . The doctor said two or three days ago that nothing but the baby would make my wife well. She is all right now, and I guess that is all.' When Margaret Clarke eventually brought her daughter to the window to show her off to the crowds below, 'a roar went up that must have been heard over in Fifth avenue. Men tossed their hats in the air and women shrieked with excitement.'

The celebrations continued across the next few days. The Clarke family was inundated with letters and flowers. Large crowds gathered outside their house, persistently calling for Marion. Her elated parents obliged when they could and Marion's appearance was greeted by loud cheers. On 3 June, Margaret and Marion featured in a mutoscope made by the American Mutoscope and Biograph Company (ill. 6.11). *The pride of the household*, made up of a series of images arranged consecutively as an early form of film, depicts Marion 'doing all of her pretty tricks', including throwing kisses to the camera and running into her mother's arms. The cameraman considered her 'a perfect little actress'. Margaret and Marion Clarke posed exclusively for *New York Journal* photographs in

MRS. ARTHUR W. CLARK AND BABY MARION, HAPPILY REUNITED, POSE FOR THE MUTOSCOPE.

(Copyrighted, 1906, by the American Mutoscope Company.)

6.11. Marion and Margaret Clarke posing for the American Mutoscope and Biograph Company.

their garden and Margaret later wrote an exclusive account of her experiences for the newspaper (ills. 6.12 and 6.13).

LITTLE MARION CLARK AND HER DOLLIES.

MRS. CLARK AND RESCUED BABY POSE FOR THE JOURNAL. The Mother Was Too Weak to Hold the Baby Up and So It Was Held on Her Lap.

6.12 and 6.13. Professional photographs of Marion and Margaret Clarke.

Half of the reward money put up by the *New York Journal* was given to postmistress Ada Bessie Carey, and the other half was placed in trust for Marion Clarke, who was considered to have 'helped to identify herself'. But the mystery was not yet over. Jennie Wilson was around the same age as Carrie Jones, but she looked nothing like her, and Arthur Clarke had confirmed that the woman in custody was not the childminder he had hired. Jennie claimed to have encountered Carrie and Marion on the street and that Carrie had given her 'a big roll of money' to take Marion to the country. But the police did not believe Jennie's account. They had one good lead that suggested Jennie Wilson had played a significantly more important role in the abduction than she had let on. A key witness, Irish-born Kate Cosgriff, had revealed to them that on the night of the kidnapping she had rented a room in her house in Brooklyn to two women, one blonde and one brunette, and a blonde-haired toddler. The blonde woman had hired the room the day before, explaining that she, her daughter and sister might stay a fortnight or a few months, depending on their circumstances. In the end, they stayed only one night. They wrote Cosgriff a note to explain that their sudden departure was because the blonde woman's husband had been seriously injured falling off a ladder. After hearing of Marion's abduction, Cosgriff's suspicions were aroused, because the women's story did not quite tally. The note was signed 'Mrs George W. Davis' but it named the injured husband as Will. Cosgriff had also noticed that the child seemed very fond of the woman who had been pre-sented as her aunt but much less so of the supposed mother. She had seen the child laugh dramatically and throw her hands in the air when asked, 'how does Mr Brown laugh?' Arthur Clarke confirmed that Mr Brown was a family friend and this was one of Marion's 'tricks'. A collar found left behind at Cosgriff's house had a laundry mark (made by a commercial laundry to ensure that it would be returned to the right customer) that matched the laundry mark on a collar belonging to Carrie Jones found at the Clarke household.

Cosgriff had overheard the two women talking about going by train to a town with 'burg' in the name, at a cost of $2.50. Detectives searching the 'burgs' were within ten miles of Marion Clarke when word of the sighting near Sloatsburg came in. Cosgriff later travelled to Rockland County Prison and identified Jennie Wilson as the blonde woman who had stayed with her in Brooklyn on the night of the abduction. By that stage Jennie's husband, James Arthur Wilson, was also in Rockland County Prison. He had returned to Haverstraw the day after her arrest and asked to be imprisoned alongside his wife.

Gradually more information filtered in about Jennie and James Arthur Wilson (ills. 6.14 and 6.15). They were in fact Addie McNally and George Barrow prior to their marriage

JENNIE WILSON OR JENNIE M'NALLY
Wife of J. Arthur Wilson.

J. ARTHUR WILSON

6.14 and 6.15. Sketches of Jennie and James Arthur Wilson (aka Addie McNally and George Barrow).

in Jersey City in February 1894, at which point Addie took her husband's surname. Addie was born in 1873 in Fishkill, New York, a typesetter by trade. Her grandfather, James J. McNally, was editor of the *Goshen News*. He talked to the press following his granddaughter's arrest: 'Addie must have been hypnotized by that man Barrow. He is a scoundrel. He boasted of his control over my granddaughter. He said he could do anything he wanted with her, and he made his boast good.' George was the 'black sheep son' of one of the wealthiest and most prominent families in Arkansas. His father, John C. Barrow, was a judge and his brother John was an attorney. He had been convicted of using dynamite to try to blow up the Little Rock Athletics Association boathouse in 1893 after the Association rejected his application for membership, though he later successfully appealed his conviction.

Addie and George Barrow had for a time rented rooms on the sixth floor of the Mills Hotel Annex at 13 Varick Street in New York City. Newspaper reporters Philip Speed of *The World* and Max J. Foster of the *New York Journal* went to the Mills Hotel, eager to speak to anyone who might have known the couple and desperate for leads on the identity or whereabouts of Carrie Jones. Their interviews revealed that the couple had lived at the hotel with a Bella Anderson, a woman who sounded suspiciously like Carrie. Bella was hired as a waitress at the hotel in January 1898. In May, she met Addie, who was also working as a waitress temporarily while her husband was looking for work. They became 'fast friends'. When Bella had to stop working due to ill-health around March 1899, the Barrows took her in as their guest in the Annex.

Fellow employees knew that Bella was from Summit, New Jersey, and the two reporters followed the trail there, tracking her family to White Oak Ridge near Summit on 3 June. Conversations with locals confirmed that Bella had been seen there in recent days. A Mrs Kelly pointed the reporters in the direction of a secluded farmhouse in the woods where Bella's aunt lived. Convinced that they had located Carrie Jones, the reporters summoned the assistance of the local Justice of the Peace and state detective, Edward Kelly. The three men burst into the farmhouse unannounced and discovered a young woman inside. Confronted with the accusations, she eventually broke down and confessed. Carrie Jones had been found.

Carrie had been born Isabella Anderson in 1877 in Hollymount, County Mayo, and had a twin brother, Samuel. Her father, John Anderson, a corporal in the 63rd Regiment in the British Army, seems to have died by the time her mother, Ellen, migrated with her children to the United States when Bella was around nine years old. They settled in New Jersey, where Ellen had relatives. Ellen later married John Donnelly, who Bella claimed ill-treated her and who locals confirmed had a bad reputation. Eventually Bella left New Jersey for New York.

Confronted with the accusation that she had instigated the kidnap of Marion Clarke, Bella made a full confession at her aunt's farmhouse. George Barrow, she explained, 'told me how I could become rich and happy; how it was possible for me, if I would do as he said, to live a life of ease'. She was to pose as a nurse, kidnap her charge and pass the child to the Barrows. They would first write a note warning the family not to contact the police, which would be followed up by a ransom request. Following payment, the plan was to return the kidnapped child safely to its parents. Bella claimed that she objected at first, 'but they were so persistent, so good to me, that at last I consented'. George Barrow assured her that he would take the blame if they got caught. The next day, Addie wrote the advertisement for the *New York Herald*, offering the services of 'Carrie Jones'. The first two families who responded had already hired childminders by the time that Bella called back. The third advertisement was answered by the Clarkes and the kidnapping plot was laid. But the plan quickly went awry after the Clarkes alerted the police, news of the kidnapping reached the press and the hunt began for the missing child and nurse.

One of the reporters who was present when Bella was arrested observed that at times she 'seemed to forget that she was a prisoner. She became again the flirt and smiled and laughed'. At other times she 'convulsed with sobs' as she told of being torn between her loyalty to the Barrows and her love for Marion Clarke and her mother, who, 'from the first, was more like my sister than my employer'. But Addie reassured Bella; Marion would only be gone for a few days, even a few hours, and the money would be easily got. 'I don't know why I did this', Bella insisted, 'except I was ill and needed money.' Arrangements were made for Addie to meet Bella in Central Park on Friday, 19 May, and for the two of them to abscond with Marion. But Margaret Clarke's sister accompanied Bella and Marion on the walk that day, thwarting the plan. On Saturday, Bella met Addie as agreed but refused to allow her to take the child. Later Bella regretted it, feeling that she 'had not treated her right after the kindness to me', and was 'determined to keep my promise' the following day. This time Bella followed through. She lifted Marion out of the pram when she spotted Addie sitting on a bench, and the two women hurried out of Manhattan with their stolen child.

The women were shocked the next day to discover that the kidnapping had made the newspapers. They realized that they could not now stay at Kate Cosgriff's house awaiting payment of the ransom money. Addie's husband, George, got the two women and Marion out of the city that afternoon. Although Bella heard many people on the train and platform talking about the missing child, nobody seemed to notice Marion in their midst.

On Friday, 26 May, Bella returned to the city with a key to the Barrows' flat. She did not go into hiding but ventured out openly, confident that New York City provided the anonymity that she required. Despite the frenzy surrounding the case and the many false sightings, she was not spotted. Bella didn't see George Barrow again until the following Thursday, when he rushed into the flat in a panicked state. His wife, he revealed, 'had queered it all'. He gave Bella $10 and advised her to 'get out of New York as fast as steam could take me'. She cycled to the railway station and caught the next train home to Summit. A journalist considered it 'incredible that this girl, hardly more than a child, had lent a hand in one of the most desperate acts ever committed in New York'.

The trial

By 8 June, following the completion of negotiations and paperwork required to extradite them from the jails in which they were being held in Rockland County and New Jersey, the three suspects were back in New York City. Bella arrived wearing 'a straw Alpine hat, with a black feather on one side, a bottle-green silk waist with cheap white lace at the throat and on the cuffs, and a dark brown and green plaid woollen skirt, much worn'. The outfit had been given to her by her aunt, the only relative who, it seems, wanted anything to do with her. Her twin brother, for his part, had refused to visit her in jail. The suspects were held in the Tombs awaiting trial. Their photographs and measurements were taken for police records and bail was set at $10,000 each (ill. 6.16).

6.16. Prisoner mugshots of George Barrow, Addie (Jennie) Barrow née McNally and Carrie Jones (aka Bella Anderson).

At trial in the Supreme Court before Justice Edgar L. Furs-
man later that month, all three defendants initially pleaded
not guilty. But, on 14 June, Bella, who had been assigned
counsel, changed her plea. She was, her defence explained,
'repentant and would throw herself upon the mercy of the
court'. She was remanded for sentencing, then returned as a
witness for the prosecution against the Barrows, having
turned State's evidence. Other witnesses included Arthur
and Margaret Clarke; Lizzie Madden, the Central Park attendant who had been left with Marion's pram; Kate Cosgriff,
who had unwittingly housed the suspects in Brooklyn; St
John's postmistress, Ada Bessie Carey; Arthur Dahl, the janitor at the Mills Hotel Annex; and Louisa Opeman, in whose
house in St John's the Barrows had stayed and Marion had
been found. Marion appeared in court briefly, for identification purposes (ill. 6.17).

The courtroom was hot that June week and many of the
legal men cast off their heavy robes. George and Addie
Barrow were permitted to sit together, and George fanned
his wife with a black handheld fan when she needed it.
(ill. 6.18.)

This may have been part of George's desire to present
himself as a loyal husband, which was the crux of his defence.
When he took to the stand, he insisted that he was innocent.
The first he had seen of Marion Clarke, he testified, was
when he met his wife, Marion and Bella in Erie railroad ter-
minal in Jersey City, just across the Hudson from lower
Manhattan, on the morning of Monday, 22 May. Addie had
explained that the baby was related to Bella. He claimed it
was only when he read about the kidnapping that he became
suspicious and confronted the two women. He did not report
them, he explained to the court, because he wanted to protect

Bella Anderson Identifies Baby Marion Clark in Court.
The nurse on the witness stand pointed to the child and said that it was the one she had stolen and turned over to Mrs. Barrow. Then she burst into tears.

6.17. Marion and Margaret Clarke in the courtroom.

his wife. His legal team also pointed to the fact that he had given himself up when he could have run. His family claimed that he was mentally unstable, the result of a severe attack of typhoid fever as a child.

But the all-male jury were unconvinced by George's account. Bella Anderson's testimony, which implicated George Barrow as the initiator of the plot, was strong. She remained steadfast under cross-examination, whereas George did not. For instance, he was asked to explain a note

6.18. Courtroom scenes.

he had written about the kidnapping that was found at his house. A journalist observed that he 'shifted about in confusion and nervously pulled at his mustache as he replied that he hadn't the slightest idea. He wrote it to kill time on the train, and was so excited he didn't know what he was doing.' Bella also identified him as the author of the 'King of the American Mafia' letter, which had been accompanied by the trinkets Marion wore around her neck. That letter relayed that the author did not desire a ransom but rather wanted to return the child without interference. George likely recognized by this point that the frenzy surrounding Marion's kidnapping was too intense to avoid getting caught, but the fact that the Barrows did not anonymously abandon Marion at some public location suggests that he might not have entirely given up hope that he might gain financially from her safe return.

On 16 June, the jury took just twenty-five minutes to find George Barrow guilty of kidnapping. The presiding judge accepted the verdict and addressed George: 'I have no doubt of your entire guilt. You instigated these two women, and you should be made an example of.' He was sentenced to fourteen years and ten months in prison, two months shy of the maximum sentence for kidnapping. He was handcuffed to a murderer who had been sentenced to life, and led away to commence his term in Sing Sing Prison, north of the city.

Following his sentence, George changed his story and tried to help his wife, claiming that she only agreed to be involved in the plot after he threatened to divorce her. In an interview with the *New York Journal*, Addie suggested that she was motivated to kidnap Marion because of her desire to replace her own dead child. Census records confirm that Addie had given birth to an infant who died, although the circumstances are unknown. She pleaded guilty to the charge of kidnapping. At sentencing, Judge Werner considered that she had 'shown none of the finer feelings of a woman'. He thought it 'necessary to make an example of her, and to demonstrate that the sex of a kidnapper does not in the least excuse the crime'. She was sentenced to twelve years and ten months in prison.

After testifying against George Barrow, Bella Anderson returned to court for sentencing. Her defence asked for mercy, 'because of her services to the State, her youth, illness and the fact that she was dominated by stronger minds'. Although it was Bella Anderson who had duped the Clarkes and taken Marion, she emerged with the lightest sentence: four years in Auburn Prison.

The fates of Carrie Jones and Addie Barrow

On 19 June 1902, three years after her conviction for the kidnap of Marion Clarke, Bella Anderson walked out of Auburn Prison, her sentence commuted. Although she was known by the name Carrie Jones in prison, she likely reverted to her own name or another pseudonym after her liberation. Around the same time, friends of Addie Barrow attempted to secure her early release by raising a petition. Addie's husband also wrote a letter from the men's prison on her behalf, pleading for her release. Early into his prison stay George was thought to have developed symptoms of insanity and was transferred to the Matteawan State Hospital for the Criminally Insane in New York. He recovered shortly thereafter and was transferred back to prison. But the efforts to secure Addie's early release failed, and she would remain behind the bars of Auburn Prison for another five years.

7. Theft and the case of Old Mother Hubbard

In 1857, Sergeant William H. Lefferts, recently appointed to New York City's detective force, began taking mugshots of local criminals for future identification. His assembled collection – known as a rogues' gallery – was lauded as a modern tool that could revolutionize policing. Policemen no longer had to commit faces to memory at the time of arrest or trial, but could instead use the photographs as visual aids to identify suspects or criminals (who often had multiple aliases). Within a few months, the collection had grown to more than 125 photographs, which policemen from across the city could access at the detective office.[1] Witnesses to crimes were also permitted to browse the rogues' gallery, to see if they recognized the culprit among the faces.[2]

A reporter from *The New York Times* who pored over the rogues' gallery in 1857 was struck by the offenders' general 'flashiness of appearance . . . Good broadcloth coats, velvet or satin vests of a conspicuous pattern, and plenty of jewelry.' The photographs seemed to offer a glimpse of the criminals' personality and success, which written physical descriptions rarely captured. They had, the journalist recounted, already led to several arrests only a few months after assembly and prompted other criminals to 'have quitted New-York for parts unknown', convinced that the images 'had put an end to their chances of success in this locality'.[3] By 1860, the collection comprised around 550 photographs, arranged largely by crime.[4]

In 1880, Thomas Byrnes was made head of New York's Detective Bureau, having moved up the ranks since joining the police force in December 1863 (ill. 7.1).[5] His ability to solve high-profile crimes and elicit confessions from suspects gained him acclaim in New York and across the US. He was, according to one journalist, 'a man widely known all over the civilized world for his unexcelled detective genius and marvellous police ability'.[6] Described by *The New York Tribune* on his retirement in 1895 as 'the most famous Chief of Police New-York ever has had', Byrnes was an Irish immigrant.[7] Born in Wicklow in June 1842, he migrated to the United States with his parents when he was a child at the height of the Great Famine.[8] His Irish background was not uncommon in the police force. During decades when the Irish were heavily represented in the jail cells of American cities, Irish-born men were also establishing themselves in large numbers in those cities' police forces.[9] By 1855, 26.5 per cent of the police force in New York City was Irish, and by 1891 the figure was around 33 per cent.[10] By the early 1860s,

7.1. Thomas Byrnes.

approximately one third of Chicago's police officers were Irish-born.[11] In Toronto, the force was 56.8 per cent Irish-born by 1881.[12] In many cases, then, when Irish-born female offenders were arrested, the arresting officer was an Irish-born man.

On his appointment, Byrnes set about elevating the status, professionalism and importance of New York City's detectives, who were until his appointment regarded as 'a troop of broken-down policemen, who worked, if they worked at all, without system or purpose'.[13] As part of these efforts, Byrnes popularized the usefulness of photography. Arrestees were to be photographed and the most notorious of these added to the rogues' gallery.[14] Duplicates were shared across the city and beyond, while the main collection filled large wooden leaves at the detective headquarters at 300 Mulberry Street. By 1894, the collection comprised more than 1,900 photographs, and another 300 photographs were awaiting filing.[15] (ill. 7.2.)

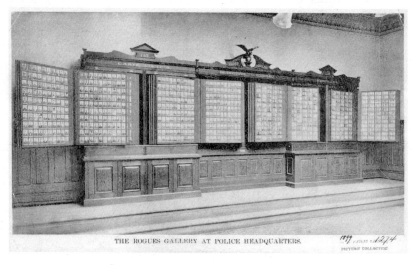

THE ROGUES GALLERY AT POLICE HEADQUARTERS.

7.2. The rogues' gallery, 1899.

But Byrnes was not content to stop at the reorganized rogues' gallery, accessible largely only to the police or victims of crime. He wrote:

Aware of the fact that there is nothing that professional criminals fear so much as identification and exposure, it is my belief that if men and women who make a practice of preying upon society were known to others besides detectives and frequenters of the courts, a check, if not a complete stop, would be put to their exploits.[16]

To that end, in 1886, the New York City detective published a book entitled *Professional criminals of America*, which reproduced the mugshots of 204 male and female criminals from the rogues' gallery, alongside details of their criminal careers and exploits. It was priced at $10 and reportedly sold 20,000 copies.[17]

Of the 204 thieves, pickpockets and frauds whose photographs feature in *Professional criminals of America*, eighteen are women. Byrnes identified six women and eleven men from the selection as having been born in Ireland. Among them was Margaret Brown, an infamous pickpocket whose criminal career was thought to span several decades and multiple US states (ill. 7.3).[18] Even by 1898, when Margaret was judged to be well into her eighties, a reporter in Texas described her as 'one of the most successful and notorious pickpockets and shoplifters in the country'. She targeted women shoppers, usually in department stores or train stations, admired their purchases, and stealthily dipped her hands into their pockets and purses. The cloak that she wore, lined with pockets to conceal her stolen loot, earned her the moniker 'Old Mother Hubbard', even though it was probably rarely bare.

7.3. Photograph of Margaret Brown, 1883.

Alongside Margaret Brown in the pages of Thomas Byrnes's *Professional criminals of America* is a photograph of another notorious Irish-born thief, Elizabeth Dillon (ill. 7.4).[19] She had

7.4. Photograph of Elizabeth Dillon, 1879.

a string of aliases, including Bridget Cole (or Cohen, or Corrigan or Rafferty), Ellen Dillon, Mary Ann Rafferty, Maggie

Riley, and Mary or Catherine Ryan. Elizabeth Dillon was thought to have migrated to the United States as a child and begun a criminal career relatively quickly. She was known as 'Queen of the dips' for her skill as a pickpocket. She frequently worked with an accomplice whom she would station nearby and to whom she would pass items that she had filched. In 1876, police detectives observed Elizabeth making 'tours of the principal retail stores' on Tremont Street in Boston, returning every few minutes to her companion and seeming to exchange something with him. When the pair were arrested, several wallets were found in their possession. Twelve years later, in 1884, Elizabeth was arrested again, with a male companion, on Tremont Street in Boston. At the police station she gave the name Bridget Rafferty, but was undone by the 'excellent picture' of her in the rogues' gallery and was sentenced to two years in prison.

Many of the offences considered in this book were crimes of passion, desperation and chaos, committed by Irish women living in poverty. This chapter, though, focuses on career criminals like Margaret Brown, Elizabeth Dillon and other Irish-born thieves who made pickpocketing and shoplifting their profession.

Mistresses of disguise

Margaret Brown was said to have been trained by Prussian immigrant Fredericka 'Marm' Mandelbaum, the notorious fence known as the 'Queen of the fences'.[20] Margaret's success as a pickpocket and shoplifter largely rested on her appearance as a harmless elderly lady. It was said that she often escaped detection because of her 'sweet face, her large hazel eyes, and her benign expression'. Historians have suggested that pickpocketing was most often carried out by young men or children, while female pickpocketing was generally associated with prostitution.[21] But older female pickpockets, who could move easily through crowds without drawing attention or suspicion, were not uncommon. Detective Thomas Byrnes explained that, in his experience, 'Women make the most patient and dangerous pickpockets. Humble in their attire, and seemingly unassuming in their demeanor, without attracting any notice or particular attention, they slip into an excited crowd in a store or in front of a shop-window.'[22]

In March 1883, Margaret Brown was sentenced to two months in Boston's House of Correction for having stolen a bag from a woman who was shopping. The clerks in the store admitted that they had considered from Margaret's physical appearance and calico dress that she was a poor, old woman and had affectionately dubbed her 'grandma'. When arrested, she was discovered to be wearing an expensive silk dress underneath her plain calico disguise.

A few years later Margaret was arrested for pickpocketing at Ridley's Store in New York in 1891. A security guard at the store recognized her from the rogues' gallery and followed her. He observed her deliberately hooking a wire from her basket onto unsuspecting shoppers. In the bustle of the department store crowd, the wire would become tangled in another woman's clothing as if by accident. Then while the victim was fumbling to get the hook out and Margaret was apologizing profusely, 'the old lady quietly and unobservedly inserts her hand in the pocket'. Margaret was also known to wear a concealed 'shoplifter's bag' around her waist into which she could slip her stolen goods. In spring 1898, she was still troubling policemen, this time in Chicago, to where she had moved.

Like Margaret Brown, Elizabeth Dillon capitalized on her age and appearance to commit crimes. Across a criminal career that spanned decades, she used to her advantage 'her famous motherly smile untarnished by time', the 'most motherly of little poke bonnets' and 'a face so benign, so free from guile and worldliness it could well be used as an advertisement for homely domesticity'. Around the turn of the century, the police realized that Elizabeth Dillon had moved away from pickpocketing on the streets and was now targeting funerals and church services. These were spaces where an older woman, dressed in mourning attire, would not attract much attention and where grieving women were not necessarily paying close attention to their belongings. In January 1900, Elizabeth was caught 'operating in a crowd' at a funeral in Boston, and while she seems to have escaped punishment on that occasion, she was found guilty of pickpocketing in May of the same year. She was back in court in August 1901, accused of pickpocketing a Mrs Ellen Doyle who had attended a friend's funeral at St Margaret's Church in Boston. As usual Elizabeth had dressed the part, 'attired in mourning with a heavy black veil shielding her features'. When questioned about her tactics, Elizabeth admitted that she favoured churches for two reasons: 'one is to steal and the other is because I am happiest there. I like to cry, and it is just as easy for me to grieve over the death of a stranger as a friend.' She went on to explain that 'no one suspects a person who cries well of being a thief'.

Elizabeth also tried to use her 'age and decrepitude' to her advantage in court. She was described in court in 1908 as being 'old and infirm and hardly able to make herself heard'.

But her career was not yet finished. When she returned to court in Boston four years later, charged with pickpocketing at a train station, she was 'Clothed in sombre black and bent with the weight of years'. A *Boston Globe* reporter observed that she 'appeared quite feeble, and her voice was faint, and it was the general opinion that she is serving her last sentence'. But the 'general opinion' underestimated Elizabeth Dillon. She was back in the Boston House of Correction in June 1913 having been sentenced to three months for picking pockets at Revere Beach. She returned to court in September of that year, this time as the first woman to be prosecuted under new legislation that allowed the arrest of anyone known to be a professional thief seen loitering in railway stations or other meeting places. When asked to explain her thieving, Elizabeth retorted that she 'had to do something in order to live. "I am an old woman now, and what can I do? I must eat and have a place to sleep"'. Crime was still clearly funding her lifestyle when she was arrested again in August 1916 for trying to steal a handbag from a department store.

'Little Annie Reilly' features alongside Margaret Brown and Elizabeth Dillon in *Professional criminals of America* (ill. 7.5). Byrnes identified her as 'the cleverest woman in her line in America. . . . She has stolen more property the last fifteen years than any other four women in America.'[23] The Ulster-born woman was described across the years as 'Beautiful but bad', a 'pretty servant girl thief', and a 'handsome blonde servant girl' having a 'fine appearance and personal bearing, pleasing manners, strictly virtuous habits, powerful physique, daring spirit and natural smartness'. A judge at Annie's trial in June 1884 addressed her: 'you have been a very dangerous thief, for the reason that your appearance is such that your success has been easy'. He acknowledged the effectiveness of her disguise, observing that 'nobody would for a moment suspect, from your appearance, that you were the kind of a character you are'.

7.5. Photograph of Annie Reilly, 1880.

Annie Reilly operated a different style of theft to Margaret Brown and Elizabeth Dillon. Her tactic was to secure employment in houses as a servant, seamstress or children's nanny, earn the trust of the family across a few days and then leave, often in the middle of the night, having plundered the valuables. In one such employment in 1881, Annie put her servant dress on over expensive clothes belonging to her employer. She then did 'the honors of dinner', serving the family their meal without them realizing that she was wearing their clothes underneath her servant attire. Following dinner, she 'slipped upstairs, put on some braids of light-colored hair . . . bedecked herself with jewels and boldly walked out'. As she was leaving, an unsuspecting passer-by complimented her on her voluminous hair and she allegedly replied: 'Yes; it is all natural'.

To catch a thief

In 1884, Margaret Brown was convicted of stealing a purse from a shopper in Macy's Department Store, New York, and sent to Blackwell's Island. Four months later, as she left her cell to join the other women about to be discharged, her time in prison complete, Detective Adams from Boston saluted her: 'How are you, Mag?' A journalist wrote: 'One glance at Detective Adams and Inspector Mountain of Boston, who accompanied him, was sufficient for her to see that she was again to be deprived of her liberty. The happy expression she had when leaving her cell, now passed away, and a dejected look took its place on her countenance.' The two Boston police officers had travelled to New York to arrest Margaret for stealing a bag containing $260 a year earlier. The familiar way in which Detective Adams spoke to Margaret and her immediate recognition of him show how well criminals and their captors got to know each other.

This is also evident in a case from 1894, when New York detectives kept a close watch on serial offender Agnes Breen, circulating in a crowd at a ceremony to celebrate the laying of the cornerstone of a new hospital. One of the detectives, Sergeant Weiser, recognized Breen as a woman he had arrested in 1882 after he saw her steal a purse from a mourner's pocket at a funeral. Breen had carried an infant on that occasion and 'looked the picture of innocence', but when arrested was found with seven purses in her possession. Now, having encountered the pickpocket again, Weiser was certain that Breen had little interest in the hospital and much more interest in the wealthy women in attendance. Fearing that she might recognize him, he held back while his colleague, Detective Reynolds, followed her. 'I've caught you this time, Ag', Reynolds pronounced as he grabbed her hand that was in a wealthy widow's pocket. 'Too soon; you can only make this an attempt at larceny', the Irish pickpocket retorted.[24]

Annie Reilly's nemesis in the police force seems to have been a Detective Keirns, who first arrested her as a teenager in 1867 for stealing from her mistress in New York. Annie was sentenced to two and a half years in Sing Sing but managed to escape after nine months, apparently the first female to do so without the help of others. On her way back to New York City, she employed her usual tactics, using her 'personal magnetism' to appeal to a wealthy family and in the 'dead of night pillaged the house from cellar to attic'. With her big basket full of stolen goods, Annie boldly went to the police station to enquire about the time of the next train to New York. She was so charming that the police captain directed one of his officers to carry her basket to the station.

Detective Keirns of the New York Police Department was less easily captivated by Annie's appearance and charisma. He managed to re-arrest her in 1869 in New York and return her to Sing Sing. In 1873, by which stage Annie had been released, Keirns was in Florida when he heard of a series of thefts in New York. He recognized Annie's trademark method of gaining employment and plundering houses, and he returned to the city 'knowing that there was but one woman capable of committing such a series of crimes'. He placed a decoy advertisement for domestic help at an address that was empty and the police waited in anticipation. Annie took the bait, and, after an attempted escape, she was captured.

An article devoted to Annie's criminal history published in

1881 describes how, while serving five years in Sing Sing for these crimes, she apparently wrote several 'beautiful' letters to her victims expressing regret for her behaviour. But they may not have been sincere. When one woman called to the prison to reclaim the expensive hair extensions that Annie had stolen from her, Annie reportedly admitted: 'I thought how funny you must have felt to get up and have no hair to put on your head'.

Annie Reilly was not the only female thief who was skilful at duping the authorities. In 1874, Mollie Holbrook, aka the 'Queen of crooks', whom Byrnes identified as Irish, was captured in New York by Detective Miller of the Chicago police force, charged with stealing $40,000 from a Chicago merchant two years earlier.[25] The detective bought tickets for the Canadian Southern Line to take Holbrook to Chicago to stand trial, but when the train stopped at Hamilton, Ontario, she jumped out of the carriage and ran to a police officer, claiming that she was being abducted to the US.[26] The Canadian magistrate before whom she was brought released her from custody.[27] Holbrook was tracked down to the residence of another famous Irish-born thief, 'Red Kate' Gorman, but Miller lost his job as a result of the incident.[28]

'Red Kate' Gorman claimed to have been a pickpocket since she was fourteen years old, and although she was regularly arrested, she had few convictions.[29] When arrested for stealing opera glasses worth around $14 from a theatregoer on Broadway in February 1865, Kate allegedly offered the police captain a diamond ring worth $600 and $400 in cash to drop the charge against her. On that occasion 'the offer was indignantly spurned', but Kate walked free from court after the legal documents mysteriously went missing.[30] In 1869, she was arrested in New York for pickpocketing. While she awaited trial, 'A delegation of politicians, bummers, pimps, and thieves, all loyal subjects of Queen Kate, repaired to the residence of the complainant, and partly by threats, partly by promises, coerced him to sign a request to the authorities withdrawing the charge.' A journalist observed: 'Lady Kate is still young and good-looking. Among thieves and criminals she is the acknowledged queen. She boasts of carrying a half dozen Judges in her dress pocket, and so she defies the authorities.'[31] 'Red Kate' and her husband, 'Red Leary', were rumoured to be in business with politician and later police court judge Bernard 'Barney' Martin. Longford-born Martin was one of the 'old guard' of Tammany Hall, the power centre of the Democratic Party in New York.[32] He was later indicted for corruption and accepting bribes but avoided conviction.[33]

As career criminals' notoriety increased, they became more easily recognizable by 'store detectives' (security guards employed by department stores) and policemen on patrol, and identifiable as previous offenders on arrest despite their string of aliases. Thomas Byrnes must have been a constant source of annoyance to the women as they tried to carry out their illegal activity in New York. Following his appointment as head of the Detective Bureau, he reorganized the force, handpicked forty men to staff the detective headquarters and established the rank of detective sergeant, whose pay ($1,600 per year) was on a par with that of police sergeants.[34] By his own admission, his work in the Detective Bureau brought him into contact with Wall Street financiers and investors, several of whom, grateful to the detective for protecting their interests by apprehending blackmailers or criminals, guided him in the purchase of stocks and investments or bought stocks on his behalf. By December 1894, Byrnes owned real estate worth almost $300,000.[35] In the following year, he published a second edition of his mugshot book, which included more than 400 images, Margaret Brown, Elizabeth Dillon and Annie Reilly still among them.

Stealing in the 'cathedrals of consumption'

In cities across Europe and North America in the mid- to late nineteenth century, dry-goods stores and general merchants gradually expanded into what would be recognized as a department store. Customers could buy a range of items from clothes, linens and haberdashery to fancy goods and jewellery, to house furnishings and kitchen utensils, all under one roof.[36] Department stores were vast spaces full of colour and light, and used new technologies to facilitate shopping, like the elaborate ventilation system at Macy's that pumped fresh air through the store.[37]

The growth and development of the large department store transformed the landscape for shoplifters and pick-pockets alike. Shopping became a female-dominated pastime. In 1904, for instance, 90 per cent of Macy's customers were women.[38] Female shoplifters and pickpockets blended in with the huge number of shoppers moving around large stores unchaperoned. The development of ready-to-wear fashion and department store displays enabled shoplifters to try on clothing and walk out wearing it.[39]

Department stores incurred huge losses to shoplifters. Silk departments alone were thought to suffer losses of $5,000 or $6,000 annually, and in 1904 it was reckoned that the big stores in Manhattan had been losing $500,000 a year to pilferage.[40] It is unsurprising, then, that department stores employed store detectives to deter shoplifting or catch shop-lifters in the act. Detectives were often women, who were better able to blend in with the crowds.[41] In 1897 the assistant superintendent of Eaton's, a vast Irish-owned department store in Toronto, was made a special police constable with powers to arrest suspects.[42]

Mary Flaherty, aged twenty-two, who worked in a paper box factory, gave her nine-year-old niece, Lottie Trayer, a rather unusual Saturday shopping trip when they went to Ridley's Stores in New York in May 1887. Mary, who had emigrated from Ireland three years earlier, was described as 'a well-dressed young Irish woman' and Lottie a 'blue-eyed and golden-haired little girl'. Mary's tactic was to take something from the counter and pass it to Lottie, who would leave the store with it. But on this occasion a store detective recognized them from the previous week. Lottie's mother went to the police station to report Lottie's disappearance that evening only to find that her daughter and sister had been arrested. A widow with four children, she denied that she knew her sister was a thief or that her young daughter 'had been used as a tool'.[43]

With department stores emerged a new type of shoplifter, the middle-class woman who was 'lacking in self-control' when faced with the variety of goods displayed on counters.[44] A clear distinction was made at this time between the shoplifter who 'deliberately and wilfully "lifts" things for a living' and the women who just happened to 'take it because inclination and impulse got together'.[45] Middle-class women who shoplifted were, unsurprisingly, treated more leniently than women of a lesser reputation or status who committed the same crime. Some middle-class women were given a warning in the stores, or their husbands were brought in to pay for the items, the owners and managers fearful of false or mistaken accusations, lawsuits and damage to the store's reputation if they took a valued customer or respected family to court.[46]

From the 1880s, the defence of kleptomania was increasingly used in court.[47] Thomas Byrnes observed:

> It does seem strange that a wife and mother whose home is an honest one, who attends religious service regularly, and who seems far removed from the world of crime, should be so carried away by her admiration of some trinket or knick-knack as to risk home, honor, everything to secure it. But the annals of metropolitan offenses are full of instances of just this kind.[48]

One such incident occurred in March 1894, when a woman named Julia Ferguson was apprehended by a detective employed in the Ehrich Brothers' multistorey department store on Sixth Avenue and Twenty-Third Street in New York.[49] The detective had 'noticed her moving from counter to counter', and while she waited on the preparation of a bottle of medicine, she shoplifted two tortoiseshell hairpins and a pair of scissors. When apprehended, she had, according to the detective, 'pretended that she had intended paying for the articles'. The stolen goods were worth $1.50 yet the woman had a cheque for $34 in her purse. On her way to the station, she tried to throw away her purse, likely realizing that the cheque therein would identify her.

A reporter described Julia Ferguson when she appeared in court charged with stealing the hairpins and scissors from Ehrich Brothers: 'The woman is about forty years old, is well dressed, and showed evidence of good breeding.' She was later determined to be Julia Horen, a wealthy Irish-born widow who lived in Tarrytown, New York, and who had clearly used an alias in an effort to avoid reputational damage. Horen's husband had worked as a liquor dealer prior to his death and left an estimated fortune of between $50,000 and $100,000. A Tarrytown lawyer argued that since his death Julia had acted 'in a queer manner'. The judge, clearly incredulous that this wealthy widow had stolen such trifling items, stated his belief that she 'was not in her right mind, or she would not have picked up a cheap pin and stuck it in her hair with the price tag still dangling from it'.

Kate White, sentenced to two and a half years in Sing Sing Prison in New York in 1867 for stealing $18,000 from a bank, claimed at a subsequent arrest for burglary:

> from my earliest remembrance I have at times been addicted to stealing; nearly always stole jewelry; sometimes could manage to overcome this desire for a year at a time; again it would come upon me with such force that there was no resisting it . . . the feeling comes over me with trembling, and if I am at work I have to leave it and steal something.[50]

But not everyone bought into the idea of addiction or compulsion. In the 1890s, Mary Plunkett, a long-serving store detective in Macy's, said: 'Do I believe in kleptomania? Hardly. Women I give into custody, I class as dishonest.'[51]

Disorganized crime

Most Irish-born female thieves were far less flamboyant and skilful than the women who feature in Byrnes's *Professional criminals of America*. They stole all sorts. In Toronto, Eva Foster stole a horse and buggy in May 1895. In September of the same year,

Mary Elliott stole plants from Riverside Park.[52] Kate Hickey, a notorious Toronto thief, was caught in 1888 stealing clothes from a clothes line.[53] In Boston, newly wed Mary McClellan seems to have had housekeeping in mind when she stole pillows, pillowcases, napkins, linen damask, quilts and a mirror from hotels, shops and eateries in 1844.[54] Sarah Fogarty embraced a shop owner in New York in relief after he gave her a discount on a candle when she found herself short. Later he noticed that his wallet, with $75 in it, had gone missing and she was later found to have been the culprit.[55] Mary Ann Couly was arrested for stealing a silver-plated candlestick off the altar of New York's Church of the Nativity.[56] Joanna Seymour went to prison in Toronto for ten days in January 1896 for stealing fish. Like Phoebe Donnelly and Bessie Cox, who stole turkeys in the city in March 1900, she might have been motivated by hunger or a desire to sell the food for money.[57]

In September 1893, twenty-year-old Mary Craig, who had migrated to Massachusetts four years earlier, explained that she was unemployed and stole because 'she was hungry and committed the theft hoping to sell the articles'.[58] Another Irish woman, Julia Barry, was, according to a *Toronto Globe* journalist, 'so impressed with the necessity of providing the Orthodox Christmas dinner', while lacking the money to do so, that she stole a goose from a Mrs Porter on Christmas Day 1873.[59] She had called at the back door of Porter's house to ask for a drink of water. It was only when Barry left that the woman realized that the goose that had been hanging up in the kitchen was also gone.[60] Barry had only just been released from prison having been convicted of stealing and then pawning a hat and coat from a hallway. The judge at her trial suggested another motive when he mused that she had 'too close an acquaintance with her old friend "rye"'.[61]

Laura Wilson, thirty-six years old, was arrested in New York in February 1904 for breaking into a house and stealing silverware and clothes. Irish-born Wilson was described as a 'chameleonic burglar' because when she robbed a house she would change out of her own clothes and leave in new stolen garments.[62] She had what were described as 'masculine habits': she drank 'rum like a sailor, smokes cigarettes and plays the races', and in each of the homes that she broke into there was a 'strong odor of liquor around and half smoked cigarettes scattered on the floors'.[63] The extent of her stealing became clear when she was taken to the police station and her victims came to retrieve the items she had stolen from them. On arrival at the police station, Laura looked like 'a woman professor' with a 'becoming tight-fitting jacket, a severe waist and a plain skirt of rich material', wearing 'gold rimmed spectacles and her hair was dressed in the fashion assumed by purely intellectual women'. But when she appeared in court the next day, she apparently looked like a 'female bum', with clothes 'that could be fished out of the cast-off pile'. Even the glasses she had worn had now been reclaimed.[64]

In December 1895, the house of Eckel Herman, at 7 Eaton Place in Boston, was burgled while the family and servants slept. Stolen items included cutlery, crockery, clothing, tableware and jewellery worth almost $150. In April of the following year, by which stage the family must have lost hope that their items would be returned, Mrs Herman, out walking, 'suddenly saw something familiar in the dress of a woman ahead of her on Leverett st'.[65] The cape worn by a young woman in front of her looked exactly like one that had been stolen from her house months previously. Herman accosted the woman, pressured her into coming to her house and summoned the police. At the police station, the woman, Catherine O'Donnell, claimed that the cape had been a present from her mother's cousin, Delia Brown. When the police went to Catherine's mother's house, they found several more items that had been reported missing after the Herman burglary. Additional items were found at the house of another of Delia Brown's relatives. The two families insisted that Delia had gifted them the goods and they knew nothing else about them. Delia was eventually tracked down and arrested.

While in police custody, Delia regaled the police with stories of her escapades. She admitted to having burgled the house at Eaton Place by using a key that she had acquired when she worked for a former occupant. Delia also admitted that when she worked in the lodging house, she stole items worth around $75 from the room of one of the lodgers after he died. This had been noticed when an inventory of the deceased man's property was drawn up but the police had never solved the case. Delia pawned some of the stolen goods for minuscule amounts of money or gave them to friends. Her husband, George, who had left his wife and children for Delia, was said to have been inconsolable in the weeks after her arrest and committed suicide by drowning.

The fate of Margaret Brown and other prominent thieves

Thomas Byrnes died at his home on West 77th Street in New York City on the night of 7 May 1910, with his wife, Ophelia, and five daughters by his side.[66] He had popularized the use of the rogues' gallery, but even at the time it was not considered a foolproof method of detection: criminals could disguise themselves or distort their faces for the photographs, the camera was not always thought to capture an exact likeness, and it could be cumbersome and time-consuming to consult vast collections of photographs. Fingerprinting technology was coming into use and eventually replaced the rogues' gallery as a policing tool. But during Byrnes's tenure at the helm of the Detective Bureau, the rogues' gallery captured public interest. And across two editions of his *Professional criminals of America* are the faces of Irish-born thieves who tested the New York City police in the nineteenth and early twentieth centuries. They were not the only Irish-born thieves to operate, as this chapter makes clear, but they were identified by Byrnes as the most notorious.

Margaret Brown seems to disappear from the records around the turn of the century. Byrnes noted in his revised edition of *Professional criminals of America* in 1895 that the 'remarkable old lady' was released from custody in Cleveland, Ohio, in December 1894, saying that she would return to New York to withdraw money from her bank account before travelling on to San Francisco. In 1967, long after her death, the *Boston Globe* stated: 'New England crime annals . . . show few such instances of single-minded devotion to the art of shoplifting as was evidenced by Margaret Brown who practiced her demeaning trade for 60 years'.

Of Annie Reilly, Byrnes noted in 1895: 'Nothing has been heard of this woman in the vicinity of New York City for a number of years.'

'Red Kate' Gorman died in poverty in Coney Island, New York, in 1896. She was considered 'one of the most daring shoplifters and all-around criminals that ever operated in this country' but had spent all her money on bail, bribes and 'high living'.[67]

Elizabeth Dillon outlived Thomas Byrnes. Her last known

whereabouts was in Boston in 1920, when a newspaper headline noted: '"Queen of Dips" now 80 gets a chance'. When Elizabeth was in court on another charge, the presiding judge, a sheriff, the arresting police officers and a probation officer agreed to set her up with a needlework job. The judge told Elizabeth that 'if she herself would assist, everything would be lovely and she would have a nice job, money and a good home in the future'. Elizabeth agreed, although a newspaper reporter judged that the old offender had in the past 'made all sorts of promises, every one of which was broken'. The judge gave Elizabeth a suspended sentence and made arrangements for her to start her new job the next day.

8. Crimes of matrimony and the case of Letitia Armstrong

On 17 April 1873, 23-year-old Letitia Armstrong got ready to leave her house in Toronto for the evening. Letitia lived on the corner of Bay Street and Richmond Street West with her 28-year-old husband, George, who was a grocer, along with their servant, Julia Pinkham, and a boarder named William Sammy. That night, Letitia's younger brother Edward Riley, a carpenter, was also sleeping in the house. Julia Pinkham had been living there for around six months when, in early April 1873, she had told Letitia of her intention to leave. But Letitia had persuaded her to stay by offering her higher wages. Julia considered herself to be on good terms with her mistress and was content to stay for another while.

Both Letitia and George were Irish-born and had immigrated when they were young, George in 1860 when he was fourteen years old and Letitia a year later in 1861 when she was ten.[1] We couldn't locate a marriage certificate for Letitia and George, but the couple are documented as having been married by the time of the 1871 census. Both were Wesleyan Methodists. Toronto, known as the 'Belfast of Canada' or the 'Belfast of [North] America', was an appealing destination for Irish Protestant emigrants.[2] From the mid-nineteenth century, when Letitia and George emigrated, the majority of the Irish arriving in Toronto came from a Protestant background. Letitia and George may have been attracted by well-established emigratory links between Ulster and Toronto, and emigration agents promoted Toronto to Ulster

Protestants as a place of opportunity alongside residents of a similar background.[3] Among the successful Irish Methodist men in the city was Timothy Eaton from County Antrim, who started out with a small shop in Toronto around the same time as George Armstrong, and went on to own the largest department store chain in Canada.[4]

On 17 April 1873, Letitia said her goodbyes as she headed out for the evening – but she did not actually leave the house. Instead, she hid and waited. A short time later, she burst into Julia's room and found her and her husband in their servant's bed. Letitia shouted: 'you take that', and shot Julia in the face with a pistol, causing her to lose her left eye. The next morning Letitia turned herself in to the Toronto police.

It is not clear how long George Armstrong and Julia Pinkham had been engaging in a sexual relationship, or how it had been initiated. Letitia blamed her servant entirely for the affair and considered that Julia had 'enticed' her husband into bed. But, as Julia's employer, George was clearly in the more powerful position. We know that Julia had been considering leaving her job, which might suggest that she also wanted to extricate herself from the sexual relationship with her married employer. We know, too, that she considered the sleeping arrangements in the house awkward because the Armstrongs had to pass through her bedroom to get to their own.

At the subsequent trial, Letitia was accused of shooting Julia with intent to do her grievous bodily harm. Although Letitia was the one on trial, George Armstrong was portrayed by the press (and the defence) as the main wrongdoer. Not only had he been having an affair, but he had run downstairs after his wife fired the shot, Julia testified, without paying any attention to his injured and bleeding paramour.

Julia also testified in court that George had only come to see her once or twice in the hospital and 'she did not get any letters from him'. Even the legal team who were prosecuting Letitia for the shooting observed: 'It would have been a more righteous act . . . if she had shot her husband, who appeared to be a man without regard either for his wife or for the decencies of society.'

A bad marriage

Letitia Armstrong's crime arose in the context of her marriage, but it was not a crime against marriage itself. There were, though, a number of offences on the books at this time that existed specifically to defend the institution of marriage. Legislation differed between Boston, New York and Toronto and across the nineteenth and early twentieth centuries, but at particular points during this period married men and women could be prosecuted for acts such as adultery, desertion, bigamy and domestic abuse.

After informally separating from her husband, Irish immigrant Alice Canning 'went with another man' in 1882 and was sentenced to a year in the Massachusetts Reformatory Prison for Women for adultery.[5] Ann Amrock was found guilty of adultery with Maggie Greyson's husband, Daniel, in 1877. Daniel, described as a 'one eyed, lame, colored man', was also found guilty and sentenced to two years in the House of Correction in South Boston.[6] Crimes of adultery by a married woman or man often only came to the attention of the authorities when reported by the scorned spouse. Adultery also affected child custody arrangements. In Ontario (Canada West) after 1855, an Act

Respecting the Appointment of Guardians and the Custody of Infants determined that custody of children under the age of twelve could be given to their mothers as the judges thought appropriate, but mothers found guilty of adultery were automatically considered unfit.[7] The same restriction did not apply to fathers who had been unfaithful to their wives.[8] This condition of fidelity on the part of mothers remained in place until 1887.[9]

A scorned spouse could also prosecute for desertion. The New York City Domestic Relations Court was established in 1910 and dealt with 'all persons charged with abandonment or non-support of wives or poor relations'. The court could enforce the payment of financial support, and anyone found guilty was adjudged to be a disorderly person and imprisoned for up to a year.[10] A wife who had committed adultery forfeited her right to support from her husband, but her children's rights were unaffected.[11] Likewise, from 1911 in Massachusetts, a wife could charge her husband with non-support of her and their children under the age of sixteen, while a husband could charge his wife with desertion of their children. The terms indicate assumptions at the time that heterosexual marriages involved male breadwinners and female dependants. Legislation and prosecutions also stemmed from the desire to relieve taxpayers or charities of having to support deserted wives or children.[12] The punishment was a fine of $200 or up to a year in prison.

In the nineteenth century, charities in New York, Boston and Toronto commented on the high numbers of deserted Irish women they had to support. In 1872, the New York Association for Improving the Condition of the Poor described the desertion of wives as a 'flagrant crime against social order' and considered it 'most frequent among our immigrant population'.[13] Irish families found themselves 'wracked by high levels of male desertion'.[14] Margaret Cummins and Mary Riley, 'two destitute immigrant women', applied for aid in November 1883 at the Castle Garden landing station, where all new immigrants were received and processed upon arrival in New York. Riley had 'left Ireland with an old man, who deserted her soon after their arrival' in the city; Cummins too was looking for her missing husband.[15] Some of the desertion may have related to men leaving in search of work, but other examples make clear that men deserted unhappy marriages or shirked family responsibilities. The physical size of Canada and the US, with their growing populations and improved transport links, meant that husbands could disappear more easily than in Ireland if they so desired.[16] Mary Donohue, who had immigrated during the American Civil War, married soon after arrival in Boston. Her husband, with whom she had three children, stole $15.62 from her and ran away with another woman.[17]

Records of charities and institutions contain descriptions of the physical abuse of Irish women at the hands of their husbands. Catherine Dillon's husband had 'been in the practice of beating her' and Mary Manning's husband had given her a 'whipping' before both women ended up in the Women's Prison Association Home in New York.[18] Annie Lucas's husband had 'always treated her cruelly', and when she was convicted of larceny in November 1887, she had 'a sore on her face . . . where he struck her with a wooden box'.[19] Johannah Kelly had a 'badly bruised' body caused by her husband, when she was sentenced to a year in the Massachusetts Reformatory Prison for Women in April 1890 for being a common drunkard.[20] Irish-born Susan Voyer was observed on conviction for drunkenness in June 1911 to have several scars on her body caused by her husband attacking her with a knife.[21]

Historian Linda Gordon found that 14 per cent of marital violence cases in Boston in the late nineteenth and early twentieth centuries involved female violence; most of these acts, she judges, were 'responsive or reactive'.[22] Irish-born Mamie Legreto insisted that she attacked her Italian husband, John, with a carving knife in New York in September 1896 in an act of self-defence. John had 'procured a sword', she explained, and so she had 'reinforced her defensive power' with the knife to protect herself from a 'murderous onslaught'. She stabbed John under the left eye and across his neck. A newspaper reporter considered that anyone who envied John for marrying 'a pure blooded Irish girl . . . the belle of the neighborhood', would have changed their minds had they seen him in the police court with his face 'swollen to the most ridiculous of proportions'.[23]

Another ethnically mixed couple in New York, John Maurer (a 'tall lean German') and his Irish-born wife, Mary Ann ('as fat and dumpy as he is long and lean'), became embroiled in a similar marital fight in 1897. After a day of drinking, John began to sing some German songs, 'much to the disgust of his Irish wife', who, according to a newspaper reporter at least, said: 'stop it, begorra, or I'll dance on your face'. John continued to sing 'until a coffee cup landed on his right eye' and then he 'smote his frau on the mouth splitting her lip'. Soon the 'husband and wife were mixed up in a wild tangle of table utensils', and with Mary Ann's 'fighting blood . . . thoroughly aroused' she kicked John's feet from under him, climbed up onto a table, launched herself off it and 'alighted squarely on his ribs'. Mary Ann 'was belabouring him with the sugar bowl' when a policeman heard the commotion and broke down the door. Initially Mary Ann's complaint of assault against John was accepted, but when he was found to have three broken ribs, Mary Ann was also summoned to the police court.[24]

In another case, John McCabe died of a stab wound to his abdomen outside his house in New York in 1881 and his wife, Bridget, was tried for his murder. A witness had heard Bridget shouting, 'you are a fine son of a bitch to leave your companion with a pair of black eyes'.[25] At her trial, Bridget pointed to the domestic abuse that she had experienced during their marriage. Her husband, she explained, had 'beaten her, breaking two of her ribs', and it was only then that she had 'held out her hand to prevent him from striking her again' and inadvertently stabbed him.[26] The jury was clearly sympathetic, convicting her not of murder but manslaughter. She was sentenced to two years' imprisonment.[27]

Across the second half of the nineteenth century, women were generally punished less severely than men for violent spousal attacks. Juries often showed themselves sympathetic to the actions of wives and the circumstances that provoked them, particularly if it involved domestic violence, desertion or infidelity.[28] Letitia Armstrong's defence would play on such attitudes when her case came to trial.

One spouse too many

The migration of a married woman or man sometimes facilitated what has been called 'divorce Irish style'.[29] And some Irish men and women committed bigamy abroad by marrying again despite having a living spouse in Ireland.[30]

Mary Bough married in 1835, and her husband, John

Dungan, later migrated to New York. His bigamous marriage to Ellen Mahony in 1845 was discovered when Mary's brother Charles recognized him on a New York street in 1848 and testified in court that Mary was alive and well in Ireland.[31] In another case, Irish-born Mary Sullivan, who was living in Liverpool, had a family member in New York keeping an eye out for her husband, John, and in June 1902, fourteen years after he had deserted her, he was spotted. Mary travelled from Liverpool to New York to see him, along with their teenage son, and found him 'living with another woman as his wife'. Vexed that he refused to acknowledge her or their marriage, she took him to court, determined 'to make him pay for his long absence from her side'.[32] Forty-year-old James McNamee, a 'dashing dry-goods clerk' from Belfast, married Katie McFaul, 'a petite brunette, handsome, about 22 years of age and very accomplished', in New York State in June 1886. Although the couple were considered a good match for each other, the hastily arranged marriage surprised their friends, as did their decision to have the ceremony in another parish. Shortly afterwards, James's employer received a letter from a woman in Belfast. She claimed to be married to James McNamee and to have five children 'in poor circumstances owing to McNamee's failing to keep up remittances'. James 'brazenly denied all knowledge of the writer of the letter' but was apparently 'dazed' when confronted with one of his own letters to his Irish-based wife.[33]

Bigamous marriages sometimes occurred even when both spouses lived in North America. In 1847, Irish-born Hannah Elizabeth Day found out after five years of marriage that her husband, William Lang, had been previously married to a woman who was still alive. She subsequently refused to live with him and he left six months before their son was born.

She reverted to using her maiden name and the baby was later placed for adoption.[34] In another case, Catherine Ryan's husband, Michael, had emigrated with her from Ireland to Halifax, Canada, in 1844. They later moved to Boston. But after being apart for two years she 'heard he had married again'.[35]

Irish women also committed bigamy. Hannah Walsh had married at sixteen but left her husband because he didn't financially support the family. She then married a sailor and had lived with him for five months before her arrest and imprisonment for three years in the Massachusetts Reformatory Prison for Women. On New Year's Eve 1884, her first husband, James, who had had her arrested, came to see her in prison. Hannah had clearly not forgiven him and refused to see him.[36]

Scorned spouses sometimes joined forces to prosecute a bigamist, as in the case of Nora McGrath, 'a winsome Irish girl of generous proportions', and Tillie Eggert, a 'pretty German girl, small but full of fight'. Together they charged Thomas Wright with bigamy in New York in 1912. Nora explained she had married Thomas in 1909, but, 'because of his propensity for liquor', she had left him in September 1911, advising him that 'whenever he thought more of her than he did of whiskey he might come back for forgiveness'. Two months later, Thomas married Tillie – but two weeks after the wedding she found out about his first wife. According to her account, she 'gave him 5 cents, told him to "beat it" and slammed the door in his face'. Thomas pleaded in court that he was 'only twenty-three, Your Honor, an' unsophisticated', and that he wanted to go back and live with Nora, who was 'the only woman I love'. He argued that Tillie had 'snared' him into marriage by giving him Scottish whiskey, 'awful strong whiskey it was – an' I think it must have had somethin' in it, for I didn't come to till two weeks after, an' found I was married'. Thomas claimed that he couldn't remember anything about the wedding ceremony, 'nor the preacher nor nothin' till I woke up an' told Tillie I had another wife'. Nora was 'willing to forgive her erring spouse' but Tillie was less forgiving, and Thomas was held for trial.[37]

Often the defence for female bigamists focused on their mistreatment at the hands of their first husbands.[38] This is evident in the case of Bridget McCool, a rare example of a female serial bigamist (ill. 8.1).[39] She had left school in Ireland when she was fifteen and migrated to the United States four years later in 1904. She worked in a laundry and a paper mill until 1907, when she married Thomas McCool. She described her marriage as 'anything but happy'. Her husband deserted her after two years, leaving her 'wandering about with no friends, food or clothing'. Later she met Walter Day, who 'took pity on her and has supported her since'. When Bridget married Walter, Thomas reported her to the authorities. Bridget was described in her prison file as 'a woman of excitable nature' who was 'terribly bitter' about her first husband bringing the charge against her. Bridget and Walter were both arrested, and it transpired that Walter too had another spouse. They were both found guilty of bigamy and adultery and sentenced to two years in prison.

Bridget's complicated love life didn't end after this conviction, and while her understanding of marital law hadn't improved, she clearly hadn't given up on marriage either. In 1921, she was arrested for marrying Arthur K. Burton despite still being married to Thomas McCool. She was returned to the Massachusetts Reformatory for Women on a second charge of bigamy. And yet still she persisted. In 1931, she

8.1. Bridget McCool, prison mugshot and admission details, 1914.

sought the annulment of her fourth marriage, which had taken place five weeks earlier. The groom was none other than Walter Day, her second husband, the couple having evidently rekindled their romance. She claimed an annulment on the basis that Walter was divorced from the first of his previous three wives and in 'consequence of her contracting a marriage with a divorced man she has been unable to continue as a member of her church'. Walter had apparently told Bridget that his three previous wives were dead, which meant that they could be married in a church, but she had since found out that his first wife was alive. Bridget's petition for an annulment was rejected. Undeterred, she filed for divorce, claiming that her husband had deceived her about his previous marriages. Her divorce was granted on the grounds of cruelty, Walter having lied to her, and Bridget was allowed to resume her former surname of McCool.

A woman scorned

In her witness statement, Julia Pinkham described the circumstances that led to her being shot by her employer Letitia Armstrong at 48 Richmond Street West in Toronto in April 1873. She went to bed about half past ten, she stated, after George Armstrong had already retired. A short while later he came into her bedroom, got into her bed and took his clothes off. Julia recounted that George had been in her room about ten minutes when she was shot in the face and, through the blinding pain, saw Letitia Armstrong standing in the doorway.

At her trial in November 1873, Letitia's defence blamed George and Julia as being 'the guilty parties' and emphasized that it was their behaviour that had motivated Letitia's violent response. She was the good and devoted wife, whereas her husband and servant had shown their disrespect for marriage. D'Arcy Boulton for the defence claimed it 'was no wonder that she had been unable to restrain her passion at the spectacle she witnessed'. He appealed to the jury to 'not proceed with too much severity against one who was only resenting an injury which the law could not sufficiently punish'. Anyone 'would have acted similarly in similar circumstances', he insisted, if they had been confronted with the situation that Letitia had encountered. He also went as far as to suggest that if Letitia 'had killed that woman at that moment she would not have been guilty of murder'.

A newspaper reporter was convinced by this, writing that Letitia 'seems to have been driven to momentary desperation by the infidelity of her husband, and resented it by shooting his paramour'. Some of the jury likely shared this view. Peter Stearns has observed that in American nineteenth-century society 'new opportunities for sexual jealousy opened up' as the idea of romantic relationships gained in popularity and the opportunities for 'rivalries, changes of mind, and disappointments grew'.[40] Women were viewed as more emotional than men and thus it was accepted at this time that a woman who had been slighted by her lover might be irrational enough to react in a violent way.[41]

Such feelings were seen to motivate 'jealous young Irish girl' Ellen McInerney in Toronto in 1886.[42] Ellen, a tailoress, had been dating Benjamin Bennett, a blacksmith's assistant, but she grew 'decidedly adverse to his taking more than passing notice of other females'. Benjamin began to 'become cool towards her' and Ellen found out that his romantic interest had shifted to a young widow named only as Mrs Jackson. On the evening of 14 January 1886, Ellen went to Jackson's house. She sent the widow's daughter out of the room, opened a bottle that she had with her and threw the contents over Jackson's face. The bottle was later determined to contain carbolic acid, and Jackson suffered severe burns that left her permanently disfigured and likely blind in her left eye.[43]

Other women focused their jealous anger on their unfaithful husbands or lovers. A *New York Times* report in August

1857, headlined 'A jealous woman stabs an unfaithful man', told how Irish-born Mary Johnson was arrested for stabbing Stephen Johnson, an oysterman. The couple were not married but had been 'living together as man and wife for some time' when Stephen had apparently 'tired of the connection' between them and suggested that they go their separate ways. Mary 'positively declined'. Stephen then deserted her and for several days and nights Mary had been searching for him. When she found him, she tried to slit his throat with a knife, and although a witness prevented her from fulfilling this aim, she managed to inflict a serious wound.[44]

Sixty-year-old Christian Davidson was less fortunate. His body was found on 17 December 1908 on board his canal boat at the bottom of Corlears Street in New York. His skull was fractured, one side of his jaw was broken, his face was cut in several places, and a few of his teeth were missing. The cabin of the boat was also in disarray with 'Broken flasks, which had contained whisky . . . on the floor and on a table were three others still half filled with the liquid.'[45] Not far from the boat, the police found 55-year-old Irish-born Mary Davidson, Christian's wife, sleeping on a park bench. She was described as a 'stout, untidy old woman whose gray hair hung in disorder over her flushed, flabby countenance'. The police managed to wake her, and although she tried to resist, they brought her to the boat to see her dead husband. On viewing Christian's body, Mary 'gave a hysterical laugh' and shouted: 'He's my husband, and I killed him.' She then 'started to laugh and fight' and was so strong that it required four policemen to restrain her and lift her into the patrol car. At the inquest it was revealed that Mary's actions were motivated by jealousy: she felt that her husband was paying too much attention to the wife of the captain of another canal boat. At her trial, Mary was found guilty of manslaughter and sentenced to two years in Auburn Prison. Her sentence was relatively light considering that Christian had died at her hands, but she likely generated sympathy because her husband's alleged infidelity was seen to provoke her to violence.

The case of another scorned Irish woman came to public attention in 1900. Irish-born Catherine Costello, aged twenty-eight, and her husband, Philip Dreiser, a 27-year-old policeman, lived at 404 East 81st Street in New York (ill. 8.2).[46] Catherine seems to have omitted to tell Philip that she hadn't yet divorced her first husband, John. When Philip found out a few months after their marriage, he left Catherine and her daughter, Nellie (from her first marriage), and began divorce proceedings. Catherine didn't react well to the news and threatened that if he 'tried to get rid of her she would kill him'. She was true to her word and on 9 February 1900 she tried to shoot Philip in the street. A newspaper reporter described how a 'glint of the sunshine on the polished barrel of a revolver' alerted Philip and he was able to jump out of the way 'just in time to save his own life'. After a struggle, Philip managed to get the gun from Catherine and then 'half carried and half dragged' her to the City Hall Police Station, where he made a complaint against her. He later refused to press charges when she was brought before the police court, and Catherine was discharged. The couple's divorce proceedings began in May 1900, and Catherine's first husband testified at the hearing. He revealed that he had married Catherine ten years earlier but had left her a week after the wedding because she 'beat him on the head with a beer bottle while he was asleep'.

8.2. Sketch of Catherine Costello.

For reasons that are not quite clear, Philip called at Catherine's apartment a few months later. Philip's brother John suggested that he had gone to pick up a portrait he had left behind at the house, while Nellie thought he had come to help her mother fit carpets. Whatever the reason, after drinking a can of beer to settle her nerves, Catherine shot Philip twice in the head. Catherine then went across the hall and told a woman who lived in a neighbouring apartment: 'I've just shot my husband', before leaving the building and making her way towards the East 51st Street Police Station, 'apparently for the purpose of giving herself up'. Philip died at the Presbyterian Hospital shortly afterwards.

Catherine reportedly told the police: 'I shot him because I loved him . . . People have tried to separate us, but now they can't do it.' The *Evening World* carried what was said to be a statement that Catherine dictated to one of its reporters, which gave a different slant to the relationship. She was quoted as saying: 'I don't feel one bit sorry for shooting my husband . . . I am glad I made a good job of it. Any man who treats a woman as he treated me deserves to be killed.' She claimed that Philip had pursued her for three years before she agreed to marry him and that he knew that she had another husband still living when he married her. Catherine further justified Philip's murder by telling the *Evening World* reporter that not long after they were married she discovered 'that he was paying attention to other women'. She came on letters from Philip to a woman called Tillie, and when she visited Tillie, she found out that Philip had been paying her rent.

Catherine was declared insane and sent to the Matteawan State Hospital for the Criminally Insane. Four years later, in January 1904, she was deemed to be cured, and upon her release from Matteawan she was re-arrested to stand trial for the murder of her husband. She was described in court as a 'little, sharp-featured woman with dark-brown hair and nervous blue eyes'. Dressed in black and 'heavily veiled', she sat 'like a little wax figure, with head bent and hands folded in her lap'. The verdict came in near midnight on 28 January. The jury found Catherine guilty of manslaughter in the second degree but recommended her to mercy. The judge took into consideration the four years that she had already spent in the asylum and sentenced her to an additional four and a half years in prison. According to a reporter, Catherine 'received the verdict coolly and without any visible sign of emotion', but considering that the penalty for the crime could have been up to fifteen years in prison, she must have felt some relief.

The fate of Letitia Armstrong

Letitia Armstrong was in a more fortunate position than many Irish female immigrants who came before the courts for crimes committed in marriage. The *Toronto Globe* reminded readers at the onset of her trial that she had 'not been suffering' behind prison bars but had instead been 'enjoying her liberty since the occurrence that caused her arrest'. Her husband, George, Andrew Fleming (a clerk of the court) and John Gavin (an insurance agent) had each posted bail of $800. In October 1873, further bail of $1,000 was posted, this time by Andrew Fleming and Tullius O'Neill, the proprietor of the King William III Hotel close to where the Armstrongs lived.[47] The men named on these bail documents were all Irish-born Protestants with well-regarded jobs. As the name indicates, the King William III Hotel was associated with the Orange Order, which wielded considerable political and social influence in Toronto at this time.[48]

Letitia Armstrong was tried in November 1873. Three witnesses testified against her: Julia Pinkham, the injured party; Dr Niven Agnew, a Scottish doctor who lived across the road from the Armstrongs and who treated Julia in the aftermath of the shooting; and George Stagg, the policeman on duty at the Toronto police station when Letitia turned herself in. There was no doubt that Letitia had shot Julia. The case hinged on whether she was seen to have been driven by impulse in a moment of desperation, or if she had carefully planned and executed the attack.

Chief Justice Hegarty, the presiding judge, seemed to show some sympathy towards Letitia when summing up the case. But he rejected the view that anyone would have reacted as Letitia had done, and insisted that to accept such a defence would 'inaugurate a system of resorting to violence on all hands' for all sorts of grievances. He also concluded that Letitia had not acted in a moment of passion but had instead 'set a trap for the other woman by pretending to go away that night and returning at an unexpected moment'.

The jury were sent to deliberate, the judge's words and guidance no doubt echoing in their minds. After three hours, they returned to the courtroom with a verdict that Letitia was guilty of wounding with intent, but that they considered that she committed the crime 'under great provocation' and strongly recommended her to mercy. Letitia was given the opportunity to respond, but according to those present she appeared to be 'very considerably agitated and seemingly alarmed, shook her head, and her lips moved, but no audible speech was heard'. Justice Hegarty took on board the jury's recommendation and sentenced her to a year in prison. Despite her defence having portrayed her as a good wife, the judge commented on Letitia's 'brutal and unwomanlike' conduct and acknowledged that the punishment was light for such a 'scandalous and abominable crime'.

It might be supposed that Letitia's crime, shooting her husband's lover in the face, or George's infidelity in sleeping with their servant in Letitia's own house, would have brought a dramatic end to the Armstrongs' marriage. But Letitia and George remained together. Perhaps they were able to forgive each other, or perhaps it was just more convenient for them to carry on living together than to separate. Over the next few years, the couple didn't move far from their home in Richmond Street West, where the shooting took place. At the time of the 1881 census, they were living just around the corner in York Street, with a nineteen-year-old Irish-born waiter, Austin Williams, presumably a boarder. By this stage George was a bailiff, a position that he held until he was in his sixties. By the 1891 census, they had moved to Adelaide Street West, in the same area of Toronto. They now had several boarders, including Rose McInty, a forty-year-old Irish Catholic, and Emma and Willie Riley, respectively the widow and son of Letitia's brother Edward. Edward had died in 1877, two years after marrying Emma, and the same year that his son Willie was born. Also boarding with the Armstrongs was Cody Edwards, an assistant bailiff.

Letitia and George Armstrong remained together until Letitia's death from typhoid pneumonia on 20 April 1904 at the age of fifty-five. Any further infidelities on George's part did not come to public attention. Perhaps his wife's response to his affair with their servant, Julia Pinkham, had proven enough of a deterrent.

9. Race, reformation and the case of the Anderson sisters

Around 7.30 on the evening of 19 January 1880, 24-year-old Stella Vannall arrived on foot at 23 Bowker Street in Boston's West End: a lodging house and brothel where she had previously lived for a time.[1] Outside the house, she spotted the person she was looking for: her sister, Ida King.[2] Almost immediately, the sisters got into a heated argument. Ida was heard to say that at least she herself did not sleep with Black men, and Stella retorted that she did. In response to whatever Ida said next – it is not recorded – Stella then pulled a three-bladed jackknife out of her pocket and stabbed her sister in the chest.

Michael Toland, who had been talking to Ida when Stella arrived, tried to intervene and was badly wounded himself.[3] He and Ida both fell to the ground. With the help of her companions, Ida was able to stagger into her lodging house, where they tried to help her until medics arrived. Josephine Fay, a friend of Ida's who had witnessed the interaction, ran onto Bowker Street for assistance. A police officer who rushed to the scene repeatedly asked Ida who had stabbed her, but she refused to answer, and eventually retorted: 'Let me alone.' Despite the best efforts of those in attendance, Ida died within an hour. A post-mortem examination would reveal that the knife had penetrated her heart.

Later that night, patrons of Doc Young's drinking saloon on nearby Sudbury Street were, according to a subsequent newspaper report, 'standing in front of the bar, discussing the murder, between drinks, when the outer door was flung wide open, and, with one leap, the murderess landed in the middle of the saloon'. Stella was well known at Doc Young's and had been drinking in the saloon earlier that day. 'All eyes were instantly rivited upon her, as, with flashing eyes, her hair streaming in all directions, she stood in the middle of the saloon vainly trying to staunch the blood which was flowing from a severe wound in her left wrist and the fingers of her left hand.' It was there in the 'low resort' of Doc Young's saloon that the policemen, with Josephine Fay in tow, found Stella washing the blood off her hands and attending to her own wounds.

Stella and Ida

Stella Vannall was born Margaret Anderson, probably in Manchester, England, around 1856. Ida King was born Elizabeth Anderson two years later in Ireland, the family having moved in the interim to Tipperary, their father's homeplace. Stella received some schooling, but Ida does not seem to have attended school at all. Stella immigrated to the United States when she was around nine or ten years old, travelling with neighbours. Ida followed a few months later with their parents, John and Ellen Anderson, and their half-brother Cornelius. The sisters gained employment at the Lyman Cotton Mill in Holyoke, Massachusetts, but their behaviour there was often censured. According to a later *Boston Globe* report, Stella especially 'developed an inclination to become wild, and her parents experienced great difficulty in keeping her within the proper limits'. She tried domestic service and hotel and factory work but had difficult encounters in various employments and never stayed long. Eventually she moved to Boston, where it was said she 'has ever since been one of the lower women that infest the neighborhood of Portland street'. According to a reporter, it was here Stella 'became intimate with the lowest people of the colored persuasion'. Following her marriage to Howard Vannall, a Black man, she became Stella Vannall.

Several journalists recounted the Anderson sisters' past histories in their reports of the circumstances surrounding Ida's death. Ida worked in mills in Holyoke for about four years, then moved to Boston around the same time as Stella, 'after some trouble with a young fellow in Holyoke'. Her half-brother seems to have evicted her from home on account of her sexual relationships. The sisters resided together for a while in Boston, until Ida, according to the *Boston Globe*, 'became disgusted with the habit the sister had of going with colored men'. A journalist for the *Boston Post* concluded that the sisters 'have rarely been on friendly terms, and the breach was widened by the habits of Stella, who, it is said, was more fond of the society of colored men than of those of her own color'.

Stella, clearly vexed by her sister's decision to essentially cut her out of her life, later told her companions that she was going to physically assault or even kill Ida. Doc Young, who kept the saloon where Stella was later arrested, claimed that she had displayed her knife when drinking in the saloon earlier that day and boasted that she planned to 'put it into her sister before the evening was out'.

Bad Bridget and race

Race permeates many of the records examined as part of the Bad Bridget project, particularly in the US. Admission registers for prisons and other institutions regularly indicate ethnicity or race. The 'color' column in Boston's House of Correction admission registers was filled in with designations such as 'B[lack]', 'C[o]l[ore]d', 'Chinaman' and 'yellow' – and left blank for white prisoners.[4] Data on annual admissions, sentences of death or acquittals, and sickness and death among inmates in Toronto Gaol were categorized by either 'M[ale]' or 'F[emale]' and 'White' or 'Black'.[5] Annual reports that compared the ethnicity of those who were aided by or incarcerated in particular institutions sometimes included 'colored' as a category distinct from 'American' or 'Canadian'. Of the 10,055 people arrested in New York from December 1857 to February 1858, 7,850 were identified as Irish, 2,468 as 'Natives of United States, (not colored)', and 255 as 'Colored Persons'.[6] Such categorization was not unique to prisons; in the same year, the *Buffalo Morning Express* noted that the nativity of residents in the Erie County Poor House in New York included 172 from the US, 550 from Ireland and twenty-eight 'Colored Persons'.[7]

Many historians have pointed to views of the Irish – the 'Celt' – as racially distinct from the Anglo-Saxon and native-born white American, particularly in the middle decades of the nineteenth century. Thirty-year-old Ellen McKilligut, who had migrated from County Kerry, was described as a 'very dull most *stupid* specimen of a celt'.[8] The *Daily Evening Transcript* commented in 1852 on the 'carelessness, improvidence and obtuseness of the Hibernians'.[9] The annual report of the New York Association for Improving the Condition of the Poor noted in 1866 that the Irish, 'though possessing many estimable traits, belong to the lowest grade of European civilisation, and know but little more of the service required of them than would a native aborigine'.[10] The Irish were also sometimes placed 'alongside black people as biological models for racial inferiority'.[11] Historian Deirdre Cooper Owens has observed that in notes and medical publications on gynaecologists' experimental treatments on patients, 'black and Irish women served as flesh-and-blood symbols of biological abnormalities linked to race'.[12] She argues that these mid-nineteenth-century male gynaecologists viewed Irish women, like Black women, as abnormally sexualized, unusually fertile, able to withstand pain, and lacking in the docility associated with native-born and other European white women.[13]

But in the racial and ethnic hierarchies of the time, Ida King's behaviour and experiences make clear the advantages that Irish women's whiteness brought them. Ida could conceal her heritage in a way that Black women could not.[14] She was recorded as American-born of American parents on admission to prison on one occasion, and this does not appear to have been questioned. Racism against Black populations was evident across the period. In 1872, the Massachusetts Infant Asylum had to hire Black wet nurses because the white women therein refused to breastfeed Black babies.[15] In 1887, the Boston Children's Aid Society bemoaned the difficulty it faced in placing Black children with foster families: 'There is a strong prejudice against the race still, and it is no easy matter to find places for them.'[16] Irish children, on the other hand, were often in demand. Even by 1910, Black children were not accepted at four of the seventeen institutions for children in Boston.[17]

Stella was not particularly unusual in marrying a Black man. In 1877, the year before her marriage to Howard Vannall, 38 per cent of Black men's and women's marriages in Boston were to white partners.[18] But US historian L. Mara

Dodge has observed that interracial marriages to Black men 'automatically marked white women as beyond the pale of respectable womanhood'.[19] Ida's decision to shun her sister because of her relationships with Black men was thus very much in keeping with contemporary racist attitudes.[20]

Reformation and repentance

Stella Vannall and Ida King were, as newspaper journalists made sure to point out in their reports of the murder, 'women of notoriously bad character' and 'not high in the social circle'. Stella was thought to have acquired the weapon with which she stabbed her sister about a week earlier, after she came out the worst in a fight with an associate nicknamed 'English Kate'. Like many of their companions, the Anderson sisters' lives were marked by violence, crime, sex work and alcohol abuse. Stella was considered to have 'always shown a vicious disposition'. On 6 August 1878, she was charged at the Springfield police court with vagrancy and sentenced to one year in the Massachusetts Reformatory Prison for Women at Sherborn. By that stage, she was already a recidivist or repeat offender, her previous convictions including thirty days in Springfield Jail, three months at the House of Correction in South Boston and two years at the Massachusetts State Workhouse at Bridgewater. She also seems to have spent time at the Palmer workhouse as a juvenile offender. The police considered Stella 'one of the most notorious of the *nymphs du pave* to be found at the West and North ends. She was continually drunk and mixed up in broils, and was looked upon as one of the worst kind of panel-thieves.'[21]

On the day after Stella's transfer in August 1878 to the

Massachusetts Reformatory Prison for Women, her sister was released from the same institution following a six-month sentence for being a common nightwalker. This wasn't Ida's first offence either; she had previously been sentenced to four months in the workhouse for being a common night-walker and thirty days in the House of Industry on Deer Island for drunkenness. Her incarceration in Sherborn did nothing to induce her to change her ways. On her release on 7 August 1878, Ida returned to a brothel 'with a bad friend', Nettie Warner. A few months later, in October 1878, a journalist for the *Boston Globe* likened Boston's 'musty old court room' to a garden, 'a sadly neglected one, it is true – in which flowers, weeds and vegetables are allowed to grow up together, regardless of form, beauty or anything save a bare existence'. Among those who featured in the courtroom on that day was Ida King, charged with being a common nightwalker. The journalist described her as 'a sort of night-blooming cereus'. She was sentenced to another year in the Massachusetts Reformatory Prison for Women and there was reunited with her sister behind bars.

Over the next few months, the punishment and reform of the Anderson sisters proved a challenge for employees at the prison. Staff observed Stella Vannall's 'violent outbursts of temper' that rendered her 'at times hardly responsible' for her own actions. Ida's friend Nettie Warner alleged that Stella had pushed her own mother down the stairs in an alter-cation from which she never recovered. Ida, for her part, was described by prison staff as 'violent and troublesome'. While in the Massachusetts Reformatory, the sisters banded together and physically assaulted a staff member, Miss Davis, for ordering Ida to wash the floor. The punishment books of the prison are replete with further evidence of their failure to adhere to the prison rules. Offences included 'trespassing on the grass', 'disrespect, disobedience', 'impertinence and disobedience in Chapel', 'disobedience and disorder', 'disobedience in Hospital', and 'insolence and threatening to strike Miss Busby'. Punishments included a restricted diet of bread and water, solitary confinement in a cell, and deprivation of outdoor exercise or other forms of recreation. Stella was released from custody on 31 July 1879 and Ida followed her a few months later on 10 October. Prison staff must have breathed a sigh of relief.

Other Irish women similarly caused problems for prison employees trying to maintain discipline and control. Staff at the Andrew Mercer Ontario Reformatory for Females in Toronto struggled with Irish-born frequent offender Tillie Robinson. Robinson, who left Ireland as a teenager around 1888, served thirty-seven prison sentences in Toronto between September 1892 and July 1904, predominantly for drunkenness but also for disorderly conduct, assault, horse stealing, trespass and being in a house of ill fame.[22] While in the Mercer, her misbehaviour included emptying her slop buckets over staff, singing and whistling when she was meant to be quiet, using what was considered to be obscene language, and threatening and abusing fellow inmates and employees. Robinson was so disruptive that Emma O'Sullivan, the superintendent at the Mercer Reformatory, refused to readmit her following a court conviction in August 1902. O'Sullivan insisted: 'It is impossible to preserve discipline wherever this woman is.' But in June 1903, when Superintendent O'Sullivan again sought to keep Robinson out of her institution following another conviction, she was unsuccessful and Robinson had to be readmitted.

Over the course of the next few months, Emma O'Sullivan's

letters to the prison inspector detail her difficulty in dealing with Tillie Robinson. The superintendent made clear 'the unsuitableness of the reformatory for this kind of prisoner'. Robinson's disruptive behaviour was seen as a threat to the reformation and rehabilitation of the women incarcerated with her. O'Sullivan also emphasized the physical threat that Robinson posed to staff. She noted: 'I believe the life of any attendant who would attempt to shut her up against her will, or cross her in any way would not be safe. I anticipate great difficulty during her incarceration in the Reformatory.' James Noxon, the prison inspector, reminded O'Sullivan that 'it is your duty to receive all prisoners regularly committed to the Reformatory on their being delivered in charge of a Bailiff or other officer'. He explained that 'so long as she conducts herself sanely and is in bodily health, you in duty will have to do the best you can with her'.

Tillie Robinson had been liberated from the Mercer Reformatory for only a few days when she returned in December 1903 to serve another six months for drunkenness. Within weeks she was on a bread-and-water diet in the so-called dungeon of the prison. The doctor who attended her recommended the revival of cold-water treatment as a punishment, which he was convinced had in the past 'invariably cured vicious women'. This involved drenching the misbehaving inmate with cold water via a hose fixed to the ceiling or wall. But the prison inspector refused to sign off on this measure, arguing that it was used in other institutions 'with deplorable consequences and excited strong public prejudice against it'. He also recommended discontinuing the bread-and-water diet: 'You know how easily the public mind is inflamed, as well as prejudiced, in regard to these matters', he warned the superintendent.

By February 1905, Tillie Robinson had been to the Mercer Reformatory eight times and yet showed no sign of reformation. Superintendent Emma O'Sullivan was clearly at her wits' end, writing to the prison inspector: 'Judging from the past she will be in the Police Court shortly after her release from here, and in a short time will be sentenced to the Mercer Reformatory. We cannot improve her here, and her example has a bad effect upon other women.' A few months later, in early September 1905, by which stage Robinson had been released and returned again, O'Sullivan's fears were realized. When attendant Maggie Mick opened Robinson's cell at six o'clock in the morning, the inmate attacked her with a pair of scissors. John Clark, the night guard, ran over and pulled Robinson off Mick, but she had been badly cut and bruised and would need time off work to recover. Robinson stated that 'she was sorry she didn't kill Mrs Mick, that she meant to kill her'. Contraband found hidden in Robinson's cell included a mirror shard, a table knife and a steel crochet needle, suggesting that she had been stockpiling potential weapons for some time. For this attack, Robinson was sent to Kingston Penitentiary in Ottawa for five years, the prison for serious offenders. Two decades later, while on duty at the Municipal Jail Farm for Women in Toronto, Maggie Mick would be killed by three female inmates (two aged sixteen and one aged twenty-one) who were attempting to escape from the prison. Two staff members found the body of the 55-year-old guard laid across the corridor with her arms tied to a waterpipe.[23]

Women like Stella Vannall, Ida King and Tillie Robinson were perceived as bad influences and a threat to control and order in the women's prisons. In custodial prisons too, where prisoners were sentenced to days or weeks behind bars, fears were commonly expressed that convicted women could leave the institution more criminal than when they had entered because of their interactions with unrepentant offenders. In 1888, the Women's Prison Association of New York condemned the workhouse as 'most corrupt', where offenders were imprisoned 'indiscriminately together – old and young – women with a first offence and confirmed "rounders" . . . It is an old story that women are ruined for life, after one visit to this pest-house.'[24] Susie Dann, 'a tall, comely young woman, with a slight Irish accent', who ended up in prison in New York charged with the theft of silver in 1896, explained her experience: 'In the Tombs, they put us in with the lowest kind of women. We heard things that were terrible to us, and were compelled to associate with women who were awful. They said things that men would not say.'[25]

Some women left prison determined (or promising at least) to demonstrate their reformation, like Mary Mahoney, who wrote to the superintendent of the Reformatory for Women in Massachusetts: 'I hope I will never have occasion to report again[.] I am so happy Mrs Hodder to think I am going to be with my dear children again and I'm going to be the best mother that ever lived with gods help.'[26] An 'out-spoken, honest, free-hearted Irish woman' who was aided by the Toronto Jail Mission in the 1860s was also perceived to be a reformed ex-prisoner. When asked about her plans on release, she responded: 'I have a pair of good honest hands, with which I intend to make a good living, as I have done in days gone by'.[27] Annie O'Donnell was imprisoned in the Massachusetts Reformatory in the late 1890s for nightwalk-ing. When her Irish-born mother, Margaret, was arrested for drunkenness seventeen years later, she told officials that

Annie, now aged forty, 'has lived well since being released from here'.[28] These examples of perceived successful rehabilitation were a sharp contrast to the repeated convictions of unrepentant recidivists Stella Vannall and Ida King.

Family tensions

The antipathy between Stella and Ida, leading eventually to murder, was unusually violent. But while narratives of Irish emigration usually emphasize chain migration and the faithful payment of remittances to family members back home, the records we examined make clear that emigration was sometimes the consequence of family tensions, and that it sometimes created or intensified such tensions. Margaret Larkin stole money from her mother and ran away to America from her County Kerry home at the age of fifteen, accompanied by her mother's female domestic servant.[29] When she was fourteen, Mary Crane married a man eleven years her senior. After 'her people disowned her for running away with him', the couple emigrated to the United States, where they went on to have eight children.[30] In 1856, Irish immigrant Bridget Isabella Laughlin, who was Protestant, fell out with her Catholic brother-in-law. He had paid her passage to Boston but since her arrival they had fought continually. Later he offered to give her a place to live 'if she would be quiet and not interfere with their religion', but she opted instead to return to Ireland.[31] In 1881, fourteen-year-old Maggie Scully, who had been in New York for six months, accused her aunt, Julia McCarthy, of abuse. Julia had sent $15 to fund Maggie's older sister's passage to America, but

Maggie had gone instead. She claimed: 'I have been most shamefully beaten and abused ever since. . . . My aunt beat me this morning with a fire poker.' A concerned passer-by encountered Maggie crying on the street and involved the New York Society for the Prevention of Cruelty to Children. The Society observed: 'Poor Maggie, who was dirty, ragged and neglected, had a rough story to tell. Her eyes were blackened, face and neck scratched, and her body looked as if she had been horsewhipped.' The Society removed her from her aunt's care and found her work as a servant, 'where she is happy and contented'.[32]

For some Irish women, it was their criminal behaviour and repeated convictions that led family members to disown them. In 1917, Mary Sweeney, convicted in Lawrence, Massachusetts, and sentenced to two years in prison for living with a man who was not her husband (ill. 9.1), wrote a pitiful letter to her sister from the Massachusetts Reformatory for Women:

> dear Sister I sent you a letter after my Poor Husband died also a coppy of his Burial But received no answer . . . I had a very nice Letter from my Aunt Sibina after Owen [husband] died wanting me to come and see her and take a rest she allso sed my uncle Pat wanted me to come their[.] well dear Sister it was Kind of them and I appricate it very mutch but had I my Preference its you my dear Sister I would like to see and I hope I will not die till I do for I think of you very offten and only wish I could see you and have a good talk with you as I am very lonesome Since my Poor Husband died . . . Please dear Sister don't forget me in your Prayers good By Please answer soon[.][33]

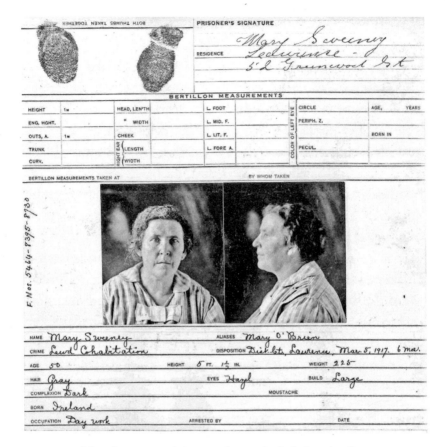

9.1. Mary Sweeney, prison mugshot and admission details, 1917.

A few days later, prison officials interviewed Sweeney's sister, Catherine Moshier, who would by then have read the letter. Moshier was described as a 'rather good looking middle-aged woman, with iron gray hair, rather stout', but 'very forcible in manner; very respectable'. Moshier made clear to officials that she was 'disgusted with her sister and disinterested in her welfare'.[34]

In another case, Stella Weymouth's aunt told the authorities in 1918: 'Stella is thoroughly bad, we have no use for her; my sons won't notice her if they meet her on the street.'[35]

Stella's sister, Mary Good, explained that she had paid for her sister's passage from Claremorris, County Mayo, to America, 'thinking she would be able to help the mother more financially'. She hosted Stella for about a week until she secured work, but Stella failed to live up to her sister's expectations. Mary cut ties with her sister after Stella became a sex worker. She made clear to the prison officials that she 'Wishes Stella could be kept at R[eformatory for] W[omen] or in some institution the rest of her life', emphasizing 'I wish she was dead, she has disgraced us all.'

The fate of Stella Vannall

The policemen who arrested Stella Vannall did not tell her of Ida's death, because they feared that she might harm herself if she knew she had killed her sister. Instead, they repeatedly reassured her that Ida 'is all right; she will come round in a few days'. Stella sought to demonstrate her affection for the sister she had stabbed. She told a journalist who interviewed her: 'I love her very much, because she is all the relation I have in the world that I care much for, and I would not do anything to harm her.'

Eventually, having learned of the outcome of the stabbing, Stella was permitted to see Ida's remains at the funeral home on Howard Street prior to burial. She was observed to express much grief at seeing her deceased sister laid out in a black walnut coffin. After a short time the hearse carried the coffin away, followed by four carriages of Ida's friends, including Sarah Evans, the head of the house on Bowker Street where Ida had lived, who was paying for the funeral.

Stella Vannall's version of events on that fateful January

day in 1880 differed dramatically from those given by witnesses. She claimed that her sister was quite drunk when she encountered her talking to Michael Toland:

> I went up to her and said 'Come, Lizzie [Ida], I want to see you; that man won't give you anything; he hasn't got anything.' With that he turned around and said, 'What in hell have you got to say about it, anyway? I will cut your bloody heart out.' I said 'Probably you will and probably you won't.' To that he replied, 'Now, before I will satisfy you by letting her go, I'll cut your bloody heart out.' All this time he had a knife in his hand, and when I said, 'No, you won't,' he caught me by the throat and forced me up against the fence. I grabbed the knife with my fingers, and when I felt the blood running down I got mad and grabbed him all the harder. Just then my sister started to go, and he said: 'Are you going to leave me?' She said, 'No;' and with that came up to me; said that the man was her man, and that she was going with him. To that, I said, 'No, you won't; he has got nothing for you' or something to that effect. He told me to shut up. I said 'I won't, she is my sister, and I will talk to her just as much as I please.'

Stella claimed that she did not want Ida to go with Michael Toland 'because I did not like the looks of him'. She insisted that she 'had never seen him before, and gave him no reason for abusing me the way he did'. Stella sought to explain her sister's injuries:

> After I told him I would talk just as much as I pleased, he said I should not talk to him, and again made a start at me with the knife in his hand. I told him that he was a dirty pimp; and, just as he rushed at me, my sister came between

us and tried to separate us, telling me he was her man; that she had known him for a long time, and she was going with him then. I was mad, because he had cut my hands, and made a grab for the knife, and twisted it out of his hands, and aimed a blow at him. I know I must have stabbed him somewhere but I know I did not cut my sister; I would not do it for the world. . . . I don't know whether he took the knife from his pocket or where it came from.

Stella had a gash on her arm which substantiated her claim that Toland had stabbed her, but the rest of her account was not believed, and she was charged with the murder of her sister. She initially pleaded not guilty to murder, but later the courts accepted her plea that she was guilty of manslaughter. She was sentenced to three years' hard labour in Boston's House of Correction.[36] In February 1883, a few weeks after her release, she was back in court again, charged with being a common nightwalker.

10. Murder and the case of Mary Farmer

When 53-year-old Patrick Brennan returned home from work on Thursday, 23 April 1908, he found his house locked up, the spare key not in its usual place, and his wife, Sarah, not at home from her dentist's appointment as he expected. He had not seen her since he'd feasted on the breakfast of eggs and ham, fried potatoes, coffee and toast that she'd made him at six o'clock that morning.[1]

The Brennans lived in Hounsfield, a very small town in upstate New York, not far from Lake Ontario. Patrick eventually got a ladder and climbed into the house through an upstairs window. While he was doing this, his neighbour James Farmer came over and relayed two puzzling pieces of information. James informed Patrick that the Brennans' house now belonged to him, and that Sarah had gone away, and if she wasn't back by four o'clock, she would not be back at all that night.

It is not clear what Patrick Brennan made of these peculiar claims, but it seems that he assumed that his wife had stayed in Watertown, where Sarah had had her dental appointment, for the night, and the following day he went to work as usual. That evening he came home from work to find that Sarah still wasn't back, and so he went to Watertown to try to find her. But he couldn't locate her anywhere.

The next morning, Saturday, Patrick Brennan left his house for a short time. When he returned, he was surprised to see his neighbours Mary and James Farmer in the house using his provisions to make their breakfast. They informed him that they now owned his house, but that as long as he was good to them, they would let him stay for free. Patrick, clearly confused about this sudden turn of events, and increasingly concerned about his wife's disappearance, finally raised the alarm. He hurried to the district attorney's office and then got a policeman involved. When they returned to his house, they found that the Farmers had moved in their belongings, with the help of several men whom they'd paid in alcohol.

Patrick stayed at a hotel over the weekend, and on Monday, 27 April, he went with the local sheriff and several others to his house. After a search of the premises, they asked Mary Farmer about a large trunk, tied with a clothes line, that was in the corner of one of the rooms. She denied that it was hers, as did her husband, James. When the clothes line was removed, and the lock broken on the trunk, they found the corpse of Sarah Brennan inside. She was fully dressed, and her head, according to a newspaper report of the case, was 'horribly mutilated by many blows from a blunt instrument'. Mary and James Farmer were both arrested and charged with the murder of Sarah Brennan.

Mary Farmer's motives

Mary O'Brien emigrated from Ireland around 1900, when she was in her early twenties, and initially worked as a domestic servant in Binghamton and Buffalo in upstate New York (ill. 10.1). There she met James D. Farmer, whom she married in the autumn of 1904. The couple moved to Brownville, James's hometown, and for the next couple of months they lived with his relatives. Mary tried keeping a boarding house in a neighbouring village, but this venture failed and in May 1907 the couple moved across the river to the town of Hounsfield. They took up residence in an old building that used to be a hotel in Paddy Hill, which may have derived its name from the large number of Irish residents living there. Their neighbours, Sarah and Patrick Brennan, had lived in a house about eighty feet away from the hotel for more than twenty years, and the house and about five acres of land belonged to Sarah. After the Farmers moved in, Mary and Sarah became close, and were regular visitors at each other's houses. Sarah also seems to have attended Mary during the birth of her son in September 1907.

10.1. Photograph of Mary Farmer.

Unknown to Sarah, her new friend was deeply jealous of her status as a homeowner with money in the bank. On 31 October 1907, having managed to get her hands on the deed to the Brennans' house, Mary Farmer went to a law office in Watertown with the document, impersonated Sarah, forged her signature, and had the deed changed to the name of her husband, James Farmer. A few days later, James and Mary Farmer asked James's sister Alice Doran to take the house deed to Watertown to have it processed. They explained to Alice that they had bought the property for $1,200; Alice thought Sarah Brennan 'must have been crazy to sell the property' for such a low price. Her suspicions were aroused even further when she read the document and spoke to the lawyer who had witnessed the signature, because the description of the woman who had signed the paperwork as Sarah Brennan sounded just like Mary Farmer. Alice told her brother that he would have to get the deed processed himself and also advised him several times to confirm the details of the sale with Sarah. In early January 1908, Mary and James Farmer took the deed to another lawyer in Watertown and had it transferred to the name of their baby son, who had been born the previous September.

It was the planned and deliberate nature of Mary Farmer's crime that drew the most condemnation. Mary had clearly schemed to get possession of Sarah Brennan's house. Not only had she stolen the documents from Sarah's home and then impersonated Sarah, but she had given careful consideration to her own debts and had the property put in her son's name instead. She had also concealed the murder after she and James had moved into the Brennan household, and then denied knowledge of the trunk in which Sarah Brennan's body was found.

Mad or bad?

After her arrest, Mary Farmer gave the police different accounts of how Sarah Brennan had died. In one version of the story, Sarah Brennan had come to her house on the morning of her death and said that she wasn't feeling very well. According to Mary, Sarah pleaded: 'She would give anything if she [Mary] would take that old axe that laid there and knock her brains out'. Mary agreed to help her friend, recalling her actions thus: 'all right, here she goes, I takes the axe and kills her.' In another account, Mary accused her husband of having committed the murder in a drunken rage, but on yet another occasion she claimed that she had acted alone and had caused Sarah's death in a fit of anger. Mary Farmer's various conflicting stories of how Sarah Brennan died clearly could not be believed.

In court, Mary's defence team tried to prove that she was insane at the time of the act and thus not responsible for causing Sarah's death. Insanity as a defence in court was based on the idea that the criminal justice system should only punish those whose mental states made them responsible for their criminal actions. During the nineteenth century, it became a medical question as well as a 'legal conundrum', and from the middle of the century psychiatrists and other medical experts were brought to court to testify for defence or prosecution teams as to the sanity or insanity of suspects.[2] Being declared insane was a matter of life and death in murder trials, because it could mean that a defendant would avoid the death penalty and instead be sent to a mental hospital or so-called insane asylum.

The defence called a number of witnesses to try to prove

that Mary Farmer's behaviour in the past suggested that she was not of sound mind. If she could be shown to have previously acted in a strange manner, or to have made irrational choices, the jury might take seriously the suggestion that she was not in her right mind at the time of the murder. Mary's family doctor, and another who was in the area temporarily, testified to seeing her talking to herself a few days before and after the birth of her son, which was viewed as abnormal behaviour. A parish priest from Brownville described interactions with Mary: she had promised him that there would be no dancing at a fundraiser event that she organized at her house but subsequently broke that promise, suggesting that she was lacking in moral fibre and was easily led by others. He also pointed to her financial issues as a potential motivation: she had borrowed money from him and she had also discussed with him her real estate dreams. He had spoken to Mary on the Monday after Sarah's murder and categorized her behaviour at that time as 'suspicious and strange'. A local shopkeeper considered Mary's purchase of three or four washtubs, multiple mops and three dustpans as evidence of an irrational mind. Another witness described how Mary had bought a portion of frozen beef, left it to defrost near her stove, and then returned it to the store claiming that it had spoilt. On a different occasion she had wanted to purchase an entire case of baking powder, actions which the storekeeper considered to be very strange. Mary also claimed that she had suffered 'fits' until she was twelve and had a family history of mental illness; and the doctors for the defence also judged that 'all of her senses [were] defective, her head illformed' and that she had 'many physical and mental evidences of degeneracy and insanity'.

But the prosecution pointed out that Mary had completed

a life insurance application prior to the murder and had not mentioned anything in it about a family history of insanity, nor of having hallucinations or seizures. The prosecution also produced witnesses who had employed Mary, each of whom insisted that she was healthy and well, and seemed to them to be 'wholly rational'. Three doctors who were 'experts in lunacy' also testified on behalf of the prosecution. They examined Mary before the trial and observed her while she was in court. They all agreed that she was 'not insane but sane and responsible for her acts'.

The medical experts' views in support of and opposition to Mary's insanity plea reveal many contemporary beliefs about mental disorder. Insanity was thought to be hereditary and could be passed down the generations. Seizures or fits were viewed as evidence of a more general brain disease that could render the sufferer ignorant of, or not responsible for, their behaviour.[3] For women, menstruation and biological circumstances relating to their reproductive systems (such as pregnancy, childbirth, lactation and menopause) were also believed to cause 'periodic instability and hysteria', and these arguments were often features of trials involving female suspects.[4]

Madeleine Z. Doty, a lawyer at the time and later a prison reformer, war reporter and peace campaigner, wrote to the editor of *The New York Times* in March 1909 on the subject of Mary Farmer's insanity plea. Doty made clear her suffragist views, arguing that 'women of today are judged by man-made laws, in which we as women have no voice, and punished by man-made punishments'. She insisted that Mary Farmer, as a woman and a mother, could not have taken 'an axe . . . hacking up a human body' unless there was a 'red twist in her brain' that made her do it. Doty believed that

Mary was 'a monster because of her heredity or environment'. She did not want Mary to be set free (because 'we do not let lions and tigers run about the streets. We fear wild beasts'), but felt that pity should be shown. She also invoked the development of James and Mary's son, suggesting that society should focus on preventing 'other criminals instead of slaying the mother'.[5] Dr Charles Pankhurst, a clergyman and social reformer, who replied to Doty's letter, agreed on the importance of heredity and environmental factors but also believed there was a 'margin of autonomy which constitutes the ground of our personal and moral responsibility'.[6] The jury's view was evidently closer to that of Dr Pankhurst than of Madeleine Doty, and Mary Farmer's insanity defence was unsuccessful.

The 'worst woman on earth'

The story of Mary Farmer was soon mostly forgotten, but some Irish women tried for murder in North America became enduringly infamous. Sixteen-year-old Grace Marks, who emigrated from Ulster to Canada around 1840, was convicted along with her fellow Irish-born servant John McDermott for the murder of Thomas Kinnear and his housekeeper and lover, Nancy Montgomery, just outside Toronto in 1843. Grace Marks's story attracted considerable attention at the time, and became the subject of Margaret Atwood's novel *Alias Grace*.[7]

Another notorious Irish murderer was Lizzie Halliday, the serial killer described by *The New York Times* on her death in 1918 as the 'worst woman on earth'. Born Elizabeth McNally in Belfast around 1864, she emigrated with her parents in

1867.[8] In September 1893, she was arrested for the murder of three people at her home in Burlingham, Sullivan County, in upstate New York: her elderly husband, Paul Halliday, and a mother and teenage daughter, Margaret and Sarah Jane McQuillan.

Lizzie had employed Margaret to do some work for her, and then summoned Sarah Jane by telling her that her mother had injured herself falling off a ladder. Neither woman was seen alive again. Their bodies were discovered only when Paul Halliday's neighbours, suspicious after he had not been seen for a while, searched the house when Lizzie was out. The neighbours found the bodies of Margaret and Sarah Jane in a barn beside the Halliday house. They had both been shot at close range at least half a dozen times. Paul was subsequently found buried under the kitchen floor, having also been shot.

Lizzie Halliday had a chequered past before her arrest for the three murders. Two of her previous husbands also died very quickly after they married her. Charles Hopkins, whom Lizzie is supposed to have married when she was fifteen, died within two years of their marriage, and Artemas Brewer, who was a war veteran and a pensioner when Lizzie married him, died within a year. Newspaper reporters at the time of her trial suggested that Lizzie may have had a hand in their deaths as well. Three additional relationships followed before she met Paul Halliday.

Lizzie also had criminal convictions. She had spent two years in the Eastern State Penitentiary in Philadelphia for arson and insurance fraud when she burnt down her own shop, along with two of her neighbours' houses in 1888. While married to Paul Halliday, she stole a team of horses and eloped with a neighbour, who then deserted her. On that occasion, Lizzie was judged to be mentally ill and sent to Middletown State Hospital, and on her release she returned to live with Paul. Shortly thereafter, Paul's house mysteriously burned down, killing his son, who had learning difficulties. Paul's family and neighbours blamed Lizzie for causing the fire but she was not prosecuted. Following her arrest for the three murders at her home, it was even proposed that Lizzie might have been Jack the Ripper, the serial killer who had killed at least five women in London in 1888.

Lizzie's defence focused on proving her insanity to avoid the death sentence rather than on proving her innocence, since the evidence against her was so overwhelming. Her behaviour while she was being held in the county jail awaiting trial pointed to serious mental health issues. She set fire to her bedclothes, and she violently attacked two doctors who visited her in the cell, kicking one in the abdomen. She attempted to bite the district attorney who was restraining her and she also tried to strangle the sheriff's wife. Lizzie made a bid as well to hang herself, and then self-harmed by cutting her throat and arms with broken glass from her cell window. She refused to eat, and was force-fed. For her own safety and that of those around her, she was kept restrained in a chair and chained to the floor in the lead-up to the trial.

Appearing for the defence, Dr Selden H. Talcott, the superintendent of the Middletown State Hospital, stated his opinion that she 'had never been of sound mind' since leaving that institution in February 1892. He 'did not think the prisoner had sufficient intelligence to feign insanity or anything else'. But not everyone was convinced. Lizzie's physical features were examined for perceived signs of insanity. She had furrows on her skin and didn't have a furry tongue, which were, it was suggested, 'symptoms that go with extreme insanity'. Dr Sol Van Etten of Port Jervis had found 'her hair soft, oily and natural' and she 'perspired naturally', signs, he argued, that 'indicated sanity'. Newspaper reports pointed out that Lizzie's 'skin was moist' while a 'lunatic's skin should not be', and her 'hair was smooth and glossy' while the 'hair of a lunatic is harsh'. A Dr Edward C. Mann pronounced on the basis of his five-minute examination of Lizzie that she was not insane. When he asked Lizzie her age, she had replied, 'nineteen skunks' and said that her residence was 'I washed your shirt'. Mann believed that her answers were 'totally unlike anything I had ever heard from a real lunatic'. Several other doctors concurred with the suggestion that Lizzie was 'simulating insanity' or 'acting a part'. The trial jury were asked to decide. Did the fact that Lizzie was able to plan the murders carry 'presumptive proof of mental responsibility' or was insanity the only explanation for her actions? Eventually the jury concluded that Lizzie had been faking her insanity and found her guilty of murder in the first degree. The following day, 22 June 1894, Judge Edwards condemned her to death by electricity, the first woman to be given such a sentence in the United Sates.

Lizzie's defence counsel appealed to the governor of New York to appoint a commission to examine Lizzie's mental condition. The commission set up the following month determined that Lizzie was insane, and Governor Flower committed her for life to the criminal asylum at Matteawan. A year later, a journalist for the *Middletown Daily Argus* reported that Lizzie seemed to be 'getting better' and had 'lost that fierce look which characterized her insanity'. But this judgement was proven to be ill-founded the following month when Lizzie and another inmate attacked Catherine Ward, one of the asylum attendants. While

Catherine survived, just over ten years later, in October 1906, nurse Nellie Wicks was not so fortunate. Lizzie stabbed Nellie over 200 times with her own scissors, motivated, it seems, by her dismay at Nellie's intention to leave the asylum (ill. 10.2).

10.2. An artist's impression of the murder of Nellie Wicks.

Portraying the murderess

Murderesses were the stuff of entertainment, and their trials were often treated as theatre. The physical appearance of women on trial for murder, their conduct in the courtroom and their reactions to their sentences filled up many newspaper column inches. The movements of accused women, what they did with their hands or where they looked were all scrutinized and reported on in detail.[9]

Mary Farmer was described in the press as a 'naturally taciturn, solid, uneducated and probably perverted creature'. After her conviction she was described as having 'dull eyes . . . misshapen lips', and the lines on her face (and that of her husband) supposedly pointed to their 'sin-sick souls'. Descriptions of Lizzie Halliday portrayed her as deranged and animalistic rather than human. Her nose was 'peculiar shaped' and 'like a pig's with a broad nostril, but pointed'. Her awareness of her crime was compared to that of 'a cowering dog . . . sensible of a fault'. When she assaulted one of the physicians assessing her mental condition, it was said that 'she fought like a tigress. Her hair fell down over her face and filled her mouth as she snapped her teeth in an attempt to bite the District Attorney' who was trying to restrain her. When she assaulted Catherine Ward in the Matteawan State Hospital, she showed her 'tigerish instinct to slay' and she attacked Nellie Wicks in 1906 with the 'fury of a tigress'. Other journalists described Lizzie as 'the wolf woman' or identified the 'wolfish ferocity of her crimes' and her singular desire of 'satiating her lust for blood'. The incomprehensibility of her actions meant that Lizzie was positioned in the press as a monster, 'a weird murderess' who was 'mentally and physically depraved' and 'probably one of the lowest types of humanity ever seen moving and dwelling among civilized people'.

Lizzie's trial in 1894 occurred at a time when scholars from a variety of disciplines were turning their attention to the 'physical and psychological differences' that set the criminal woman apart.[10] Italian criminologist Cesare Lombroso, writing at the end of the nineteenth century, popularized the idea that female crime was biologically determined and that a propensity for crime could be detected in a woman's physical appearance[11] (ills. 10.3 and 10.4).

10.3 and 10.4. Sketches of Lizzie Halliday.

Lizzie Halliday's appearance was juxtaposed against descriptions of her victims. Sarah Jane McQuillan was 'beautiful', an 'especially attractive girl of about nineteen', and it was considered particularly shocking that 'pretty Sarah Jane McQuillan had died at the hands of this sallow faced woman'. Catherine Ward, whom Lizzie attacked in 1895, was a 'comely, intelligent, altogether attractive young woman'. Nellie Wicks, Lizzie's final murder victim, was 'a graceful and pretty young woman'. Lizzie was also positioned against the femininity of the 'women in delicious summer gowns of gingham, lawn and the like' who came in large numbers to watch her trial.

Another Irish woman accused of murder in this period was portrayed more positively in the press.[12] After Edward

MacTavish, aged twenty-four, was found dead in his room at Hotel Florence in Cambridge, Massachusetts, in July 1909, having been shot and hit with an axe, Elizabeth Richmond, the 45-year-old proprietor, was arrested and tried for his murder (ill. 10.5).

10.5. Photograph of Hotel Florence.

Elizabeth Richmond grew up in Cork (ill. 10.6). Her father was an engineer and she described her family as 'well-to-do'. At the age of sixteen, she married William James Byrne, then a policeman in the Royal Irish Constabulary, who was around ten years her senior. Since policemen could not be stationed where they or their wives were from, William was subsequently transferred to Wexford.[13] He was discharged from the force in July 1893, which Elizabeth attributed to his drinking. She subsequently left him, migrating to the US with their four young daughters. She remarried after she heard of his death, and had two more daughters. But her second husband was also intemperate and, by her account, 'has done little for her'.

By the time of her arrest for the murder of Edward Mac-Tavish, Elizabeth's financial affairs were described as being 'in a pitiful way'. She had several properties with 'mortgage piled on mortgage', but she had fallen behind with the payments and had been pawning jewellery to try to make up the shortages. In his closing statement, the assistant district attorney described Elizabeth's 'sordid motives' and noted that 'immediately after the killing of MacTavish, Mrs Richmond was in possession of money which she did not have on her own account'. Edward's valuables, including a ring and a gold watch and chain, as well as his cigars, were found in Elizabeth's room.

Elizabeth Richmond's actions appeared to have been unplanned and may have been fuelled by the whiskey she had been drinking in the days before the murder. She was, according to the *Boston Globe*, 'a woman of large proportions and pleasing appearance' who was 'neatly dressed in black satin and wore a becoming black hat'. Elizabeth was described as if she were attending a social function rather than her trial, and as it progressed 'exchanged the heavy satin waist worn during the two previous days for a white peekaboo waist, which made her look almost girlish'. A journalist observed how 'her complexion indicated that nearly a year of jail regime had done little to impair her good looks'. Several days earlier the *Boston Globe* had also suggested that Elizabeth showed 'very little trace of the effect of confinement in prison. There was considerable color in her cheeks, her eyes were bright and she seemed as unconcerned as anyone in the court.' On the day of her sentencing, she was described as 'quite an attractive figure, especially for a woman of her years, as she walked across the street from the court room to the jail to enter on her lifelong sentence in prison'. Perhaps because of her relatively high socio-economic status, Elizabeth also seems to have been afforded privileges not given to other Irish-born women on trial for murder mentioned in this chapter.[14] As a 'matter of courtesy', for example, she did not have to sit in the metal cage often reserved for murder suspects in court.

10.6. Photograph of Elizabeth Richmond.

Female murder defendants came under intense scrutiny not just for their appearance but for their body language.[15] Mary Farmer was described in court as being 'immobile as a statue' and as having her hands clasped and her 'eyes almost constantly fixed on the green carpet' before her. One reporter observed that although she was pale, 'there is not the slightest sign of nervousness'. When she was found guilty of Sarah Brennan's murder and sentenced to death in March 1909,

Mary was 'wide-eyed and calm'; showing a 'remarkable exhibition of nerve' she 'listened with unmoved face and erect figure', and 'with eyes staring straight ahead of her, and unfaultering step, she walked back to her cell'. Her lack of reaction was noted, and one local journalist seemed disappointed that she had shown no 'outburst of tears, no expression of horror, no weakening of any kind'. Mary's calmness, her lack of engagement in the proceedings, and her failure to respond emotionally in a way expected of a woman in her predicament meant that she generated little sympathy.[16]

Lizzie Halliday was similarly observed to be 'completely composed, and if it were not for occasional twitching's [sic] of her mouth no one would suspect that she understood that anything unusual was going on'. She sat with her 'head bent forward, her chin on her breast, her eyes half closed, her waxy fingers picking, constantly picking, at her sleeves near the shoulder'. The previous day 'her fingers picked at a handkerchief', her lips 'moved incessantly and her head nodded for five minutes, then turned slowly for five minutes, then nodded again'. When Lizzie was found guilty, 'She looked down, and if she heard, she said nothing. She had covered her head with her handkerchief and continually rapped her face with her hands.'

Elizabeth Richmond's emotional state also invited press comment. She smiled and laughed throughout her trial and 'did not seem to be affected to any extent by the terrible position in which she is placed'. Her 'three pretty daughters' attended court each day and they too, 'judging by their demeanor ... do not consider their mother's life in imminent peril'. Mary Farmer, for her part, had allegedly not 'expressed the slightest wish' to see her infant son while in prison. She was perceived instead as 'devoid of motherly instinct or sentiment'. Elizabeth's display of emotion, and her clear affection for her daughters, may well have humanized her. The jury found her guilty of murder in the second degree, saving her from execution by the electric chair. She was sentenced to life in prison, and 'Neither by the twitch of a muscle or the wink of an eyelid' did she 'betray any trace of emotion or fear'.

Mary Jennings expressed more conventionally elevated emotions when she was tried for murder in New York (ill. 10.7). In the summer of 1901, Mary lost her job in the supply kitchen of the Childs restaurant chain in Greenwich Village, following a fight with a fellow employee, Kate McVeight.[17] While Kate had managed to get her job back, Mary had not. Mary returned to the supply kitchen a few days later, and when the manager, Fredrick Van Dorn, heard a commotion in the kitchen he ran in to find Kate lying on the floor, covered in blood. Kate was sufficiently conscious to say that Mary had stabbed her with a knife and that she'd had to 'pull it out myself'. Kate died soon after at St Vincent's Hospital. Mary was arrested, and when she heard of Kate's death reportedly claimed it was 'none of my doing', that she 'had the knife in my hand and she came at me like she was crazy and I held my hand to keep her off, and the knife was in it, which I forgot. If she had not run on it it wouldn't have hurt her.'

In court, Mary's defence similarly argued that this was an accident, although the story had changed somewhat. Mary now claimed that she had gone to the kitchen to get the key to a closet to pick up her clothes. She had in her hand 'the knife with which I used to peel potatoes, and as I stepped on a box to reach the key my foot slipped. Kate was sitting right near. I fell and the knife went into her heart.' Some of the

10.7. Photograph of Mary Jennings.

women who had testified against Mary during the trial had to stifle their laughter when they heard this implausible story, and Mary 'looked at them with an expression of utter helplessness'. Mary Booth, another employee in the kitchen, testified that Mary Jennings had 'deliberately thumped Kate McVeight with her hand', causing the death.

Mary Jennings was found guilty of the murder of Kate McVeight in the second degree and sentenced to life imprisonment. On hearing her sentence, Mary, according to one journalist, 'sank to her knees sobbing, and it became necessary to half carry her from the room. The sound of her wild sobbing was heard long after she had passed out of sight.' Mary's court proceedings were also rather dramatic and journalists revelled in the emotion. When the blood-stained knife with which Kate McVeight had been killed was produced in court, Mary screamed: 'Oh my God! . . . Oh my God! Take it away!' and then fainted. Later, while on her way to Auburn

Prison, Mary tried to throw herself out of the car and was taken to a police station, where 'she went raving mad' and had to be carried in 'shrieking and kicking'. Newspaper journalists feared 'that her mind has given way permanently'. An ambulance took her to Bellevue Hospital, where doctors judged that she would not live more than a year. But prison records show that Mary Jennings remained behind bars for fifteen years until she was pardoned in December 1916.

The prosecuting district attorney at Mary Jennings's trial maintained that hers 'was a premeditated, cold-blooded murder, done for revenge'. He urged the jury to ignore her gender, insisting: 'She ought not to be permitted to escape the penalty of her crime because she is a woman.'[18] The assistant district attorney in Elizabeth Richmond's trial likewise told the jury: 'this is not a romantic murder. It is a gross murder. And if you are satisfied that the prisoner at the bar committed it, then the fact that she is a woman must not prevent you from declaring her guilty of the crime.'[19] A woman's gender might not necessarily have prevented her being found guilty, but, as shown in this chapter, her gender had a significant impact on how she was portrayed in the newspapers that covered these trials so voraciously.

The poisoners

The crime of poisoning was frequently associated with women.[20] Not only was it 'carried out secretly, within the home, behind closed doors', but it was usually orchestrated by someone who was in close contact with the victim.[21] Poisoning required planning, and the poisoner needed to have access to the food, drink or medicine of the victim, which women, in their roles as caregivers, often had within households.[22] In the last two decades of the nineteenth century, two Irish-born women made the headlines in Massachusetts accused of poisoning members of their family.

Sarah Jane Robinson, forty-nine years old, was arrested in August 1886 for the murder of her 23-year-old son, William (ill. 10.8). One of the doctors treating William sent a sample of his green vomit to the renowned chemist and toxicologist Dr Edward S. Wood at Harvard Medical School.[23] Wood determined that arsenic was present, and suspicion grew about the number of other members of Sarah Jane's family who had also died. Following her arrest for William's murder, officials exhumed the bodies of her brother-in-law Prince Arthur Freeman, who had died in June 1885, and her daughter Lizzie, who had died eight months later in February 1886. Traces of arsenic were found. The police then exhumed the bodies of Sarah Jane's husband, Moses Robinson, who had died in July 1882; her sister Annie, who had died in February 1885; her nephew, Tommy Freeman, Annie and Prince's son, who had died in July 1886; and her elderly landlord, Oliver Sleeper, who had died in August 1881. All the bodies were found to contain traces of arsenic.

Sarah Jane was initially charged with her son William's murder alongside Thomas Smith and Dr Charles C. Beers, two men with whom she had had relationships. But the charges against them were dropped and she stood trial alone. The prosecution was not permitted to reveal the details of the other suspicious deaths at this trial. The *Boston Globe* observed that everyone 'thought the woman guilty, but that her guilt was not proved'. Sarah Jane was then charged with the murder of her brother-in-law, and on this occasion the court allowed her sister Annie's death to be discussed as well.

MRS. SARAH J. ROBINSON.

10.8. Sketch of Sarah Jane Robinson at her trial.

At the trial in February 1888, the prosecution argued that Annie's murder was part of Sarah Jane's scheme to get Annie's husband's life insurance. The court was shown considerable evidence of Sarah Jane's debts and the way she benefited from insurance policies taken out by family members who had died. Sarah Jane had nursed them all, and in doing so had a clear opportunity to poison them. She maintained her innocence, pleading ignorance of both poisons and insurance policies. The defence offered up witnesses, including her remaining son, Charlie, aged nineteen, who spoke of her love for her family. After deliberating for fourteen hours, the jury found Sarah Jane guilty of murder in the first degree. She was sentenced to die on 16 November 1888.

Sarah Jane Tennant had emigrated from Ulster in the 1850s

aged fifteen, along with her younger sister, Annie, following their parents' deaths. Their brother was already in Cambridge, Massachusetts. Sarah Jane worked as a seamstress before her marriage to Moses Robinson, also a native of Ulster, when she was nineteen. They went on to have eight children, two of whom died as infants, and the family struggled financially. Like other accused murderesses in this chapter, Sarah Jane's behaviour in court did not fit gendered expectations.[24] Her calmness caused disquiet, and it was observed that when she was found guilty 'not a muscle' of her face moved, 'not a twitch or a tremor . . . a statue could not have shown less feeling'.

Sarah Jane's death sentence generated public sympathy, and a petition of over 500 'leading citizens', including suffragists, clergymen and seven of the original jurors, pleaded for a commutation. The suffragist influence is clear in the argument that it would be a 'disgrace to the Commonwealth to hang a woman' because 'her sex has no power in making the laws'. The petition also argued that for a woman to commit such 'unnatural crimes', she must have been 'laboring under uncontrollable impulses, called homicidal mania, and is not responsible for her acts'. The arguments were made at a public hearing in Boston on 31 October 1888, and on 12 November Sarah Jane's execution was commuted to solitary life imprisonment. She is alleged to have said after learning of the commutation: 'I should so much rather have had the sentence [of death] carried out, for then I should be free, and now I shall never know freedom again.' She spent eighteen years in solitary confinement before her death from heart failure at the age of sixty-eight in 1906. She was buried in the family grave, alongside her son, William, daughter, Lizzie, and husband, Moses.

Insurance policies were also thought to be at the heart of the case against Irish-born Margaret Kane, who was arrested in December 1893 for giving her 73-year-old mother-in-law, Ellen Kane, whiskey poisoned with Paris green, an arsenic compound that was used as an insecticide (ill. 10.9). Margaret had been married to Ellen's son James for thirteen years and the couple had one son.[25] Margaret claimed that she and her husband had 'always lived happily'. He was a fisherman and spent much time away from home, leaving Margaret to care for his mother. Tension between the two women seems to have developed after Margaret stole around $30 that had been 'tucked in the old lady's bosom'. Ellen threatened to call the police if Margaret did not return the money. Margaret had also taken out two insurance policies on Ellen's life.

MARGARET KANE.

10.9. Sketch of Margaret Kane at her trial.

Ellen Kane's nineteen-year-old grandson, Miles, testified in court that, on 16 December 1893, his Aunt Margaret arrived at the house where he, his father and brothers lived with his grandmother. The boys' father was also a fisherman and spent much time away from home. They had moved in with Ellen following the death of their mother. Ellen had a bad cold or flu, and Margaret sent Miles out for alcohol, telling him that 'a warm drink of whisky would do my grandmother good'. The next day, Margaret returned to the house. She prepared a tumbler of whiskey for her mother-in-law and, handing it to Ellen, said: 'It is time for you to take your medicine.' The boys later noticed green powder on Ellen's tongue and false teeth and at the bottom of the glass, and an anxious Ellen allegedly asked: 'Oh, Mag, are you going to poison me?' When Miles accused Margaret of poisoning his grandmother, she tried to grab him by the throat and dropped some of the green powder on the floor and on her clothing. Miles called an upstairs neighbour and ran for the doctor. Dr David Collins found the house 'in an uproar' on his arrival and he saw a patch of green powder on Margaret's dress. Ellen was sick while he was there, and he ordered the boys to scoop up a sample of the 'greenish vomit' while he went for some medicine to treat her.

Ellen Kane died three days later. Dr Edward S. Wood, the chemist and toxicologist at the Harvard Medical School who had been involved in Sarah Jane Robinson's trial, tested the tumbler, vomit, false teeth, soiled clothing and some packaging, and determined the presence of Paris green. Wood testified that 'In the small amount of vomit there was nearly sufficient poison to kill a human being'. Poison was also found in the dead woman's stomach and liver. But the quantity of poison in the organs was considered too small to have caused Ellen's death and an autopsy pointed to heart disease, pneumonia and chronic bronchitis. Margaret was thus judged to have hastened Ellen's death but not to have killed her.

At her trial in February 1894, Margaret 'looked decidedly troubled and worn when brought into court. Her eyes were sunken, and deep lines marked her face.' A journalist observed that she 'was evidently greatly affected, as she was constantly moving in her chair, and frequently moaned', and at one point she fainted. The defence argued that the 'two women were deeply attached to each other' and that Margaret was too drunk at the time to know what she was doing. But after a short deliberation the jury found her guilty of 'administering poison with intent to kill'. Margaret was sentenced to seven years in the Reformatory Prison for Women in Massachusetts. After serving her sentence, Margaret reunited with her husband, James, who seems to have forgiven her attempt to poison his mother.

The fate of Mary Farmer

Mary Farmer's date of execution by the electric chair was set for 29 March 1909, her efforts to appeal her sentence having failed. Her husband had also been tried for Sarah Brennan's murder and sentenced to death.

The evening before Mary was due to be executed, she and James were allowed to meet for an hour, 'separated in their parting interview by heavy bars and an impenetrable screen'. When the time came for the 'final parting', Mary is reported to have said: 'Good bye, Jim. If I don't see you in this world, I will in the next.' Following this 'last good bye, the weeping husband returned to his cell and the hapless woman was led down the narrow corridor'. But Mary did one last thing before she died. She made a statement to her priest, Fr John J. Hickey, in which she exonerated James from having any part in Sarah Brennan's murder:

> My husband, James D. Farmer, never had any hand in Sarah Brennan's death nor never knew anything about it till the trunk was opened. I never told him anything what had happened. I feel he has been terribly wronged. James D. Farmer was not at home the day the affair happened, neither did James D. Farmer ever put a hand on Sarah Brennan after her death. Again I wish to say as strongly as I can that my husband, James D. Farmer, is entirely innocent of the death of Sarah Brennan, that he knowingly had no part in any plans that led to it and that he knew nothing whatever about it.

On the strength of this statement, James was granted a new trial and was acquitted in March 1910. He returned to his son in Brownville and moved in with his sister Alice and her family. He died in 1934 of heart failure, and the press described him as the 'husband in the trunk murder case' whose death 'closes the book on one of the most celebrated murder cases in the country's annals'.

Patrick Brennan, Sarah's husband, remarried seven months after her death. Following his death in 1918 he was buried with Sarah, and their daughter, Mamie, who had predeceased her mother.

Mary Farmer was 'resigned to her fate' in the days leading up to her execution. She was reported to have said that she hoped her 'baby will be happy and that no cruel person will ever tell him of the end his parents came to'. Fr Hickey, who had spent much time with Mary before her death, insisted that her mental condition should have prevented her from being executed, and her attorney, Robert Wilcox, continued to claim that she was mentally unwell and the death penalty thus 'a judicial murder and a most serious error on the part of the State of New York'. The execution generated huge public interest, with 'many morbid curiosity seekers' pleading with the prison warden to watch the execution. She would be the seventh woman executed for murder, and the second to be electrocuted, in the state of New York.

The morning of 29 March 1909 was chilly and grey when Mary Farmer, dressed in a plain black blouse and skirt with her hair pulled tightly into two plaits, was led to the electric chair in Auburn Prison shortly before six o'clock. She held a crucifix in her hands, and Fr Hickey stood beside her, offering prayers as she was strapped into the chair. Mary murmured to herself: 'Jesus, Mary and Joseph have mercy on my soul.' A dozen witnesses were present, including three women, two of whom were nurses who assisted in the attachment of the electrodes to Mary's skin. Dr John Gerin, the prison doctor, said that Mary died after the first electric shock, but as there was a 'tremor of muscular reaction' two more shocks were given and she was pronounced dead at 6.15 a.m. In her own words, she went quietly, 'like a queen going to God's high court to atone for my sins'.

A note on sources

The Bad Bridget project is based on years of archival research largely in New York State, Massachusetts and Toronto. We searched for Irish-born girls and women in original manuscript sources like court records, petitions for clemency, institution admission and discharge books, correspondence, prison files, and state, church and charitable society material, and in published sources like annual reports, pamphlets and contemporary writings. The appetite for stories of crime meant that Bad Bridget cases were often reported in newspapers, particularly those that involved career criminals or notorious crimes like kidnapping or murder. Newspaper reports, although sometimes written in a sensational manner or with conflicting details, offer a useful insight into contemporary attitudes and are used alongside manuscript material.[1]

Our focus is on Irish-born girls and women. Many records do not indicate nationality, and thus we had to exclude many individuals with Irish-sounding names for lack of proof that they were in fact Irish-born. Some records deliberately omitted names. The annual reports of the Association for the Protection of Roman Catholic Children in Boston, for instance, excluded surnames 'lest the children, when grown up, might be brought to unmerited shame by the revelation of the misconduct of their parents'.[2] Some of the archives and records we used had particular access policies and where required we have anonymized the individuals involved. We have regularly used first names in this book to refer to individuals rather than surnames. This is not intended to be infantilizing or overfamiliar, but rather to ease understanding, particularly when cases involve more than one person of the same surname.

Our research often involved piecing together diverse records. Many Irish girls and women changed their names in North America to assimilate, to conceal their Irish heritage or just as part of their new adventure. And many criminal women used multiple aliases or provided conflicting details when arrested or imprisoned, which can make it difficult to trace their activities in North America or their origins in Ireland.[3] Some refused to give any information about themselves. Catherine Lynch, who emigrated to New York when she was around twenty, ended up in the Massachusetts Reformatory Prison for Women in 1900 for stealing. Officials recorded that she 'will not give her peoples names. Does not want to disgrace them.'[4] Common first names and surnames, incorrect transcriptions of Irish names in North American records and women's practice of changing their surnames on marriage also complicated our efforts.[5] Despite these challenges, the archives we used revealed thousands of cases of Irish-born girls and women who found themselves in trouble at some point in their lives in North America.

References

Introducing Bad Bridget

1 A thirteenth pregnancy ended in miscarriage. This case study is based on Case file of Stella Weymouth (Delia (Bridget) Jones) (Massachusetts Archives, Massachusetts Reformatory for Women, Inmate case files, HS9.06/series 515, #11095). The Massachusetts Reformatory Prison for Women dropped the word 'prison' from its title in 1911, and thus references to the institution after 1911 also exclude the word 'prison'. Endnotes for the entire period refer to the Reformatory for Women in line with Massachusetts Archives guidelines.

2 Caitriona Clear, *Social change and everyday life in Ireland, 1850–1922* (Manchester, 2007), p. 57.

3 Donald Harman Akenson, *Ireland, Sweden and the great European migration, 1815–1914* (Liverpool, 2012), p. 16.

4 David Fitzpatrick, *Irish emigration, 1801–1921* (Dublin, 1984), p. 3; K. A. Miller, *Emigrants and exiles: Ireland and the Irish exodus to North America* (Oxford and New York, 1985), p. 291.

5 Donald Harman Akenson, *The Irish diaspora: a primer* (Belfast, 1996); Maureen Fitzgerald, *Habits of compassion: Irish Catholic nuns and the origins of New York's welfare system, 1830–1920* (Chicago, IL, 2006), p. 55; Pauline Jackson, 'Women in 19th-century Irish emigration' in *International Migration Review*, 18, no. 4 (1984), pp. 1004–20; Janet Nolan, *Ourselves alone: women's emigration from Ireland, 1885–1920* (Lexington, KY, 1989), pp. 48–9.

6 Chad C. Heap, *Slumming: sexual and racial encounters in American nightlife, 1885–1940* (Chicago, IL, 2009), p. 27; Akenson, *Ireland, Sweden and the great European migration*, p. 240.

7 Kevin Kenny, *The American Irish: a history* (London, 2016), p. 151; Nolan, *Ourselves alone*, p. 51.

8 Nolan, *Ourselves alone*, p. 49; Grace Neville, 'Dark lady of the archives: towards an analysis of women and emigration to North America in Irish folklore' in Mary O'Dowd and Sabine Wichert (eds.), *Chattel, servant or citizen: women's status in church, state and society* (Belfast, 1995), p. 201.

9 Donna Gabaccia, *From the other side: women, gender, and immigrant life in the U.S., 1820–1990* (Bloomington and Indianapolis, IN, 1994), p. 30.

10 *Thirty-first annual report of the Children's Aid Society, November 1883* (New York, 1883), p. 25.

11 *The New York Times*, 30 April 1897.

12 Entry for Mary Ward, #327 (Massachusetts Archives, Massachusetts Board of State Charities, Histories of alien residents of almshouses and other institutions, vol. 3, HS3/series 539x).

13 Tyler Anbinder, *City of dreams: The 400-Year Epic History of Immigrant New York* (Boston and New York, 2017), pp. 138–9; Deirdre Cooper Owens, *Race, gender, and the origins of American gynecology* (Athens, GA, 2017), pp. 90–91.

14 J. Sheridan to Vere Foster, 2 October 1881 (Public Record Office of Northern Ireland (hereafter PRONI), Vere Foster Papers, D3618/D/15/53).

15 Mary E. Daly, 'Famines and famine relief, 1740–2000' in Eugenio F. Biagini and Mary E. Daly (eds.), *The Cambridge social history of modern Ireland* (Cambridge, 2017), p. 45.

16 Clear, *Social change and everyday life*, pp. 64–5.

17 Fitzpatrick, *Irish emigration*, pp. 18–20; Peter Gray, '"Shovelling out your paupers": the British state and Irish famine

migration, 1846–50' in *Patterns of Prejudice*, 33, no. 4 (1999), pp. 47–65; Hidetaka Hirota, *Expelling the poor: Atlantic seaboard states and the nineteenth-century origins of American immigration policy* (Oxford, 2017); Kenny, *The American Irish*, p. 100; Dympna McLoughlin, 'Superfluous and unwanted deadweight: the emigration of nineteenth-century Irish pauper women' in Patrick O'Sullivan (ed.), *Irish women and Irish migration* (London and New York, 1995), pp. 66–88; Gerard Moran, *Sending out Ireland's poor: assisted emigration to North America in the nineteenth century* (Dublin, 2004); PRONI, Vere Foster Papers, D3618.

18 Entry for Margaret Haley, #256 (Massachusetts Archives, Massachusetts Board of State Charities, Histories of alien residents of almshouses and other institutions, vol. 3, HS3/ series 539x).

19 Nell Irvin Painter, *The history of white people* (New York, 2011), p. 138.

20 Kenny, *The American Irish*, p. 131.

21 Painter, *The history of white people*, p. 139.

22 Hidetaka Hirota, '"The great entrepot for mendicants": foreign poverty and immigration control in New York State to 1882' in *Journal of American Ethnic History*, 33, no. 2 (2014), pp. 5–32; Gerardine Meaney, Mary O'Dowd and Bernadette Whelan, *Reading the Irish woman: studies in cultural encounter and exchange, 1714–1960* (Liverpool, 2013), p. 94.

23 *The New York Times*, 22 August 1856.

24 Donald MacKay, *Flight from famine: the coming of the Irish to Canada* (Toronto, 1990); William Jenkins, *Between raid and rebellion: the Irish in Buffalo and Toronto, 1867–1916* (Montreal, 2013), p. 36.

25 Akenson, *The Irish diaspora*, pp. 261–2; Jenkins, *Between raid and rebellion*, p. 5.

26 Miller, *Emigrants and exiles*, p. 191.

27 Jenkins, *Between raid and rebellion*, pp. 42–3.

28 See for example, Akenson, *The Irish diaspora*; E. Margaret Crawford (ed.), *The hungry stream: essays on emigration and famine* (Belfast, 1997); Sophie Cooper, *Forging identities in the Irish world: Melbourne and Chicago, 1840–1922* (Edinburgh, 2022); Enda Delaney, *Demography, state and society: Irish migration to Britain, 1921–1971* (Liverpool, 2000); Hasia Diner, *Erin's daughters in America: Irish immigrant women in the nineteenth century* (London, 1983); Patrick Fitzgerald and Brian Lambkin, *Migration in Irish history, 1607–2007* (Basingstoke, 2008); Fitzpatrick, *Irish emigration*; Ruth-Ann Harris, ' "Come you all courageously": Irish women in America write home' in *Éire–Ireland*, 36, no. 1 (2001), pp. 166–84; Suellen Hoy, 'Discovering Irish nuns in the nineteenth-century United States: the case of Chicago' in Rosemary Raughter (ed.), *Religious women and their history: breaking the silence* (Dublin, 2005), pp. 50–62; Jackson, 'Women in 19th-century Irish emigration'; Kenny, *The American Irish*; Don MacRaild, *The Irish diaspora in Britain* (London, 2010); Miller, *Emigrants and exiles*; Nolan, *Ourselves alone*; Jennifer Redmond, *Moving histories: Irish women's emigration to Britain from Independence to Republic* (Liverpool, 2018); Gender, migration and madness research project: treating the Irish in the Canadian colonial lunatic asylums, 1841–68, available at gendermigrationandmadness.ca (last accessed 10 December 2021). For a comprehensive historiographical account, see Bernadette Whelan, 'Women on the move: a review of the historiography of Irish emigration to the USA, 1750–1900' in *Women's History Review*, 24, no. 6 (2015), pp. 900–916.

29 *The Tablet*, 31 January 1914.

30 Andrew Urban, 'Irish domestic servants, "Biddy" and rebellion in the American home, 1850–1900' in *Gender and History*, 21, no. 2 (2009), pp. 263–86.

31 *Irish Standard,* 30 June 1915.

32 Interview with Mary Good, 11 April 1918 (Massachusetts Archives, Massachusetts Reformatory for Women, Inmate case files series, HS9.06/series 515, #11095).

33 House of Correction, register of inmates, 1882–1905, vols. 135–41 (Boston City Archives, House of Corrections records, Collection 8502.001). There are some gaps in these records, most notably from November 1892 to April 1898.

34 Statistics of the Toronto Gaol, 1853–63 (Archives of Ontario, Correctional services, RG 20-100-3).

35 *Third annual report of the Commissioners of Public Charities and Correction, New York for the year 1862* (New York, 1863), p. 113.

36 Statistics of the Toronto Gaol, 1860–74 (Archives of Ontario, Correctional services, RG 20-100-3).

37 Peter Oliver, '"To govern by kindness": the first two decades of the Mercer Reformatory for Women' in Jim Phillips, Tina Loo and Susan Lewthwaite (eds.), *Crime and criminal justice* (Toronto, 1996), p. 546.

38 *Third annual report of the Commissioners of Public Charities and Correction, New York for the year 1862* (New York, 1863), p. 113.

39 *Seventeenth annual report of the New York Association for Improving the Condition of the Poor for the year 1860* (New York, 1860), p. 50.

40 *Twenty-fifth annual report of the New York Association for Improving the Condition of the Poor for the year 1868* (New York, 1868), p. 36.

41 *The New York Times,* 24 May 1867.

42 William Vaughan and A. J. Fitzpatrick, *Irish historical statistics: population, 1821–1971* (Dublin, 1978), pp. 261–3.

43 *Boston Globe,* 18 March 1919; M. Alison Kibler, *Censoring racial ridicule: Irish, Jewish, and African American struggles over race and representation, 1890–1930* (Chapel Hill, NC, 2015), chapter 2.

44 Sarah Deutsch, *Women and the city: gender, space, and power in Boston, 1870–1940* (Oxford, 2000), pp. 87–8; Jennifer Duffy,

Who's your Paddy? Racial expectations and the struggle for Irish American identity (New York, 2013), pp. 70–72; L. Mara Dodge, *'Whores and thieves of the worst kind': a study of women, crime, and prisons, 1835–2000* (DeKalb, IL, 2002), p. 115; Heap, *Slumming*; Chris McNickle, 'When New York was Irish, and after' in R. H. Bayor and T. J. Meagher (eds.), *The New York Irish* (Baltimore, MD, 1996), p. 337; Gunja SenGupta, *From slavery to poverty: the racial origins of welfare in New York, 1840–1918* (New York, 2009), pp. 197–203; Bronwen Walter, *Outsiders inside: whiteness, place and Irish women* (Abingdon, 2001), p. 61.

1. Prostitution and the case of Marion Canning

1 The sources on which this case study is based include: Case of Marion Canning, 1891 (New York Municipal Archives, District attorney cases, Court of General Sessions New York County, Grand jury indictments, box 443, folder 4082); Case of Marion Canning (New York State Archives (hereafter NYSA), New York (State) Governor, Executive clemency and pardon case files, A0597-78, box 44, folder 45); US census, 1880, available at ancestry.com (last accessed 28 January 2022).

2 Tyler Anbinder, *Five Points: the 19th-century New York City neighborhood that invented tap dance, stole elections, and became the world's most notorious slum* (New York, 2001), p. 176.

3 Timothy Gilfoyle, *City of Eros: New York City, prostitution and the commercialization of sex, 1790–1920* (New York, 1992), p. 215.

4 Jacob Riis, *How the other half lives: studies among the tenements of New York* (New York, 1890), p. 17.

5 Anbinder, *Five Points*, p. 367.

6 Riis, *How the other half lives*, p. 3.

7 *The New York Times*, 10 August 1889; *Brooklyn Daily Eagle*, 18 August 1891; *Evening World*, 27 November 1894.

8 The sources on which this case study is based include: *Brooklyn Times Union*, 13 May 1892; *Standard Union*, 13 May 1892; *The World*, 14 May 1892.

9 Tyler Anbinder, ' "We will dirk every mother's son of you": Five Points and the Irish conquest of New York politics' in Kevin Kenny (ed.), *New directions in Irish-American history* (Madison, WI, 2003), p. 105.

10 *Sixth annual report of the Children's Aid Society, February 1859* (New York, 1859), p. 34.

11 *The New York Times*, 21 January 1866.

12 William Wallace Sanger, *The history of prostitution: its extent, causes, and effects throughout the world* (New York, 1858), pp. 460–61.

13 Barbara Hobson, *Uneasy virtue: the politics of prostitution and the American reform tradition* (New York, 1987), pp. 89–90.

14 Constance Backhouse, 'Nineteenth-century Canadian prostitution law: reflection of a discriminatory society' in *Histoire Sociale – Social History*, 18 (1986), p. 400.

15 See, for example, Maria Luddy, *Prostitution and Irish society, 1800–1940* (Cambridge, 2007), pp. 53–4.

16 *Democrat and Chronicle*, 4 May 1910.

17 Anbinder, *Five Points*, p. 213.

18 *The New York Times*, 4 January 1885.

19 The sources on which this case study is based include: Entries for Mary Ann Murphy, 5 July, 19 July 1883; 2 February, 5 April 1888; 14 July, 13 August 1893 (Archives of Ontario, Toronto Gaol Registers, 1853–1908, Correctional services, RG 20-100-1); *Queen* v. *Mary Ann Murphy*, 1872 (Archives of Ontario, Criminal assize clerk criminal indictment files, York County, RG 22-329-0-7067); *Queen* v. *Mary Ann Murphy*, 1873 (Archives of Ontario, Criminal assize clerk criminal

indictment files, York County, RG22-329-0-7168); *Toronto Globe*, 31 October 1870; 10 May 1876. To avoid confusion with the *Boston Globe*, we have identified *The Globe* (Toronto) in the text and endnotes as *Toronto Globe*.

20 Inmate's own story, 14 February 1914 (Massachusetts Archives, Massachusetts Reformatory for Women, Inmate case files, HS9.06/series 515, #10515).

21 Inmate's own story, 29 January 1914 (Massachusetts Archives, Massachusetts Reformatory for Women, Inmate case files, HS9.06/series 515, #10267).

22 Gilfoyle, *City of Eros*, p. 62.

23 The sources on which this case study is based include: *Atchison Daily Patriot*, 16 December 1872; *Bellows Falls Times*, 20 December 1872, 24 January 1873; *Brooklyn Daily Eagle*, 12–13, 16, 21 December 1872, 1 May 1873; *Buffalo Commercial*, 10 May 1873, 4 March 1874; *Buffalo Evening Post*, 12 December 1872, 14 May 1873; *Buffalo Morning Express*, 14 December 1872; *Buffalo Weekly Courier*, 18 December 1872; *Democrat and Chronicle*, 16 December 1872; *New York Herald*, 8, 26, 29 April, 1, 7 May 1873; *The New York Times*, 9–14 December 1872, 8, 26 April, 1–8 May 1873; *New York Tribune*, 12 December 1872; *Rutland Independent*, 28 December 1872; *The Sun*, 11–12 December 1872, 9 April, 3 May 1873.

24 *Toronto Daily Star*, 7 June 1906.

25 Five Points Mission Adoption Journal, 28 January 1861 (United Methodist Church Archives and History Center, Drew University, New Jersey, Five Points Mission, Adoption records, 2129-4-7: 2).

26 Inmate's own story, 3 March 1918 (Massachusetts Archives, Massachusetts Reformatory for Women, Inmate case files, HS9.06/series 515, #11095).

27 Fitzgerald, *Habits of compassion*, p. 68.

28 Sanger, *The history of prostitution*, pp. 461–2.

29 *Fifth annual report of the Toronto Magdalene Asylum, 1859* (Toronto, 1859), p. 6; *Seventh annual report of the Toronto Magdalene Asylum, 1861* (Toronto, 1861), p. 4.

30 *The New York Times*, 9 October 1856.

31 Ibid., 24 October 1869.

32 Andrew Urban, *Brokering servitude: migration and the politics of domestic labor during the long nineteenth century* (New York, 2018), pp. 29–30.

33 Cited in ibid., p. 48.

34 Five Points Mission Adoption Journal, 19 April 1857 (United Methodist Church Archives and History Center, Drew University, New Jersey, Five Points Mission, Adoption records, 2129-4-7: 2).

35 *Third annual report of the Toronto Magdalene Asylum, 1857* (Toronto, 1857), pp. 7–8.

36 Urban, *Brokering servitude*, p. 49.

37 Constance Backhouse, *Petticoats and prejudice: women and law in nineteenth-century Canada* (Toronto, 1991), p. 232.

38 Five Points Mission Adoption Journal, 12 April 1857 (United Methodist Church Archives and History Center, Drew University, New Jersey, Five Points Mission, Adoption records, 2129-4-7: 2).

39 Five Points House of Industry, *Monthly Record*, June 1860.

40 See, for example, Ruth Rosen, *The lost sisterhood: prostitution in America, 1900–1918* (Baltimore, MD, 1983); Carolyn Strange, *Toronto's girl problem: the perils and pleasures of the city, 1880–1930* (Toronto, 1995).

41 US Senate document, no. 753, *Importation and harboring of women for immoral purposes* (61st Congress, Washington, DC 1911), p. 25.

42 Fitzgerald, *Habits of compassion*, p. 62. See also Maureen Murphy, 'Charlotte Grace O'Brien and the Mission of Our Lady of the Rosary for the Protection of Irish Immigrant Girls' in *Mid-America: An Historical Review*, 74, no. 3 (1992), pp. 253–70.

43 Minutes of the Charitable Irish Society quarterly meeting, 17 December 1883 (Massachusetts Historical Society, Charitable Irish Society, vol. 5).

44 Case of Mary Cotton, 1848 (New York Public Library (hereafter NYPL), Astor, Lenox, and Tilden Foundations, Manuscripts and Archives Division, Women's Prison Association of New York).

45 Case of Honora Maxwell, 1848 (NYPL, Astor, Lenox, and Tilden Foundations, Manuscripts and Archives Division, Women's Prison Association of New York).

46 Case of Bridget Scanlin, 1848 (NYPL, Astor, Lenox, and Tilden Foundations, Manuscripts and Archives Division, Women's Prison Association of New York).

2. *Unmarried motherhood and the case of Rosie Quinn*

1 *The Sun*, 11 January 1904.

2 *The New York Times*, 26 September 1907.

3 US census, 1900, available at ancestry.com (last accessed 21 October 2021).

4 The sources on which this case study is based include: Case of Rosie Quinn (NYSA, New York (State) Governor, Executive clemency and pardon case files, A0597-78, box 68, folder 19); Entry for Rosie Quinn, 30 April 1903 (NYSA, State Prison for Women at Auburn, Register of female inmates discharged, 1893–1906, B0055); *Baltimore Sun*, 28 November 1902; *Brooklyn Citizen*, 10 March, 8 April 1903; *Brooklyn Daily*

Eagle, 7, 17 April 1903, 14 December 1904; *Brooklyn Times Union*, 17 April 1903, 14 December 1904; *Buffalo Enquirer*, 22 December 1904; *Buffalo Times*, 14 December 1904; *Butte Miner*, 24 April 1903; *Courier Post*, 17 April 1903; *Democrat and Chronicle*, 18 April 1903; *Evening Standard*, 11 April 1903; *Evening World*, 9 April 1903, 16 December 1904; *The New York Times*, 18 April 1903, 15 December 1904; *New York Tribune*, 15 December 1904; *Post Standard*, 15–17 December 1904.

5 Sanger, *The history of prostitution*, p. 459.

6 Report of the Investigative Society for the Aid of Friendless Women and Children, 1877, series iii, vol. 286 (New York Historical Society (hereafter NYHS), Leake and Watts Children's Home Records).

7 Report of aid given to destitute mothers and infants, 1878, p. 3 (University Archives & Special Collections Department, Joseph P. Healey Library, University of Massachusetts Boston (hereafter UMB), Society for Helping Destitute Mothers and Infants, box 1).

8 *Boston Globe*, 13 March 1884.

9 Entry for Winifred Ruane, 15 August 1893 (Massachusetts Archives, Massachusetts Reformatory for Women, Inmate registers, HS9.06/series 824).

10 Interview with Elizabeth McGetterick, 15 March 1917 (Massachusetts Archives, Massachusetts Reformatory for Women, Inmate case files, HS9.06/series 515, #10813).

11 Statement of Constable James Burrows, 23 June 1870 (Archives of Ontario, Criminal assize clerk criminal indictment files, York County, *Queen* v. *Ellen McCarty* RG 22-392-0-6860).

12 Florence White to Mrs Sauborn, December 1915 (Massachusetts Archives, Massachusetts Reformatory for Women, Inmate case files, HS9.06/series 515, #10679).

13 Inmate's own story, 22 November 1915 (Massachusetts Archives, Massachusetts Reformatory for Women, Inmate case files, HS9.06/series 515, #10679).

14 Report of the Investigative Society for the Aid of Friendless Women and Children, 1876, series iii, vol. 286 (NYHS, Leake and Watts Children's Home records).

15 *Thirteenth annual report of the Toronto Prison Gate Mission and The Haven* (Toronto, 1891), p. 5. Emphasis in the original.

16 The Haven Letterbook, 9 February 1898, p. 369, cited in John R. Graham, 'The Haven, 1878–1930: a Toronto charity's transition from a religious to a professional ethos' in *Histoire Sociale–Social History*, 25, no. 50 (1992), p. 293.

17 Entry for James Haley Brennan, 8 May 1869 (University Archives & Special Collections Department, Joseph P. Healey Library, UMB, Massachusetts Board of State Charities, Infant Asylum admission register, 1868–72).

18 The sources on which this case study is based include: Case of Kate Sullivan, 1886 (New York Municipal Archives, District attorney cases, Court of General Sessions New York County, Grand jury indictments, Kate Sullivan, box 239, folder 2331); *Brooklyn Daily Eagle*, 24 November 1886; *The New York Times*, 26 March, 27 April 1887; *The Sun*, 26 March 1887.

19 *Buffalo Daily Republic*, 22 September 1852.

20 *Brooklyn Evening Star*, 24 February 1844.

21 *New York Herald*, 11 February 1844.

22 Stephen Robertson, 'Making right a girl's ruin: working-class legal cultures and forced marriage in New York City, 1890–1950' in *Journal of American Studies*, 36, no. 2 (2002), pp. 199–230.

23 Record of Catherine Kelly, 2 January 1866 (Massachusetts Archives, Massachusetts Board of State Charities, Histories

of alien residents of almshouses and other institutions, vol. 4, part 1, HS3/series 539x).

24 Record of Margaret Murphy, #1430 (Massachusetts Archives, Massachusetts Board of State Charities, Histories of alien residents of almshouses and other institutions, vol. 3, HS3/series 539x).

25 Deutsch, *Women and the city*, p. 61; Karen Dubinsky, *Improper advances: rape and heterosexual conflict in Ontario, 1880–1929* (Chicago, IL, 1993), pp. 52–4; Lindsay R. Moore, *Women before the court: law and patriarchy in the Anglo-American world, 1600-1800* (Manchester, 2019), pp. 73–4.

26 Dorothy Eddis notes, January 1918 (City of Toronto Archives, Dorothy Glen Papers, 143656).

27 *Forty-first annual report of the Boston Children's Aid Society, 1904–1905* (Boston, 1905), p. 11.

28 *Boston Globe*, 25 November 1905.

29 Outside investigation, 15 March 1917 (Massachusetts Archives, Massachusetts Reformatory for Women, Inmate case files, HS9.06/series 515, #10813).

30 Case notes, 16–18 June 1919 (University Archives & Special Collections Department, Joseph P. Healey Library, UMB, MSPCC, box 106, #51099).

31 Inmate's own story, 18 November 1914 (Massachusetts Archives, Massachusetts Reformatory for Women, Inmate case files, HS9.06/series 515, #10948).

32 Entry for Ellen O'Neil, 13 July 1900 (Massachusetts Archives, Massachusetts Reformatory for Women, Inmate registers, HS9.06/series 824).

33 George Deshon, *Guide for Catholic young women: especially for those who earn their own living* (New York, 1871), pp. 292, 303.

34 Peter Ward, 'Unwed motherhood in nineteenth-century English Canada' in *Historical Papers*, 16, no. 1 (1981), p. 42. For Ireland, see Maria Luddy, *Matters of deceit: breach of promise to marry cases in nineteenth- and twentieth-century Limerick* (Dublin, 2011).

35 Julie Miller, *Abandoned: foundlings in nineteenth-century New York City* (New York, 2008), p. 49.

36 *Boston Evening Transcript*, 14 November 1911.

37 *Fifty-second annual report of the Boston Children's Aid Society for the year ending September 30, 1916* (Boston, 1916), p. 10.

38 Karen Bridget Murray, 'Governing "unwed mothers" in Toronto at the turn of the twentieth century' in *Canadian Historical Review*, 85, no. 2 (2004), p. 267.

39 Robertson, 'Making right a girl's ruin', p. 219.

40 Constance Backhouse, 'Involuntary motherhood: abortion, birth control and the law in nineteenth-century Canada' in *Windsor Access to Justice Yearbook*, 3 (1983), pp. 65–72.

41 Leslie J. Reagan, *When abortion was a crime: women, medicine, and law in the United States, 1867–1973* (Berkeley and Los Angeles, CA, 1997), p. 11.

42 Backhouse, *Petticoats and prejudice*, p. 149.

43 *Berkshire County Eagle*, 24 December 1858.

44 *The New York Times*, 19 April 1856.

45 Ibid., 11 December 1857.

46 *Brooklyn Daily Eagle*, 23 November 1864.

47 Cara Delay, 'Pills, potions, and purgatives: women and abortion methods in Ireland, 1900–1950' in *Women's History Review*, 28, no. 3 (2019), pp. 476–99.

48 *The New York Times*, 31 May 1876.

49 Cited in Linda Gordon, *The moral property of women: a history of birth control politics in America* (Urbana and Chicago, IL, 2002), p. 25.

50 Backhouse, *Petticoats and prejudice*, chapter 4; Elaine Farrell, 'A most diabolical deed': infanticide and Irish society, 1850–1900

(Manchester, 2013); Mark Jackson (ed.), *Infanticide: historical perspectives on child murder and concealment, 1550–2000* (Aldershot, 2002).

51 *New York Tribune*, 27 April 1895.

52 Marcela Micucci, '"Another instance of that fearful crime": the criminalization of infanticide in Antebellum New York City' in *New York History*, 99, no. 1 (2018), pp. 76–7.

53 The sources on which this case study is based include: *Forty-ninth annual report of the Boston Children's Aid Society, 1913* (Boston, 1913), p. 15; Passenger list for the SS *Mauretania*, 13 September 1908, available at ancestry.com (last accessed 4 April 2021); *Boston Globe*, 7 October 1913, 15 April 1914; *Limerick Leader*, 24 August 1925; 31 August 1946.

54 *Evening Star*, 11 February 1898.

55 *Toronto Globe*, 15 February 1898.

56 Statement of Theresa McNally, 13 July 1886 (New York Municipal Archives, District attorney cases, Court of General Sessions New York County, Grand jury indictments, Theresa McNally, box 216, folder 2218).

57 Entry for Catherine Wilson, 25 February 1909 (Massachusetts Archives, Massachusetts Reformatory for Women, Inmate registers, HS9.06/series 824).

58 Entry for Mary Cunningham, 15 February 1901 (Massachusetts Archives, Massachusetts Reformatory for Women, Inmate registers, HS9.06/series 824).

59 Entry for John Bosworth, 12 September 1868 (University Archives & Special Collections Department, Joseph P. Healey Library, UMB, Massachusetts Board of State Charities, Infant Asylum admission registers, 1868–72).

60 Entry for James Knowles, 21 May 1869 (University Archives & Special Collections Department, Joseph P. Healey Library, UMB, Massachusetts Board of State Charities, Infant Asylum admission registers, 1868–72).

61 'An appeal in behalf of Destitute Mothers and Infants', 1874, p. 4 (University Archives & Special Collections Department, Joseph P. Healey Library, UMB, Society for Helping Destitute Mothers and Infants, 8/1).

62 Report of aid given to destitute mothers and infants, 1883, p. 2 (University Archives & Special Collections Department, Joseph P. Healey Library, UMB, Society for Helping Destitute Mothers and Infants, box 1).

63 *Annual report of the New York Infant Asylum, 1872* (New York, 1872), p. 1.

64 *Fifteenth annual report of the board of managers of the Infants' Home and Infirmary* (Toronto, 1925).

65 Russ Lopez, *Boston's South End: the clash of ideas in a historic neighborhood* (Boston, 2015), p. 33. For how Irishwomen negotiated maternity services in New York and Boston, see Ciara Breathnach, 'Immigrant Irishwomen and maternity services in New York and Boston, 1860–1911' in *Medical History*, 66, no. 1 (2022), pp. 3–23.

66 Entry for Catherine O'Donnell, 22 May 1889 (Massachusetts Archives, Massachusetts Reformatory for Women, Inmate registers, HS9.06/series 824).

67 *Boston Globe*, 23 May 1889.

68 Janice Harvey, 'The Protestant Orphan Asylum and the Montreal Ladies' Benevolent Society: a case study in Protestant child charity in Montreal, 1822–1900' (PhD thesis, McGill University, 2001), p. 154; Reagan, *When abortion was a crime*, p. 28.

69 Case notes, 19 March 1918 (University Archives & Special Collections Department, Joseph P. Healey Library, UMB, MSPCC, box 101, #49212).

70 *Thirteenth annual report of the Toronto Prison Gate Mission and The Haven* (Toronto, 1891), p. 5. Emphasis in the original.

71 *Eighty-second annual report of the New England Moral Reform Society, Talitha Cumi Maternity Home, 1918* (Concord, 1918), p. 14.

72 Murray, 'Governing "unwed mothers" in Toronto', p. 264.

73 Ibid., p. 265.

74 *Fifty-fourth annual report of the Boston Children's Aid Society for the year ending September 30, 1918* (Boston, 1918), pp. 13–14.

75 *The New York Times*, 1 October 1907.

76 *Clarion-Ledger*, 3 January 1883.

77 *Buffalo Times*, 14 December 1904; Entry for Sarah Silvermeister, 15 December 1904 (NYSA, State Prison for Women at Auburn, Register of female inmates discharged, 1893–1906, B00055).

78 *Washington Herald*, 27 September 1907; Green-wood Cemetery Civil War Project, available at https://www.green-wood.com/2015/civil-war-biographies (last accessed 16 February 2022).

79 *New York Tribune*, 7 April 1908.

3. Child neglect and the case of Annie Young

1 The sources on which this case study is based include: Case notes, 12 October 1908–12 June 2014 (University Archives & Special Collections Department, Joseph P. Healey Library, UMB, MSPCC, box 44, #32062); Annie Young to C. C. Carstens, 4 November 1910 (University Archives & Special Collections Department, Joseph P. Healey Library, UMB, MSPCC, box 44, #32062); Admission record of Annie and Mary Farry or Young, 5 July 1907 (Boston City Archives, Temporary Home for Women and Children, vol. 29, Collection 8720.001); *Boston Globe*, 16 November 1923, 3 September 1930; Marriages registered in the City of Boston, 1905, available at ancestry.com (last accessed 6 May 2021); UK and

Ireland incoming passenger lists, 1878–1960, available at ancestry.co.uk (last accessed 12 May 2021); Birth records of the Furey family, available at Irishgenealogy.ie (last accessed 20 April 2021); Censuses of Ireland, 1901 and 1911, available at census.nationalarchives.ie (last accessed 10 January 2022).

2 Linda Gordon, *Heroes of their own lives: the politics and history of family violence* (London, 1989), p. 21. See also Linda M. Shoemaker, 'The gendered foundations of social work education in Boston, 1904–1930' in Susan L. Porter (ed.), *Women of the Commonwealth: work, family, and social change in nineteenth-century Massachusetts* (Amherst, MA, 1996), pp. 99–117.

3 Mary Pond to Mary R. Martin, 2 February 1908 (University Archives & Special Collections Department, Joseph P. Healey Library, UMB, MSPCC, box 42, #31451).

4 Case notes, 15 May 1908 (University Archives & Special Collections Department, Joseph P. Healey Library, UMB, MSPCC, box 42, #31718).

5 Case notes, 10 June 1912 (University Archives & Special Collections Department, Joseph P. Healey Library, UMB, MSPCC, box 45, #32135).

6 US census, 1910, available at ancestry.com (last accessed 1 November 2021).

7 Doris Weatherford, *Foreign and female: immigrant women in America, 1840–1930* (New York, 1995), p. 54.

8 *The New York Times*, 14 August 1874.

9 Case notes, 5 June 1908 (University Archives & Special Collections Department, Joseph P. Healey Library, UMB, MSPCC, box 43, #31833).

10 Gordon, *Heroes of their own lives*, p. 60.

11 Case notes, 8 October 1908 (University Archives & Special Collections Department, Joseph P. Healey Library, UMB, MSPCC, box 45, #32219).

12 Case notes, 23 April 1919 (University Archives & Special Collections Department, Joseph P. Healey Library, UMB, MSPCC, box 102, #49706).

13 Lopez, *Boston's South End.*

14 Albert Benedict Wolfe, *The lodging house problem in Boston* (Boston, 1913).

15 Case book, 3 July 1888 (University Archives & Special Collections Department, Joseph P. Healey Library, UMB, MSPCC, collection 2, box 4, #7982).

16 Case notes, 28 February 1908 (University Archives & Special Collections Department, Joseph P. Healey Library, UMB, MSPCC, box 42, #31530).

17 Case notes, 24 March 1908 (University Archives & Special Collections Department, Joseph P. Healey Library, UMB, MSPCC, box 42, #31628). Emphasis in the original.

18 Case notes, 27 January 1914 (University Archives & Special Collections Department, Joseph P. Healey Library, UMB, MSPCC, box 45, #32135).

19 Timothy W. Guinnane, Carolyn M. Moehling and Cormac Ó Gráda, 'The fertility of the Irish in America in 1910', Economic Growth Center Yale University working paper series, no. 848, October 2002, p. 7.

20 'The condition of the children of laborers on public works' in *Common School Journal*, 2, no. 4 (1840), p. 49. See also Cooper Owens, *Race, gender, and the origins of American gynecology*, p. 98.

21 Elsa G. Herzfeld, *Family monographs: the history of twenty-four families living in the middle west side of New York City* (New York, 1905), p. 94.

22 Fitzgerald, *Habits of compassion*, p. 67.

23 Deutsch, *Women and the city*, p. 298, n. 23.

24 Herzfeld, *Family monographs*, p. 135.

25 Ibid., pp. 64–7.

26 Entry for Mary Scarlett, 16 October 1858 (University Archives & Special Collections Department, Joseph P. Healey Library, UMB, Gwynne Temporary Home for Children, general register, vol. 4).

27 Entry for John Henry and Mary Elizabeth King, 10 June 1898 (University Archives & Special Collections Department, Joseph P. Healey Library, UMB, Gwynne Temporary Home for Children, general register, vol. 15).

28 Mary R. Martin to C. C. Carstens, 3 April 1908 (University Archives & Special Collections Department, Joseph P. Healey Library, UMB, MSPCC, box 42, #31461).

29 Wolfe, *The lodging house problem in Boston*, p. 67.

30 Ibid., p. 68.

31 Ibid., p. 63.

32 Peter C. Holloran, *Boston's wayward children: social services for homeless children, 1830–1930* (Cranbury, NJ, 1989), p. 205.

33 Ibid., p. 92.

34 Ibid., p. 102.

35 Winifred Murphy to Mr Ewers, 10 March 1909 (University Archives & Special Collections Department, Joseph P. Healey Library, UMB, MSPCC, box 47, #32840).

36 Mary Mahoney to Mrs James Cooney, n.d. (Massachusetts Archives, Massachusetts Reformatory for Women, Inmate case files, HS9.06/series 515, #10212).

37 *Eleventh annual report for the Massachusetts Society for the Prevention of Cruelty to Children, 31 December 1891* (Boston, 1892), p. 12.

38 Case notes, 29 October 1910 (University Archives & Special Collections Department, Joseph P. Healey Library, UMB, MSPCC, box 43, #31785).

39 Client register, 1833–1858 (University Archives & Special Collections Department, Joseph P. Healey Library, UMB,

Boston Children's Friend Society, box 3, #71). Emphasis in
the original.

40 *Annual report of the Boston Society for the Care of Girls* (Boston,
1918), p. 6.

41 Marriage certificate of John Gilmore and Mary McGovern,
available at ancestry.com (last accessed 20 May 2021).

42 Susan L. Porter, 'A good home: indenture and adoption in
nineteenth-century orphanages' in E. Wayne Carp (ed.), *Adoption in America: historical perspectives* (Ann Arbor, MI, 2004), p. 28.

43 Peter L. Tyor and Jamil S. Zainaldin, 'Asylum and society: an
approach to institutional change' in *Journal of Social History*,
13, no. 1 (1979), p. 28.

44 Cited in Helen Campbell, *Darkness and daylight, or, lights and
shadows of New York life* (New York, 1891), p. 389.

45 Census of Ireland, 1901, available at census.nationalarchives.
ie (last accessed 16 December 2021).

46 Catherine Harrigan to Katherine O'Rourke, 10 April 1910
(University Archives & Special Collections Department,
Joseph P. Healey Library, UMB, MSPCC, box 42, #31649).

47 Cited in Anbinder, *Five Points*, p. 263.

48 Five Points House of Industry, *Monthly Record*, June 1865.

49 Charles R. Henderson, 'Juvenile offenders in Canada' in *Journal of the American Institute of Criminal Law and Criminology*, 4,
no. 5 (1914), p. 766.

50 *Third annual report for the Massachusetts Society for the Prevention of
Cruelty to Children, 31 December 1883* (Boston, 1884), p. 17.

51 Case notes, 18 June–28 October 1908 (University Archives &
Special Collections Department, Joseph P. Healey Library,
UMB, MSPCC, box 42, #31664).

52 Catherine Conboy to Jessie Donaldson Hodder, 14 September
1915 (Massachusetts Archives, Massachusetts Reformatory
for Women, Inmate case files, HS9.06/series 515, #10464).

4. Rebel girls and the case of Ellen Nagle

1 The sources on which this case study is based include: Entry for Ellen Nagle, 13 May 1903 (Massachusetts Archives, Massachusetts Reformatory for Women, Inmate registers, H59.06/series 824); Birth records of the Nagle family, available at Irishgenealogy.ie (last accessed 20 April 2021); Marriages registered in the city of Boston, 1906, available at ancestry.com (last accessed 20 May 2021); US censuses, 1900, 1910, available at ancestry.com (last accessed 20 May 2021); *Boston Post*, 3, 6 April 1902.

2 Holloran, *Boston's wayward children*, p. 248.

3 Annual admissions for 1903 (Massachusetts Archives, Massachusetts Reformatory for Women, Commitment register, 1877–1906, HS9.06/series 299x).

4 See also the Incorrigibles transmedia project, which focuses on delinquent girls in New York since 1904 (Incorrigibles. org, last accessed 1 February 2022).

5 Ruth M. Alexander, *The 'girl problem': female sexual delinquency in New York, 1900–1930* (New York, 1995), p. 50.

6 Strange, *Toronto's girl problem*, p. 55.

7 *Tenth annual report of the Secretary of the Board of State Charities, 1872–1873* (Boston, 1874), p. 228.

8 Barbara M. Brenzel, *Daughters of the state: a social portrait of the first reform school for girls in North America, 1865-1905* (Cambridge, MA, 1983), p. 80.

9 See, for example, Joy Damousi, *Depraved and disorderly: female convicts, sexuality and gender in Colonial Australia* (Cambridge, 1997); Dodge, *'Whores and thieves of the worst kind'*; Elaine Farrell, *Women, crime and punishment in Ireland: life in the nineteenth-century convict prison* (Cambridge, 2020); Estelle B. Freedman, *Their sisters' keepers: the origins of female corrections in America* (New York,

1976); Nicole Hahn Rafter, *Partial justice: women in state prisons, 1800–1935* (Boston, 1985); Lucia Zedner, *Women, crime, and custody in Victorian England* (Oxford, 1991).

10 Freedman, *Their sisters' keepers*, pp. 50–55; Home for Friendless Women and Children, 27 January 1876 (Boston Public Library, Massachusetts Charitable Societies records, MS Acc. 825-64).

11 Emory Washburn, *Reasons for a separate state prison for women* (Boston, 1874), p. 4.

12 Elizabeth Gurney Fry, *Observations on the visiting, superintendence and government of female prisoners* (London, 1827).

13 Entry for Hannah Sullivan, 7 November 1877 (Massachusetts Archives, Massachusetts Reformatory for Women, Inmate history logbooks, HS9.06/series 821x).

14 *Third annual report of the Bureau of Prisons of Massachusetts, including reports of all prison matters; with statistics of arrests and of criminal prosecutions, for the year 1918* (Boston, 1919), p. 72.

15 *First annual report of the Commissioners of Prisons on the Reformatory Prison for Women, 1878* (Boston, 1879), p. 17.

16 *Third annual report of the Bureau of Prisons of Massachusetts, including reports of all prison matters; with statistics of arrests and of criminal prosecutions, for the year 1918* (Boston, 1919), p. 163.

17 Robert Pickett, *House of refuge: origins of juvenile reform in New York State, 1815–1857* (Syracuse, NY, 1969), p. 6.

18 *The greatest reform school in the world: a guide to the records of the New York House of Refuge* (New York, 1989), p. 4.

19 Entry for Bridget Meuldary, January 1858 (NYSA, New York House of Refuge inmate case histories, A2064).

20 Strange, *Toronto's girl problem*, p. 132.

21 Entry for Mary Dean, 7 October 1882; Entry for Maria Thornton, 12 April 1889 (Archives of Ontario, Ontario Industrial Refuge for Girls register, 1880–1905, vol. 1, p. 2).

22 Strange, *Toronto's girl problem*, p. 132.

23 Eric C. Schneider, *In the web of class: delinquents and reformers in Boston, 1810s–1930s* (New York, 1992), p. 76.

24 Ibid., p. 79.

25 Entry for Margaret O'Brien, 14 August 1878 (Massachusetts Archives, Massachusetts Reformatory for Women, Inmate history logbooks, HS9.06/series 821x).

26 Holloran, *Boston's wayward children*, pp. 111–14.

27 Fitzgerald, *Habits of compassion*, p. 79.

28 Katherine E. Conway, *In the footprints of the Good Shepherd: New York, 1837–1907* (New York, 1910), p. viii.

29 Holloran, *Boston's wayward children*, pp. 129–32.

30 Cited in Conway, *In the footprints of the Good Shepherd*, p. 92.

31 Brenzel, *Daughters of the state*, p. 82; Leanne McCormick, *Regulating sexuality: women in twentieth-century Northern Ireland* (Manchester, 2009), chapter 3.

32 Regina Kunzel, *Fallen women, problem girls: unmarried mothers and the professionalization of social work, 1890–1945* (New Haven, CT, 1993), p. 52.

33 Mary Odem, *Delinquent daughters: protecting and policing adolescent female sexuality in the United States, 1885–1920* (Chapel Hill, NC, 1995), pp. 12–13.

34 Deutsch, *Women and the city*, p. 61.

35 Stephen Robertson, *Crimes against children: sexual violence and legal culture in New York City, 1880–1960* (Chapel Hill, NC, 2005), p. 76.

36 *Boston Globe*, 2 April 1908; Schneider, *In the web of class*, chapter 8.

37 Strange, *Toronto's girl problem*, p. 132; Amanda Glasbeek, *Feminized justice: the Toronto Women's Court, 1913–1934* (Vancouver, BC, 2009), p. 27.

38 Anne Meis Knupfer, *Reform and resistance: gender, delinquency, and America's first juvenile court* (London, 2001), p. 92.

39 Women's Night Court, New York, January 1911 (New York City Municipal Archives, Magistrates' Court, 9th District Manhattan, Women's Night Court docket books, 1907–1930).

40 Glasbeek, *Feminized justice*, p. 4.

41 Eileen Murphy, Colm Donnelly and Dave McKean, 'In a city of mills and canals: mortality among pre-teen and teenage Irish workers in mid-nineteenth-century industrial Lowell, Massachusetts' in *Childhood in the Past*, 12, no. 2 (2019), pp. 120–21.

42 Wolfe, *The lodging house problem in Boston*, p. 32.

43 *Second annual report of the Children's Aid Society, February 1855* (New York, 1855), pp. 33–4. Emphasis in the original.

44 Odem, *Delinquent daughters*, p. 22.

45 Entry for Mary Sheridan, February 1859 (NYSA, New York House of Refuge inmate case histories, A2064).

46 Entry for Ellen Morrissey, August 1879 (NYSA, New York House of Refuge inmate case histories, A2064).

47 Entry for Bridget Burns, 17 March 1882 (Massachusetts Archives, Massachusetts Reformatory for Women, Inmate history logbooks, HS9.06/series 821x).

48 Dennis P. Ryan, *Beyond the ballot box: a social history of the Boston Irish, 1845–1917* (Boston, 1983), p. 29.

49 *Toronto Star*, c.1916 clipping (City of Toronto Archives, General subject and correspondence of Children's Aid Society and Infants' Home of Toronto, 1877–1968, 143655).

50 Entry for Maggie Miskelley, 6 June 1896 (Massachusetts Archives, Massachusetts Reformatory for Women, Inmate registers, HS9.06/series 824).

51 Entry for Mary Scott, 17 August 1896 (Massachusetts Archives, Massachusetts Reformatory for Women, Inmate registers, HS9.06/series 824).

52 Another sibling was born in Massachusetts.

53 Sources on which this case study is based include: case file of Elizabeth Fingliss (Massachusetts Archives, Massachusetts Reformatory for Women, Inmate case files, HS9.06/series 515, #10559); Entry for Elizabeth Fingliss, 10 April 1915 (Massachusetts Archives, Massachusetts Reformatory for Women, Inmate registers, HS9.06/series 824); *Fall River Daily Globe*, 8–9 April 1915.

54 Odem, *Delinquent daughters*, p. 55.

55 Kathy Peiss, 'Charity girls and city pleasures' in *OAH Magazine of History*, 18, no. 4 (2004), p. 14. See also Ruth True, *The neglected girl* (New York, 1911), p. 72.

56 Elizabeth Alice Clement, *Love for sale: courting, treating, and prostitution in New York City, 1900–1945* (Chapel Hill, NC, 2006), p. 52.

57 Glasbeek, *Feminized justice*, p. 98.

58 Entry for Catherine Holmes, 13 May 1901 (Massachusetts Archives, Massachusetts Reformatory for Women, Inmate registers, HS9.06/series 824).

59 Entry for Bridget Kennedy, 18 August 1896 (Massachusetts Archives, Massachusetts Reformatory for Women, Inmate registers, HS9.06/series 824).

60 *Tenth annual report of Board of State Charities of Massachusetts, January 1874* (Boston, 1874), p. 79.

5. Drink and the case of the Toronto Drunks

1 The sources on which this case study is based include: *Toronto Globe*, 23 May 1865; Toronto Gaol Registers, 1853–1908 (Archives of Ontario, Correctional services, RG 20-100-1).

2 George T. Denison, *Recollections of a police magistrate* (Toronto, 1920), p. 178.

3 *Toronto Globe*, 18 May 1865.

4 Ibid., 1 February 1865.

5 Jenkins, *Between raid and rebellion*, p. 80.

6 Robert Ernst, *Immigrant life in New York City, 1825–1863* (New York, 1949), p. 204.

7 *Fifth annual report of the Board of Police Justices of the City of New York* (New York, 1876), p. 21.

8 Theodore N. Ferdinand, 'Criminality, the courts, and the constabulary in Boston: 1702–1967' in *Journal of Research in Crime and Delinquency*, 17, no. 2 (1980), pp. 200–201.

9 A pastoral letter of Archbishop John Joseph Lynch regarding Ireland, the Irish people, and ways of preserving the faith and nationality of the Irish, 17 March 1875, p. 4 (Archives of the Roman Catholic Archdiocese of Toronto, Archbishop John Joseph Lynch fonds, LAA11.22).

10 *The New York Times*, 13 November 1881. See also Lawrence J. McCaffery, 'Forging forward and looking back' in Bayor and Meagher (eds.), *The New York Irish*, p. 221.

11 Kenny, *The American Irish*, p. 202.

12 Boston House of Correction register of inmates, 1882–1915, vols. 135–43 (Boston City Archives, House of Corrections records, Collection 8502.001). Gaps in these records include November 1892–February 1898, and July 1909–April 1911.

13 Toronto Gaol Registers, 1853–1908 (Archives of Ontario, Correctional services, RG 20-100-1). This sample includes annual admissions at five-year intervals from 1853 to 1908, excluding 1863.

14 Women's Night Court, New York, January 1911 (New York City Municipal Archives, Magistrates' Court, 9th District Manhattan, Women's Night Court docket books, 1907–1930). The records were sampled for January and May for each year, 1911–18.

15 *Seventeenth annual report of the New York Association for Improving the Condition of the Poor for the year 1860* (New York, 1860), p. 51.

16 Herzfeld, *Family monographs*, p. 12.

17 Thomas Colley Grattan, *Civilized America* (London, 1859), vol. ii, p. 8.

18 John Francis Maguire, *The Irish in America* (New York, 1868), pp. 281, 286.

19 Richard Stivers, *Hair of the dog: Irish drinking and its American stereotype* (New York and London, 2000), pp. 176–7.

20 Kenny, *The American Irish*, p. 145; Diner, *Erin's daughters in America*, pp. 112–13.

21 Deshon, *Guide for Catholic young women*, p. 295.

22 Kenny, *The American Irish*, pp. 145–7.

23 Diner, *Erin's daughters*, p. 114; Stivers, *Hair of the dog*, p. 188.

24 Five Points House of Industry, *Monthly Record*, July 1865, p. 41.

25 Ibid., p. 42.

26 Campbell, *Darkness and daylight*, p. 109.

27 *Thirty-sixth annual report of the New York Association for Improving the Condition of the Poor for the year 1879* (New York, 1879), pp. 67–8.

28 Oscar Handlin, *Boston's immigrants* (Cambridge, MA, 1959), p. 121.

29 Max Berger, 'The Irish emigrant and American nativism: as seen by British visitors, 1836–1860' in *Dublin Review*, 219, no. 439 (1946), p. 177.

30 Murray W. Nicolson, 'Peasants in an urban society: the Irish Catholics in Victorian Toronto' in Robert Harney (ed.), *Gathering place: peoples and neighbourhoods of Toronto, 1834–1945* (Toronto, 1985), p. 58.

31 Roy Rosenzweig, *Eight hours for what we will: workers and leisure in an industrial city, 1870–1920* (Cambridge, 1983), p. 41.

32 Deutsch, *Women and the city*, p. 16.

33 Toronto Gaol Registers, 1858–1908 (Archives of Ontario, Correctional services, RG 20-100-1); Toronto Police Service,

Register of criminals, 1861–1893 (Toronto City Archives, Toronto Police Service, fonds 38, series 94, subseries 4).

34 Entry for Mary Downey, Toronto Gaol Registers, 1858–1908 (Archives of Ontario, Correctional services, RG 20-100-1); *Toronto Globe*, 14 September 1880.

35 Entry for Annie Sexton, Toronto Gaol Registers, 1858–1908 (Archives of Ontario Correctional services, RG 20-100-1); *Toronto Globe*, 19 July 1878.

36 Deutsch, *Women and the city*, p. 85.

37 *Toronto Globe*, 18–19 May 1865.

38 Entry for Mary Fitzpatrick, 19 August 1896 (Massachusetts Archives, Massachusetts Reformatory for Women, Inmate registers, HS9.06/series 824).

39 Ernst, *Immigrant life in New York City*, p. 57.

40 Denison, *Recollections of a police magistrate*, p. 178.

41 *Toronto Globe*, 23 May 1865.

42 *Third annual report of the Board of Police Justices of the City of New York* (New York, 1874), pp. 16–17; Fitzgerald, *Habits of compassion*, p. 71.

43 Glasbeek, *Feminized justice*, p. 124.

44 *Toronto Globe*, 26 July 1881.

45 Lorna R. McLean and Marilyn Barber, 'In search of comfort and independence: Irish immigrant domestic servants encounter the courts, jails, and asylums in nineteenth-century Ontario' in Marlene Epp, Franca Iacovetta and Frances Swyripa (eds.), *Sisters or strangers? Immigrant, ethnic, and racialized women in Canadian history* (Toronto, 2004), pp. 142–4.

46 *Tenth annual report of the Women's Prison Association and Home* (New York, 1854), p. 8.

47 *Fifty-sixth annual report of the Women's Prison Association and Home* (New York, 1900), p. 20.

48 Ibid.

49 Toronto Gaol Registers, 1858–1908 (Archives of Ontario, Correctional services, RG 20-100-1).

50 *Fourteenth annual report of the Women's Prison Association and Home* (New York, 1858), pp. 6–7.

51 *Fifty-sixth annual report of the Women's Prison Association and Home* (New York, 1900), p. 22.

52 Glasbeek, *Feminized justice*, p. 124.

53 Catherine Murdock, *Domesticating drink: women, men, and alcohol in America, 1870–1940* (Baltimore, MD, 1998), p. 171.

54 Entry for Ellen McGuire, April 1848 (NYPL, Astor, Lenox, and Tilden Foundations, Manuscripts and Archives Division, Women's Prison Association of New York).

55 Entry for Ellen O'Neil, May 1848 (NYPL, Astor, Lenox, and Tilden Foundations, Manuscripts and Archives Division, Women's Prison Association of New York).

56 *Report of the Jail Mission Work, Toronto, from December, 1867, to August, 1869* (Toronto, 1869), pp. 15–16.

57 Toronto Gaol Registers, 1868 (Archives of Ontario, Correctional services, RG 20-100-1).

58 *Meridan Daily Journal*, 15 March 1905.

59 *Boston Globe*, 15 March 1905.

60 Entry for Minnie O'Connor, 13 March 1905 (Massachusetts Archives, Reformatory for Women, Inmate history logbooks, HS9.06/series 821x); *Meridan Daily Journal*, 15 March 1905.

61 SenGupta, *From slavery to poverty*, p. 185.

62 Entry for Margaret Wilson, 3 September 1891 (Massachusetts Archives, Massachusetts Reformatory for Women, Inmate registers, HS9.06/series 824).

63 Entry for Julia Murphy, 12 March 1892 (Massachusetts Archives, Massachusetts Reformatory for Women, Inmate registers, HS9.06/series 824).

64 Entry for Elizabeth Pierce, May 1848 (NYPL, Astor, Lenox, and Tilden Foundations, Manuscripts and Archives Division, Women's Prison Association of New York).

65 Inmate's own story, 17 May 1917 (Massachusetts Archives, Massachusetts Reformatory for Women, Inmate case files, HS9.06/series 515, #10464).

66 Christine Stansell, *City of women: sex and class in New York, 1789–1860* (Champaign, IL, 1987), p. 199; Fitzgerald, *Habits of compassion*, p. 65.

67 Entry for Catherine Ryan, May 1848 (NYPL, Astor, Lenox, and Tilden Foundations, Manuscripts and Archives Division, Women's Prison Association of New York).

68 Entry for Annie Proud, 20 February 1892 (Massachusetts Archives, Massachusetts Reformatory for Women, Inmate registers, HS9.06/series 824).

69 Entry for Mary Connor, 19 February 1892 (Massachusetts Archives, Massachusetts Reformatory for Women, Inmate registers, HS9.06/series 824).

70 Entry for Mary Mountjoy, 27 October 1910 (Massachusetts Archives, Massachusetts Reformatory for Women, Inmate registers, HS9.06/series 824).

71 Entry for Mary Mountjoy, 27 November 1914 (Massachusetts Archives, Massachusetts Reformatory for Women, Inmate registers, HS9.06/series 824).

72 Conor Reidy, *Criminal Irish drunkards: the inebriate reformatory system, 1900–1920* (Dublin, 2014), p. 161.

73 *Third annual report of the Children's Aid Society, February 1856* (New York, 1856), pp. 6, 29.

74 Case notes, 12 March 1908 (University Archives & Special Collections Department, Joseph P. Healey Library, UMB, MSPCC, box 42, #31624).

75 *Sixth annual report of the New York Society for the Prevention of Cruelty to Children* (New York, 1881), pp. 99–100.

76 Sarah R. May to E. A. W. Quincy, Secretary of the Children's Friend Society, 9 December 1841 (University Archives & Special Collections Department, Joseph P. Healey Library, UMB, Children's Friend Society, Clients' correspondence).

77 Entry for Mary O'Connor, 3 July 1899 (Massachusetts Archives, Reformatory for Women, Inmate history logbooks, HS9.06/series 821x).

78 *Brooklyn Times Union*, 31 August 1891.

79 Case notes, 15 May 1908–3 June 1919 (University Archives & Special Collections Department, Joseph P. Healey Library, UMB, MSPCC, box 44, #31945).

80 Case notes, 24 March 1909 (University Archives & Special Collections Department, Joseph P. Healey Library, UMB, MSPCC, box 43, #31738).

81 Entry for Mary Greene, 26 September 1905 (Massachusetts Archives, Reformatory for Women, Inmate history logbooks, HS9.06/series 821x).

82 *The New York Times*, 2 July 1858.

83 *Toronto Globe*, 23 September 1857.

84 Ibid., 31 July 1900.

85 *The New York Times*, 11 May 1885.

86 *Boston Globe*, 27 September 1885.

87 The sources on which this case study is based include: Entry for Bridget Hennessy, 16 October 1885 (Boston City Archives, Boston House of Correction register of inmates, vol. 135, Collection 8502.001); *Boston Evening Transcript*, 28 September 1885; *Boston Globe*, 27–29 September, 2, 14–16 October 1885.

88 The sources on which this case study is based include: *Boston Evening Transcript*, 2 March 1889; *Boston Globe*, 2 March, 10 September 1889.

89   *Toronto Globe*, 29 June 1881.

90   Ibid., 25 August 1881.

91   Ibid., 7 April 1882.

92   Ibid., 24 December 1879.

93   Ibid., 25 November 1880.

94   Ibid., 26 January 1881.

95   *The New York Times*, 8 September 1860.

96   Susan Stryker, *Transgender history* (Berkeley, CA, 2008), p. 31.

97   Emily Skidmore, *True sex: the lives of trans men at the turn of the twentieth century* (New York, 2017), p. 5.

98   *The New York Times*, 5 June 1876.

99   *Toronto Globe*, 1 February 1865.

100 *Brooklyn Times Union*, 21 September 1903.

101 *Toronto Globe*, 23 May 1865.

102 Ibid., 7 January 1890.

103 *Brooklyn Daily Eagle*, 21 July 1885.

6. The hired help and the case of Carrie Jones

1   The sources on which this case study is based include: *American Mutoscope and Biograph Company picture catalogue* (New York, 1902), p. 218; Birth record of Isabella and Samuel Anderson, 29 November 1877, available at civilrecords.genealogy.ie (last accessed 12 May 2021); Entries for Carrie Jones, 19 June 1902 and Addie Barrow, 23 September 1907 (NYSA, State Prison for Women at Auburn, Register of female inmates discharged, 1893–1919, B0055); US census, 1900, available at ancestry.com (last accessed 12 May 2021); *Arkansas Democrat*, 16 June 1899; *Baltimore Sun*, 17 June 1899; *Barre Evening Telegram*, 26 May 1899; *Boston Daily Advertiser*, 5, 9 June 1899; *Boston Globe*, 15 June 1899; *Brooklyn Citizen*, 2 June 1899; *Brooklyn Daily Eagle*,

2 June 1899; *Brooklyn Times Union*, 27 June 1899; *Buffalo Commercial*, 26 May, 3 June 1899, 14 May 1902; *Buffalo Courier*, 16 June 1899, 7 January 1900; *Buffalo Enquirer*, 29 May 1899; *Buffalo Evening News*, 29 May 1899; *Buffalo Morning Express*, 27–28 May 1899; *Buffalo Times*, 28–29 May 1899; *Chicago Tribune*, 26 May, 2–3 June 1899; *Daily Arkansas Gazette*, 7 September 1894, 13 June 1899; *Daily Iowa Capitol*, 19 June 1899; *Democrat and Chronicle*, 27, 29 May, 11 June 1899; *Fall River Daily Globe*, 15 June 1899; *Mining Times*, 26 May 1899; *Montgomery Advertiser*, 20 June 1902; *New York Journal*, 23–29 May, 3–5, 8, 17 June 1899; *The New York Times*, 23–31 May, 2–4, 15–16 June 1899; *New York Tribune*, 3, 16 June 1899; *Pawtucket Times*, 15 June 1899; *Philadelphia Enquirer*, 28 May 1899; *Philadelphia Times*, 3 June 1899; *Pittsburgh Press*, 29 May, 26 June 1899; *Reading Times*, 29 May 1899; *San Francisco Examiner*, 30 May 1899; *Star Gazette*, 31 May, 1 June 1899; *The Sun*, 3 July 1896; *Wilkes-Barre Semi-Weekly Record*, 26 May 1899; *Wilkes-Barre Times Leader*, 29 May 1899; *Yonkers Statesman*, 18 July 1899. Journalists wrote the family's name as both 'Clark' and 'Clarke'. We have used 'Clarke' in this chapter, which is the spelling that Arthur and Margaret used in other sources.

2 Margaret Lynch-Brennan, 'Ubiquitous Bridget: Irish immigrant women in domestic service in America, 1840–1940' in J. J. Lee and Marion R. Casey (eds.), *Making the Irish American: history and heritage of the Irish in the United States* (New York, 2006), pp. 332–53.

3 *The New York Times*, 24 May 1867.

4 Cited in April Schultz, 'The Black Mammy and the Irish Bridget: domestic service and the representation of race, 1830–1930' in *Éire–Ireland*, 48, no. 3–4 (2013), pp. 180–81.

5 Kenny, *The American Irish*, p. 152.

6 Holloran, *Boston's wayward children*, p. 64.

7 Kenny, *The American Irish*, p. 152.

8 *New York Herald*, 14 February 1860.

9 Walter, *Outsiders inside*, p. 36; Currency converter, 1270–2017, available at Currency converter: 1270–2017 (nationalarchives. gov.uk) (last accessed 29 January 2022).

10 Meaney, O'Dowd and Whelan, *Reading the Irish woman*, p. 99.

11 Deutsch, *Women and the city*, pp. 55–6.

12 *Irish Canadian*, 29 September 1869.

13 *Evening Post*, 28 July 1829.

14 *New York Tribune*, 18 March 1851.

15 *Brooklyn Daily Eagle*, 6 August 1899.

16 *Boston Evening Transcript*, 13 November 1873. See also Catherine Healy, 'Ethnic jokes: mocking the working Irish woman' in *Journal of Victorian Culture*, 27, no. 1 (2022), pp. 1–14; Diane M. Hotten-Somers, 'Relinquishing and reclaiming independence: Irish domestic servants, American middle-class mistresses, and assimilation, 1850–1920' in Kenny (ed.), *New directions in Irish-American history*, pp. 227–43; Maureen Murphy, 'Bridget and Biddy: images of the Irish servant girl in *Puck* cartoons, 1880–1890' in Charles Fanning (ed.), *New perspectives on the Irish diaspora* (Carbondale, IL, 2000), pp. 152–75; Peter O'Neill, *Famine Irish and the American racial state* (New York, 2017), pp. 154–9.

17 *Daily Evening Transcript*, 5 February 1852. Emphasis in the original.

18 *Daily Evening Transcript*, 7 February 1852.

19 *The New York Times*, 4 July 1860.

20 Entry for Mary Leyden, 12 December 1900 (Massachusetts Archives, Massachusetts Reformatory for Women, Inmate history logbooks, HS9.06/series 821x).

21 *Toronto Globe*, 8 August 1865.

22 *Boston Globe*, 22 October 1907.

23 Fitzgerald, *Habits of compassion*, p. 67.

24 Entry for Jane Mills, April 1848 (NYSA, New York House of Refuge inmate case histories, A2064).

25 *The New York Times*, 3 February 1895.

26 *Boston Globe*, 23, 24 November 1875; 23 November 1877.

27 *The New York Times*, 20 November 1882.

28 *Philadelphia Inquirer*, 14 July 1874.

29 *Journal News*, 8 September 1994.

7. Theft and the case of Old Mother Hubbard

1 *New York Tribune*, 23 February 1858.

2 *New York Herald*, 7 January 1860.

3 *The New York Times*, 5 December 1857.

4 Ibid., 5 September 1860.

5 *New York Tribune*, 28 May 1895; *Evening World*, 8 December 1893.

6 *The World*, 13 June 1890; 11 December 1893.

7 *New York Tribune*, 28 May 1895.

8 John Oller, *Rogues' gallery: the birth of modern policing and organized crime in Gilded Age New York* (New York, 2021), p. 19.

9 Hasia Diner, '"The most Irish city in the Union": The era of the great migration, 1844–1877' in Bayor and Meagher (eds.), *The New York Irish*, p. 97; William Jenkins, 'Patrolmen and peelers: immigration, urban culture, and "the Irish police" in Canada and the United States' in *Canadian Journal of Irish Studies*, 28/29, no. 2 (2002), p. 23.

10 *New York Herald*, 21 March 1855; Campbell, *Darkness and daylight*, p. 506.

11 Dodge, *'Whores and thieves of the worst kind'*, p. 115.

12 Jenkins, 'Patrolmen and peelers', p. 21.

13 *Evening World*, 27 May 1895.

14 Oller, *Rogues' gallery*, p. 94.

15 *Buffalo Courier*, 11 March 1894.

16 Thomas Byrnes, *Professional criminals of America* (New York, 1886), preface.

17 *The New York Times*, 1 October 1886; J. North Conway, *The big policeman: the rise and fall of Thomas Byrnes, America's first, most ruthless, and greatest detective* (Guilford, CT, 2010), p. 190.

18 The sources on which this case study is based include: Entries for Margaret Brown, 31 March 1883, 20 July 1884 (Boston City Archives, Boston House of Correction register of inmates, vol. 135, Collection 8502.001); Byrnes, *Professional criminals of America* (1886); Thomas Byrnes, *Professional criminals of America: new and revised edition* (New York, 1895); *Boston Globe*, 2–3 July 1884, 7 November 1893, 29 January 1967; *Buffalo Enquirer*, 26 June 1891; *Buffalo Times*, 4 December 1898; *Buffalo Weekly Express*, 18 October 1894; *Evening Messenger*, 1 April 1898; *San Francisco Call*, 15 July 1891; *Wilmington Morning Star*, 24 June 1893; *Windsor Star*, 17 March 1898.

19 The sources on which this case study is based include: Entry for Elizabeth Dillon, 11 September 1908 (Boston City Archives, Boston House of Correction register of inmates, vol. 141, Collection 8502.001); Entry for Lizzie Dillon, 1 June 1913 (Boston City Archives, Boston House of Correction register of inmates, vol. 142, Collection 8502.001); Byrnes, *Professional criminals of America* (1886); Byrnes, *Professional criminals of America* (1895); *Boston Evening Transcript*, 15 April 1876, 9 August 1884, 17 May 1900, 10 September 1908; *Boston Globe*, 25 July 1884, 24 May 1895, 19 January 1900, 10 September 1908, 22 August 1912, 24 September 1913, 12 August 1916, 25 May 1920, *Boston Post*, 13 August 1901; *Fitchburg Sentinel*, 13 August 1901.

20 *The New York Times*, 31 July 1884.

21 Timothy Gilfoyle, *A pickpocket's tale: the underworld of nineteenth-century New York* (New York, 2006), p. 64; Alana Piper, 'Victimization narratives and courtroom sexual politics: prosecuting male burglars and female pickpockets in Melbourne, 1860–1921' in *Journal of Social History*, 51, no. 4 (2018), p. 764.

22 Byrnes, *Professional criminals of America* (1886), p. 35.

23 The sources on which this case study is based include: Byrnes, *Professional criminals of America* (1886); Byrnes, *Professional criminals of America* (1895); *Brooklyn Daily Eagle*, 16 June 1884; *Brooklyn Union*, 27 June 1884; *The New York Times*, 27 June 1875; *Sedalia Weekly Bazoo*, 9 August 1881; *The Sun*, 7 October 1869.

24 *Brooklyn Daily Eagle*, 23 October 1894; *Brooklyn Times Union*, 23 October 1894.

25 Byrnes, *Professional criminals of America* (1886), p. 195; *Buffalo Times*, 22 February 1884. Byrnes listed Holbrook as Irish but prison registers identify her as being from Salem, Massachusetts (Entry for Mary Williams alias Molly Hoy, 22 March 1883 (Boston City Archives, Boston House of Correction register of inmates, vol. 135, Collection 8502.001)).

26 *Boston Post*, 6 March 1874; *Buffalo Times*, 22 February 1884.

27 *Boston Post*, 25 April 1874.

28 *Boston Globe*, 18 July 1874.

29 *New York Herald*, 23 February 1865.

30 Ibid.; *The Sun*, 7 September 1869.

31 *The Sun*, 7 October 1869.

32 *Evening World*, 10 August 1914.

33 *The New York Times*, 7 November, 23 November 1894; *The Sun*, 10 May 1890.

34 Oller, *Rogues' gallery*, p. 91; Conway, *The big policeman*, p. 190.

35 *Report and proceedings of the investigation of the New York City Police, 11–29 December 1894*, vol. 5, Testimony of Thomas Byrnes at the Lexow Committee, p. 5711.

36 Sarah Elvins, 'History of the department store' in Jon Sto-
bart and Vicki Howard (eds.), *Routledge companion to the history
of retailing* (London, 2018), p. 136.

37 Ibid., p. 137.

38 Elaine Abelson, 'The invention of kleptomania' in *Signs*, 15,
no. 1 (1989), p. 136.

39 Kerry Segrave, *Shoplifting: a social history* (Jefferson, NC, 2001),
p. 15.

40 *The New York Times*, 24 July 1884; 11 December 1904.

41 Elaine Abelson, *When ladies go a-thieving: middle-class shoplifters
in the Victorian department store* (Oxford, 1989), p. 130.

42 Seagrave, *Shoplifting*, p. 16.

43 *New York Tribune*, 16 May 1887; *The Sun*, 16 May 1887.

44 Elvins, 'History of the department store', p. 143.

45 Abelson, *When ladies go a-thieving*, p. 161.

46 Ibid., pp. 115, 161.

47 Ibid., p. 192.

48 Byrnes, *Professional criminals of America* (1886), p. 31.

49 The sources on which this case study is based include:
Evening World, 13 March 1894; *The New York Times*, 15
March 1894. See also Abelson, *When ladies go a-thieving*, pp.
170–71.

50 *New York Herald*, 3 January 1870; *The New York Times*, 2 June
1867.

51 *The New York Times*, 11 April 1895.

52 Criminal Registers of the Detectives' Department: 'B', 1895–
1903 (City of Toronto Archives, Toronto Police Service,
fonds 38, series 171, file 3).

53 *Toronto Globe*, 6 August 1888.

54 *Daily Atlas*, 27 April 1844.

55 *The New York Times*, 17 August 1860.

56 Ibid., 12 February 1856.

57 Criminal Registers of the Detectives' Department: 'B', 1895–1903 (City of Toronto Archives, Toronto Police Service, fonds 38, series 171, file 3).

58 Entry for Mary Craig, 27 September 1893 (Massachusetts Archives, Massachusetts Reformatory for Women, Inmate registers, HS9.06/series 824).

59 *Toronto Globe*, 26 December 1873.

60 Ibid., 29 December 1873.

61 Ibid., 27 December 1873.

62 *Evening World*, 2 February 1904.

63 *Brooklyn Times Union*, 2 February 1904.

64 *Evening World*, 2 February 1904.

65 The sources on which this case study is based include: Entry for Delia Brown, 11 May 1896 (Massachusetts Archives, Massachusetts Reformatory for Women, Inmate registers, HS9.06/series 824); *Boston Globe*, 22–24 April, 5, 12 May 1896.

66 *New York Tribune*, 8 May 1910.

67 *The Sun*, 6 December 1896.

8. Crimes of matrimony and the case of Letitia Armstrong

1 The sources on which this case study is based include: *Queen vs Letitia Armstrong*, York Fall Assizes 1873 (Archives of Ontario, Criminal assize clerk criminal indictment files, York County, RG 22-392-0-7105); Censuses of Canada, 1871, 1881, 1891, 1901, available at Libraries and Archives Canada, https://www.bac-lac.gc.ca/eng/census/Pages/census.aspx (last accessed 12 November 2021); *C. E. Anderson & Co.'s Toronto city directory for 1868–9: containing a complete street directory, an alphabetical directory of the citizens, a subscriber's business*

classification and an appendix of useful information (Toronto, 1868); Toronto City Directories, 1878–1908, available at https://www.torontopubliclibrary.ca/history-genealogy/lh-digital-city-directories.jsp (last accessed 10 November 2021); Ontario, Canada, Marriages, 1826–1938, available at ancestry. com (last accessed 10 November 2021); Ontario, Canada, Deaths and deaths overseas, 1869–1948, available at ancestry. com (last accessed 10 November 2021); *Toronto Globe*, 5 November 1873. We are grateful to Elizabeth Mathew of the United Church of Canada Archives and genealogist Melissa J. Ellis for their assistance in trying to locate a marriage certificate for George and Letitia Armstrong.

2 Jenkins, *Between raid and rebellion*, p. 35; Miller, *Emigrants and exiles*, p. 323.

3 Jenkins, *Between raid and rebellion*, pp. 42–3.

4 Ibid., pp. 61–2.

5 Entry for Alice Canning, 9 October 1882 (Massachusetts Archives, Massachusetts Reformatory for Women, Inmate history logbooks, HS9.06/series 821x).

6 Entry for Ann Amrock, 10 September 1877 (Massachusetts Archives, Massachusetts Reformatory for Women, Inmate history logbooks, HS9.06/series 821x).

7 Backhouse, *Petticoats and prejudice*, p. 203.

8 Ibid.

9 Ibid., pp. 203–4.

10 Anna R. Igra, 'Likely to become a public charge: deserted women and the family law of the poor in New York City, 1910–1936' in *Journal of Women's History*, 11, no. 4 (2000), pp. 63–4.

11 Charles Zunser, 'The Domestic Relations Courts' in *Annals of the American Academy of Political and Social Science*, 124, no. 1 (1926), p. 118.

12 Igra, 'Likely to become a public charge', p. 59. See also Martha May, 'The "problem of duty": family desertion in the Progressive Era' in *Social Service Review*, 62, no. 1 (1988), pp. 40–60.

13 *Twenty-ninth annual report of the New York Association for Improving the Condition of the Poor for the year 1876* (New York, 1872), p. 40.

14 Diner, *Erin's daughters in America*, p. 59.

15 *The New York Times*, 28 November 1883.

16 Beverly Schwartzberg, '"Lots of them did that": desertion, bigamy, and marital fluidity in late nineteenth-century America' in *Journal of Social History*, 37, no. 3 (2004), p. 584.

17 Entry for Mary Donohue, 12 June 1891 (Massachusetts Archives, Massachusetts Reformatory for Women, Inmate registers, HS9.06/series 824).

18 Entry for Catherine Dillon, 5 April 1848; Entry for Mary Manning, 18 January 1855 (Astor, Lenox, and Tilden Foundations, Manuscripts and Archives Division, Women's Prison Association of New York).

19 Entry for Annie Lucas, 17 November 1887 (Massachusetts Archives, Massachusetts Reformatory for Women, Inmate registers, HS9.06/series 824).

20 Entry for Johannah Kelly, 10 April 1890 (Massachusetts Archives, Massachusetts Reformatory for Women, Inmate registers, HS9.06/series 824).

21 Entry for Susan Voyer, 2 June 1911 (Massachusetts Archives, Massachusetts Reformatory for Women, Inmate registers, HS9.06/series 824).

22 Gordon, *Heroes of their own lives*, p. 274.

23 *Brooklyn Daily Eagle*, 19 September 1896.

24 *The Sun*, 18 October 1897.

25 *People vs Bridget McCabe*, 22 September 1881 (New York Municipal Archives, District attorney cases, Court of General

Sessions New York County, Grand jury indictments, box 508, folder 4631).

26 *The Sun*, 28 October 1881.

27 Ibid., 1 November 1881.

28 Martin Wiener, *Men of blood: violence, manliness and criminal justice in Victorian England* (Cambridge, 2004), pp. 130–34; Ginger Frost, *Living in sin: cohabiting as husband and wife in nineteenth-century England* (Manchester, 2013), p. 37.

29 Sarah-Anne Buckley, 'Desertion and "divorce Irish style" (1937–97)' in Salvador Ryan (ed.), *Marriage and the Irish: a miscellany* (Dublin, 2019), pp. 198–201; Diane Urquhart, 'Ireland and the Divorce and Matrimonial Causes Act of 1857' in *Journal of Family History*, 38, no. 3 (2018), p. 315.

30 Maria Luddy and Mary O'Dowd, *Marriage in Ireland, 1660–1925* (Cambridge, 2020), p. 292.

31 *New York Herald*, 14 July 1848; Timothy Gilfoyle, 'The hearts of nineteenth-century men: bigamy and working-class marriage in New York City, 1800–1890' in *Prospects*, 19 (1994), p. 142.

32 *Brooklyn Daily Eagle*, 4 June 1902.

33 *Sunday Truth*, 2 October 1886.

34 Entry for George H. Lang, 16 May 1868 (University Archives & Special Collections Department, Joseph P. Healey Library, UMB, Massachusetts Infant Asylum records, Admission Committee, 1868–72).

35 Entry for Catherine Ryan, #1164 (University Archives & Special Collections Department, Joseph P. Healey Library, UMB, Massachusetts State Board of Charities, Histories of Alien Residents, HS3/539x vol. 3).

36 Entry for Hannah Walsh, 13 June 1882 (Massachusetts Archives, Massachusetts Reformatory for Women, Inmate history logbooks, HS9.06/series 821x).

37 *Evening World*, 13 March 1912.

38 Mélanie Méthot, 'Bigamy in the Northern Alberta judicial district, 1886–1969: a socially constructed crime that failed to impose gender barriers' in *Journal of Family History*, 31, no. 3 (2006), p. 260.

39 The sources on which this case study is based include: Entry for Bridget McCool, 21 October 1914 (Massachusetts Archives, Massachusetts Reformatory for Women, Inmate registers, HS9.06/series 824); *Fitchburg Sentinel*, 28 October 1914, 28 October 1921, 13 June, 20 July, 5 September 1931.

40 Peter Stearns, *Jealousy: the evolution of an emotion in American history* (New York, 1989), pp. 21, 25.

41 Ginger Frost, '"She is but a woman": Kitty Byron and the English Edwardian criminal justice system' in *Gender and History*, 16, no. 3 (2004), p. 547.

42 *Angola Record*, 21 January 1886.

43 *Buffalo Morning Express*, 16 January 1886.

44 *The New York Times*, 17 August 1857.

45 The sources on which this case study is based include: Entry for Mary Davidson, 24 May 1911 (NYSA, State Prison for Women at Auburn, Register of female inmates discharged, 1893–1919, B0055); *Brooklyn Daily Eagle*, 17 December 1908; *Evening World*, 17, 20 December 1908; *New York Tribune*, 12 May 1909; *Star Gazette*, 17 December 1908.

46 The sources on which this case study is based include: Entry for Catherine Dreiser, 20 May 1907 (NYSA, State Prison for Women at Auburn, Register of female inmates discharged, 1893–1919, B0055); *Democrat and Chronicle*, 10 February 1900; *Evening World*, 12 May 1900, 25–29 January 1904; *The New York Times*, 12 May 1900, 26–29 January 1904; *New York Tribune*, 12–13 May 1900, 29–30 January 1904; *Standard Union*, 29 January 1904; *The Sun*, 12–13 May 1900, 29–30 January 1904.

47 Toronto City Directories, 1873, available at https://www.
torontopubliclibrary.ca/history-genealogy/lh-digital-city-
directories.jsp (last accessed 10 November 2021).

48 Jenkins, *Between raid and rebellion*, p. 165.

9. Race, reformation and the case of the Anderson sisters

1 Stella's surname is interchangeably written in the sources as
Varnell, Varnall and Vannall. For consistency, the text of this
chapter uses the spelling as given in the court papers.

2 The sources on which this case study is based include: *Com-
monwealth of Massachusetts vs Stella Vannall*, February 1880
(Massachusetts Supreme Judicial Court Archives, Boston
Superior Criminal Court); Entries for Ida King, 11 February
and 17 October 1878 (Massachusetts Archives, Massachu-
setts Reformatory for Women, Inmate history logbooks,
HS9.06/series 821x); Entry for Ida King, 11 February 1878
(Massachusetts Archives, Massachusetts Reformatory for
Women, Recommitment register, HS9.06/series 301x); Entry
for Stella Varnall, 6 August 1878 (Massachusetts Archives,
Massachusetts Reformatory for Women, Inmate history
logbooks, HS9.06/series 821x); Entry for Stella Varnall, 6
August 1878 (Massachusetts Archives, Massachusetts Reformatory for Women, Inmate registers, HS9.06/series 824);
Punishment register, 1877–1912 (Massachusetts Archives,
Massachusetts Reformatory for Women, HS9.06/series
302x); Boston Cemetery records, available at Bostoncemetery.
com (last accessed 1 November 2021); *Boston Globe*, 20 January, 7 May 1880; *Boston Herald*, 20 January 1880; *Boston Post*,
20 January 1880; *Buffalo Weekly Courier*, 28 January 1880; *Intel-
ligencer Journal*, 21 January 1880.

3 Michael's surname is written as Toland and Tolan. For consistency, this chapter uses the spelling as given in the court papers.

4 Boston House of Correction register of inmates, 1882–1915, vols. 135–43 (Boston City Archives, House of Corrections records, Collection 8502.001).

5 Statistics of the Toronto Gaol, 1866–74 (Archives of Ontario, Correctional services, RG 20-100-3).

6 *The New York Times*, 11 February 1858.

7 *Buffalo Morning Express*, 15 December 1858.

8 Entry for Ellen and Catherine McKilligut, #1428 (Massachusetts Archives, Massachusetts Board of State Charities, Histories of alien residents of almshouses and other institutions, vol. 2, HS3/series 539x). Emphasis in the original.

9 *Daily Evening Transcript*, 7 February 1852.

10 *Twenty-third annual report of the New York Association for Improving the Condition of the Poor for the year 1866* (New York, 1866), p. 57.

11 Cooper Owens, *Race, gender, and the origins of American gynecology*, p. 90. See also Dubinsky, *Improper advances*, pp. 140–42; Duffy, *Who's your Paddy?*, p. 3; Catherine M. Eagan, '"White," if "not quite": Irish whiteness in the nineteenth-century Irish-American novel' in Kenny (ed.), *New directions in Irish-American history*, pp. 140–55; Hirota, *Expelling the poor*, pp. 138–40; Noel Ignatiev, *How the Irish became white* (New York, 1995); Kibler, *Censoring racial ridicule*; O'Neill, *Famine Irish and the American racial state*; Painter, *The history of white people*, pp. 140–2; Schultz, 'The Black Mammy and the Irish Bridget', pp. 181–2.

12 Cooper Owens, *Race, gender, and the origins of American gynecology*, p. 100.

13 Ibid., pp. 96–102, 106.

14 Racial passing was not unheard of in the nineteenth century, for those who were light-skinned enough to do it. See Nik

Ribianszky, *Generations of freedom: gender, movement, and violence in Natchez, 1779–1865* (Athens, GA, 2021), chapter 7.

15 Deutsch, *Women and the city*, p. 88.

16 *Twenty-third report of the Executive Committee of the Boston Children's Aid Society, from June 1886, to June 1887* (Brookline, MA, 1887), p. 24.

17 Deutsch, *Women and the city*, p. 42.

18 Ibid., p. 87.

19 Dodge, *'Whores and thieves of the worst kind'*, p. 187.

20 See also Kibler, *Censoring racial ridicule*, pp. 30–33, 46–7.

21 Emphasis in the original.

22 The sources on which this case study is based include: Case file of Tillie Robinson (Archives of Ontario, Andrew Mercer Ontario Reformatory for Females, Case file #2786, RG20-50-5); Census of Canada, 1911, available at findmypast.co.uk (last accessed 5 April 2022); *Toronto Globe*, 19 September 1905; *Weekly British Whig*, 21 September 1905.

23 *Ottawa Citizen*, 26 May 1925; *Times Colonist*, 26 May 1925.

24 *Forty-fourth annual report of the Women's Prison Association and Home* (New York, 1888), pp. 31–2.

25 *The New York Times*, 1 February 1896.

26 Mary Mahoney to Jessie Hodder, n.d. (Massachusetts Archives, Massachusetts Reformatory for Women, Inmate case files, HS9.06/series 515, #10212).

27 *Report of the Jail Mission Work, Toronto, from December 1867 to August 1869* (Toronto, 1869), pp. 17–18.

28 Entry for Margaret O'Donnell, 29 September 1914 (Massachusetts Archives, Massachusetts Reformatory for Women, Inmate registers, HS9.06/series 824).

29 Entry for Margaret Larkin, 30 September 1905 (Massachusetts Archives, Massachusetts Reformatory for Women, Inmate registers, HS9.06/series 824).

30 Case notes, 6 April 1908 (University Archives & Special Collections Department, Joseph P. Healey Library, UMB, MSPCC, box 43, #31745).

31 Record of Bridget Isabella Laughlin, 24 December 1856 (Massachusetts Archives, Massachusetts Board of State Charities, Histories of alien residents of almshouses and other institutions, vol. 1, HS3/series 539x).

32 *Seventh annual report of the New York Society for the Prevention of Cruelty to Children, 1881* (New York, 1881), p. 36.

33 Mary Sweeney to Catherine Moshier, 8 July 1917 (Massachusetts Archives, Massachusetts Reformatory for Women, Inmate case files, HS9.06/series 515, #10948).

34 Outside investigation, 16 July 1917 (Massachusetts Archives, Massachusetts Reformatory for Women, Inmate case files, HS9.06/series 515, #10948).

35 Interview with Mary Good, 11 April 1918 (Massachusetts Archives, Massachusetts Reformatory for Women, Inmate case files, HS9.06/series 515, #11095).

36 She was probably sent to this prison rather than the Massachusetts Reformatory Prison for Women because she was a repeat offender who had committed a serious offence.

10. Murder and the case of Mary Farmer

1 The sources on which this case study is based include: *People vs Farmer*, 196 N.Y. 65, 89 N.E. 462 (New York, 1909); *People vs Farmer*, 194 N.Y. 251, 87 N.E. 457 (New York, 1909); U.S. find a grave index, 1600s–current, available at ancestry.com (last accessed 1 December 2021); US censuses, 1920, 1930, available at ancestry.com (last accessed 1 December 2021); U.S. Social Security Death Index, 1935–2014, available at

ancestry.com (last accessed 1 December 2021); New York county marriage records, 1847–1849, 1907–1936 available at ancestry.com (last accessed 1 December 2021); *Binghamton Press*, 27 February 1909; *Bisbee Daily Review*, 31 March 1909; *Brooklyn Citizen*, 27 December 1908, 28–29 March 1909; *Brooklyn Daily Eagle*, 29 March 1909; *Brooklyn Times Union*, 25–31 March 1909; *Buffalo Courier*, 9 May, 21 June 1908, 10, 14 February, 4, 22, 28–31 March 1909; *Buffalo Enquirer*, 26, 29 March, 20 October 1909; *Buffalo Evening News*, 26–29 March, 1 April, 4 June 1909; *Buffalo Times*, 28–29 March 1909; *Evening World*, 22, 27–29 March 1909; *The New York Times*, 27–30 March 1909; *Pittsburgh Sun–Telegraph*, 3 July 1934; *Post Standard*, 8, 25 November 1909, 28 February, 2, 15 March 1910; *Poughkeepsie Eagle News*, 29 March 1909, 2 March 1910; *Star Gazette*, 3 June 1909; *Watertown Daily Times*, 30 April, 4 May 1908; *Watertown Re-union*, 6 May, 13, 24 June 1908; *Wilkes-Barre Times Leader*, 10 November 1908.

2 Lawrence Friedman, *Crime and punishment in American history* (New York, 1992), p. 143.

3 Karen Halttunen, *Murder most foul: the killer and the American Gothic imagination* (Cambridge, MA, 1998), pp. 231–3.

4 Cara Robertson, 'Representing Miss Lizzie: cultural convictions in the trial of Lizzie Borden' in *Yale Journal of Law and the Humanities*, 8, no. 2 (1996), pp. 287–90, 412. See also John B. Tuke, 'Cases illustrative of the insanity of pregnancy, puerperal mania, and insanity of lactation' in *Edinburgh Medical Journal*, 12 (1866–7), pp. 1083–101; Joel Peter Eigen, *Witnessing insanity: madness and mad-doctors in the English court* (New Haven, CT, 1995); Pat Gibbons, Niamh Mulryan and Art O'Connor, 'Guilty but insane: the insanity defence in Ireland, 1850–1995' in *British Journal of Psychiatry*, 170, no. 5 (1997), pp. 467–72; Judith Walzer Leavitt (ed.), *Women and*

health in America: historical readings (2nd edn, Madison, WI, and London, 1999), pp. 405–22; Hilary Marland, *Dangerous motherhood: insanity and childbirth in Victorian Britain* (New York, 2004).

5 *The New York Times*, 29 March 1909.

6 Madeleine Z. Doty, *One woman determined to make a difference: the life of Madeleine Zabriskie Doty*, ed. Alice Duffy Rinehart (Cranbury, NJ, 2001), p. 73.

7 Margaret Atwood, *Alias Grace* (London, 1996).

8 The sources on which this case study is based include: Entry for Elizabeth Halliday, 23 July 1894 (NYSA, State Prison for Women at Auburn, Register of female inmates discharged, 1893–1919, B0055); *Abbeville Press and Banner*, 31 October 1906; *Alexandria Gazette*, 28 September 1906; *Altoona Tribune*, 22 October 1906; *Buffalo Evening News*, 15 November 1893; 22 June 1894; *Daily Item*, 21 June 1894; *Daily Telegram*, 24 October 1906; *Daily Tribune*, 21 July 1894; *Evening World*, 19–21 June 1894; *Helena Independent*, 29 December 1893; *Hot Springs Weekly Star*, 13 July 1894; *Long Beach Telegram*, 24 October 1906; *Los Angeles Herald*, 25 June 1894; *Lowell Sun*, 22 June 1894; *Middletown Daily Argus*, 21 June 1894, 21 August 1895; *Morning Post*, 22 June 1894; *The New York Times*, 9–10, 19, 29 June 1894, 29 June 1918; *New York Tribune*, 9 September 1893; *Pottsville Republican*, 20 June 1894; *The Press*, 22 June 1894; *Tunkhannock Republican*, 22 June 1894; *Washington Bee*, 7 September 1895; *Wilkes-Barre News*, 29 June 1894; *Windham County Reformer*, 29 June 1894; *Wood County Reporter*, 26 October 1893; *York Daily*, 19 September 1893.

9 Judith Knelman, *Twisting in the wind: the murderess and the English press* (Toronto, 1998), p. 250; Cara Anzilotti, *She-devil in the city of angels: gender, violence, and the Hattie Woolsteen murder case in Victorian era Los Angeles* (Santa Barbara, CA, 2016), chapter 6.

10 Arthur Griffiths, 'Female criminals' in *North American Review*, 161, no. 465 (1895), p. 141.

11 Cesare Lombroso and Guglielmo Ferrero, trans. Nicole Hahn Rafter and Mary Gibson, *Criminal woman, the prostitute, and the normal woman* (Durham, NC, 2004), pp. 4–8.

12 The sources on which this case study is based include: Entry for Elizabeth Richmond, 28 May 1910 (Massachusetts Archives, Massachusetts Reformatory for Women, Inmate registers, HS9.06/series 824); Marriage record of Elizabeth Daly and William Byrne, 4 July 1880, available at civilrecords. genealogy.ie (last accessed 12 May 2021); Record of William James Byrne, #38964, Royal Irish Constabulary Service Records, 1816–1922, available at findmypast.co.uk (last accessed 5 April 2022); *Boston Globe*, 24–26 July, 1–4 August, 21 September 1909, 23–29 May 1910; *Evening World*, 29 March 1910; *Fall River Daily Globe*, 31 May 1910; *Fall River Evening News*, 3 August 1909, 26–28 May 1910; *Fitchburg Sentinel*, 4 August, 17, 21 September 1909, 31 May 1910.

13 Brian Griffin, 'The Irish police: love, sex and marriage in the nineteenth and early twentieth centuries' in Margaret Kelleher and James H. Murphy (eds.), *Gender perspectives in nineteenth century Ireland* (Dublin, 1997), pp. 170–73.

14 Lizzie Seal, *Women, murder and femininity: gender representations of women who kill* (Basingstoke, 2010), p. 168.

15 Katie Barclay, 'Narrative, law and emotion: husband killers in early nineteenth-century Ireland' in *Journal of Legal History*, 38, no. 2 (2017), p. 215.

16 Shani D'Cruze, Sandra Walklate and Samantha Pegg, *Murder: social and historical approaches to understanding murder and murderers* (Cullompton, 2006), p. 57.

17 The sources on which this case study is based include: Entry for Mary Jennings, 1 December 1916 (NYSA, State Prison

for Women at Auburn, Register of female inmates discharged, 1893–1919, B0055); *Evening World*, 11, 14, 21, 25 October 1901; *New York Tribune*, 26 October 1901; *The Sun*, 16 July 1901.

18 *Evening World*, 11 October 1901.

19 *Boston Globe*, 24 May 1910.

20 Ann Jones, *Women who kill* (Boston, 1996), p. 103.

21 Mark Essig, 'Poison murder and expert testimony: doubting the physician in late nineteenth-century America' in *Yale Journal of Law and the Humanities*, 14, no. 1 (2002), p. 181.

22 Linda Stratmann, *The secret poisoner: a century of murder* (New Haven, CT, 2016), p. 260.

23 The sources on which this case study is based include: *Boston Evening Transcript*, 3 August, 7 September, 4 November, 24 December 1886, 15 January, 15 June, 13–15 December 1887, 7 February, 31 May, 29 June, 31 October, 15 November 1888; *Boston Globe*, 18–22, 26–27 August 1886, 15 December 1887, 9–12 February, 12, 29 June, 13 November 1888, 23 December 1905, 5–7 January 1906; *Fall River Daily News*, 5 March 1887, 29 May, 1, 13 November 1888, 5 January 1906; *Post Star*, 16 November 1888; *Sioux City Journal*, 13 November 1888. See also Jones, *Women who kill*, pp. 121–8.

24 Jones, *Women who kill*, pp. 125–6.

25 The sources on which this case study is based include: Entry for Margaret Kane, 31 January 1894 (Massachusetts Archives, Massachusetts Reformatory for Women, Inmate registers, HS9.06/series 824); Entry for Margaret Kane, 31 January 1894 (Massachusetts Archives, Massachusetts Reformatory for Women, Inmate history logbooks, HS9.06/series 821x); Massachusetts marriage records, 1840–1915, available at ancestry.com (last accessed 30 November 2021); US census, 1920, available at ancestry.com (last accessed 1 December

2021); *Boston Evening Transcript*, 18 December 1893, 8, 31 January 1894; *Boston Globe*, 18 December 1893, 31 January, 1 February 1894; *Boston Post*, 1 February 1894.

A note on sources

1 We accessed newspapers in libraries and repositories, and through online databases, including America's Historical Newspapers; 19th-Century British Library Newspapers; Irish Newspaper Archives; Newspapers.com; Library of Congress; and ProQuest Historical Newspapers.

2 *First annual report of the Association for the Protection of Roman Catholic Children, in Boston, from Jan. 1, 1865, to Jan. 1, 1866* (Boston, 1866), p. 5.

3 This is also recognized by Wolfgang Helbich and Walter D. Kamphoefner, 'The hour of your liberation is getting closer and closer . . .' in *Studia Migracyjne-Przegląd Polonijny*, 35, no. 3 (2009), p. 45.

4 Entry for Catherine Lynch, 11 May 1900 (Massachusetts Archives, Massachusetts Reformatory for Women, Inmate registers, HS9.06/series 824).

5 Neville, 'Dark lady of the archives', p. 211.

Illustrations

Index